The Soul of Art

Number Twenty

CAROLYN AND ERNEST FAY SERIES
IN ANALYTICAL PSYCHOLOGY

Michael Escamilla, General Editor

The Carolyn and Ernest Fay book series, based on the Fay Lecture Series in Analytical Psychology, was established to further the ideas of C. G. Jung among students, faculty, therapists, and other citizens and to enhance scholarly activities related to analytical psychology. The lecture and book series address topics of importance to the individual and to society. Both series were generously endowed by Carolyn Grant Fay, the founding president of the C. G. Jung Educational Center in Houston, Texas. The series are in part a memorial to her husband, Ernest Bel Fay. Carolyn Fay has planted a Jungian tree carrying both her name and that of her husband, which will bear fruitful ideas and stimulate creative works from this time forward. The Jung Center, Houston, and all those who come in contact with the growing Fay Jungian tree are extremely grateful to Carolyn Grant Fay for what she has done. The Frank N. McMillan Jr. Scholar at the Jung Center, Houston, functions as the general editor of the Fay Book Series.

The Soul of Art

ANALYSIS AND CREATION

Christian Gaillard

Translation by Anita Conrade

Foreword by David H. Rosen

Texas A&M University Press • College Station

First edition

This paper meets the requirements of ANSI/NISO Z39.48-1992
(Permanence of Paper).
Binding materials have been chosen for durability.
Manufactured in the United States of America

LIBRARY OF CONGRESS CATALOGING-IN-PUBLICATION DATA

Names: Gaillard, Christian, 1942– author. | Conrade, Anita, translator. | Rosen, David H., 1945– writer of foreword.
Title: The soul of art: analysis and creation / Christian Gaillard ; translation by Anita Conrade; foreword by David H. Rosen.
Other titles: Carolyn and Ernest Fay series in analytical psychology; no. 20.
Description: First edition. | College Station: Texas A&M University Press, [2017] | Series: Carolyn and Ernest Fay series in analytical psychology; number twenty | Includes bibliographical references and index.
Identifiers: LCCN 2016046611 | ISBN 9781623495251 (book/cloth: alk. paper) | ISBN 9781623495268 (ebook)
Subjects: LCSH: Art—Psychology. | Emotions in art. | Psychoanalysis and art. | Art therapy. | Jung, C. G. (Carl Gustav), 1875–1961—Knowledge—Art.
Classification: LCC N72.P74 G3313 2017 | DDC 700/.453—dc23 LC record available at https://lccn.loc.gov/2016046611

A list of titles in this series is available at the end of the book.

Contents

Foreword

The Soul of Art is deep. It goes back to our beginnings. It is aboriginal and archetypal. Cave people were artists, and as so eloquently described in this text, we honor their creative capacities and ours. Cave paintings also are seen in Africa, Texas, and in other locations around the world. When I lived in Texas, I remember visiting Panther Cave, near Del Rio, and standing in awe of the beautiful, magnificent panther depicted on the wall. This book cites the French cave paintings at Lascaux, with which the author is keenly familiar. I was astonished by the way Gaillard explores this and was filled with wonder. Some speculate that these cave paintings were made in an altered state of consciousness. This same theory has been advanced by Harry J. Shafer in *Ancient Texans.*[1] Nevertheless, they appear childlike, and we encourage our analysands to drop the ego and produce similar kinds of creative artwork.

All of this follows Jung, who embodied the soul and spirit of art. Throughout his life, Jung maintained that he was not an artist, but it is clear that he was able to paint from the depth of the collective unconscious. When I was in Texas, I wanted to know more about these paintings, and now we can all learn from this magnificent book about those same stick figures, shamanic priests, and designs—specifically the ever-present mandala. What was striking to me then and in this book is how humans are characterized as stick figures, the animals appear more lifelike, and the shamans seem larger than life.

Through revelatory analysis, Gaillard explores the meaning of these ancient paintings and their modern descendants. He doesn't limit his exploration of art to paintings, but includes literature and religion—*Ulysses* and Moses, for example. Since Jung's technique of active imagination brings forth these aboriginal symbols, Gaillard starts out his work in the analyst's consulting room. There is an early "encounter in Herculaneum" in the first century BC, and then we move forward to the time of the Roman Empire, specifically to the wonderful center of art at Pompeii. Those images can be seen today as they were painted at that time. This is followed by "Whatever Happened to Paradise?" Gaillard covers art from Dürer to Cranach, focusing on melancholy in black and red. Then we are on an excursion with Picasso, Caravaggio, and Ovid. Next is an exciting adventure with Bluebeard, and then on to Jackson Pollock and Kiefer.

The fact that the prehistoric cave paintings resemble the art of children and active imagination is a truism. As we know, these are creative products that analysts and our analysands produce that link us with our archetypal past, as well as with our divine child archetype. In a real way, we are like the first artists, and we should never lose touch with our inner divine child archetype. Let us remember that the soul of art can be expressed in many ways: painting, sculpting, dancing, and the joy of life itself, which is the most important form of art.

Christian Gaillard helps us to appreciate and value the art that springs forth from the collective unconscious. I commend him for writing this treatise. Art makes us human and preserves the wellspring of creativity in all of us.

David H. Rosen
Eugene, Oregon

Introduction

ONWARD AND UPWARD?

The psychoanalyst with a taste for all the arts has an advantage over the art historian. He is under no obligation to become a scholarly specialist, an expert in a certain artistic period or place. He travels freely through time and space, stopping where he pleases. Rather, he finds himself stopped inadvertently when he encounters a certain work of art.

It may be one that he has only glimpsed and knows little about, or, on the contrary, one that everyone knows too well. This work of art may either impose itself, or it may allow itself to be skimmed over and forgotten. But it will return and insist on facing him, outwardly and inwardly, until he finally yields to it, observes it, gets to know it more intimately, wondering about what is happening when he contemplates it: something that is unexpected and yet expected and unforeseen, but intuited.

It is likely that one of the functions of art is to make us experience and recognize something we usually overlook: something that, unbeknownst to us, dwells inside and haunts us, or carries us forward to some other becoming—if we are finally willing to lend it the attention it awaits and demands.

The works that form the subject of this book often confronted me in this way. Often I initially put off any dalliance with them, being busy with the tasks of the moment for years or even decades. Finally, I returned to these pieces—or, in actuality, finally they were so insistent and imposing that I was forced to deal with them. I had to find out what they were presenting and representing to me with such insistence and consistency that it would have been indecent to avoid them, to forget them, or to dismiss them by telling myself that enough was already known about them.

Rather oddly, these works commanded my attention helter-skelter, causing me to spend several months, even years, grappling with the Middle Ages, on the brink of leaping into the discoveries and upheavals of the Renaissance, or embarking on a perilous and possibly mortal adventure with a piece from the twentieth century or perhaps ancient Rome. I even faced some mute enigmas of prehistory. I accepted this charge with amazement. These encounters made me very happy, and so did the discoveries I made as I wandered and wondered into museums and libraries, while also teaching at the French National Academy of Fine Arts in Paris.

As I was publishing in journals and essay collections, or in books I wrote, or for lectures I was asked to give at various universities or congresses, for a long time, I lacked the motivation to sit down with all of these pieces of writing and build something that could be called a coherent, intelligent whole.

Gradually, I wondered and wandered, experimenting with these essays, attempts to express what I had noticed and what had struck my eye. Little by little, I realized that something was emerging from this jumble of impressions and discoveries, something inchoate, groping, and uncertain at first—something new that I had to dig out to grasp it better and share it with others.

David Rosen's friendly invitation to teach at his university's Fay Lectures series came just at the right time. It helped me put the puzzle together into a sort of archipelago. A map was emerging in the vast ocean, a way to sail through the journey without drowning in it.

Therefore, the book is not the result of a plan. It is an assemblage of essays, a reflection under way that is still forming and wants to be heard—by me and by others who might be attuned to this type of journey.

What can I say about this reflection and research to introduce this book? I'll offer just a few clues to open some perspectives and guide you from one chapter to another, or one part to the next, of this book.

It's worth noting that if the imaginary galleries and rooms we will visit are arranged in chronological order, that order was not preconceived. Nor is it a mere artifice shaped by the needs of this publication.

The history to which these works belong, our collective history, from the origins of time until today, is the long-hidden path that finally emerged, the red thread that connected the subjects of my research and reflection.

Amazingly, humans gradually discovered who they were—an altogether unique phenomenon of the living world, different from the animals and nature surrounding them. At the dawn of humanity, there is astonishment. What an awakening! The traces of it remain: the earliest artworks in caves. They are powerful and impressive even today, and they are largely puzzling to us. We know nothing of the rituals and myths of our origins, aside from the drawn, painted, or carved representations, and a few objects spared by the ravages of time.

Today, some scholars assert that if we assume that there was a primal religion, such as shamanism, we will be enlightened. Should we believe them?

More generally, what should an analyst make of belief? The question of belief looms over our approach to each of the pieces studied herein, from the dawn of history up to Anselm Kiefer, one of our most creative contemporary artists. Likewise, the question is constantly raised by our psychoanalytical practice and the theoretical reflection to which it gives birth. Is individuation compatible with belief? Isn't the reliance on psychoanalysis, our psychoanalysis in particular, a form of belief?

The question deepens and engages us. It is more than disturbing. Jung spent years grappling with it, using colors, pencils, and brushes, largely at his expense, unsure of what he could think of it and what he was becoming, not to mention whether he was fated to meet a power that would be his doom.

Individuation is an adventure—a long-haul journey involving individual and collective risks. Do we always go forward? Do we sometimes regress? It is evident, perhaps today more than ever, that we experience crisis moments. At this turning point, one does not know if the road will lead to some relief—another perspective that will enable us to breathe freer.

On the scale of the history of a culture as well as that of an individual, these moments are indeed critical, in both senses of the word. They challenge all that we have taken for granted, even our most dearly cherished, established certainties. They are so critical and painful that it is hard for us to say if they are leading us to our collapse, or to another, brighter future, a becoming.

For the relationship to the unconscious is at stake. It does not always lead to awakening, emergence, and progress. It is an experience consisting of events that very often prove to be terrible ordeals, which endanger us to the core.

The point is that the emergences and transformations that delight us have an opposite, a movement that is just as strong in the other direction. Perhaps it's a nosedive, a fall toward a reality that, for all practical purposes, has never changed. It's enduring and active, with its own rhythms and powers.

Down there, drowning is a threat. One may get lost. At one end, at the dawn of time, we are awed by Lascaux. At the other, we find Pollock, who died smashed into a tree.

Might we see two sides to this coin? A form of bipolarity? No, because the whole point of the endeavor, from the beginning, has been the art and manner of shaping, and representing—and thereby confronting—sights that make us flinch, insights we would rather ignore. But they demand to be heard and often at the most inconvenient times. Art channels them.

Art is not the matter of artists alone. We are all involved in the adventure, the outcome of which sometimes appears to be, or really is, totally uncertain. As analysts and analysands, we are even more committed than others.

In fact, you will have noticed that the term "unconscious" surfaced briefly, in the lines I have just written. The unconscious, as a vivid, largely innate, and uncontrollable reality, is really at the heart of our work as clinicians.

In this book, I will use as little jargon as possible, as academic language contains many obvious traps. I want to create a particular way of thinking. I hope to show that that was one of the issues with Jung's commitment to his *Red Book.* Now it is my turn to press forward, to make my own attempt in the field of the arts to give shape to a thought.

It is an analyst's thought, and as such, it accompanies the works. Interrogative, exploratory, and, therefore open to the unexpected, to the unplanned event or chance meeting, to the provocation of what is unfolding and it's attentive to what is ineluctably fading. I hope it attests to my taste for following the ongoing matters we conduct in our personal lives, and also those of our collective history, of which we are all the subjects.

For now, I will say no more. We will see how the ideas I have just mentioned, in the form of hypotheses, are fleshed out, in the journey from one artwork to another. We will see how they are challenged and affirmed, or infirmed, unless they will be renewed.

So let's go forward together and see.

1

From the Analyst's Consulting Room to Prehistoric Caves

"Rien n'est jamais acquis à l'homme"
"Man can take nothing for granted."
LOUIS ARAGON

I love my life and my work as an analyst, the protected and protective space of my consulting room.

And yet, I occasionally dream of another life or lives for myself: that of the paleoanthropologist, particularly. This desire was sharpened when I discovered more about the work and research of Denis and Agueda Vialou at Paris' National Museum of Anthropology.[1] My interest for prehistory became even keener when I visited the dig they are in charge of as archeologists and paleoanthropologists in Brazil, at La Cidade de Petra (The Stone City), near Manaus, in Amazonia.[2]

My interest in prehistoric man was also inspired by an encounter with the work of another paleoanthropologist, Professor David Lewis-Williams, who teaches at the University of Witwatersrand, South Africa. Lewis-Williams is a distinguished researcher of San art and the Upper Paleolithic. He developed a thesis on the shamanic rituals that, according to him, would have been performed in the caves before language was written.[3]

In the summer of 2007, I met him, when I invited him to present his research as part of a panel I set up at an International Association for Analytical Psychology international congress in Cape Town, South

Africa. His ideas were discussed by analysts from various schools: two were Freudians; I was one of two Jungian analysts.[4]

Methodological discipline

In making a methodological remark, I should note that, at first, I wondered if it was wise to apply the same approach to European Upper Paleolithic sites and relatively more recent South African ones. They are quite distant from each other in time and space. I finally overcame my reluctance to adopt what initially appeared to be a somewhat unorthodox approach, thanks to prior work of paleoanthropologists who also proceed in this way.[5]

As an analyst, I meticulously check all of my statements and ideas with scholars specializing in the field where I have ventured, regarding the facts and methods on which they are recognized experts. They tell me what has been established in the past and what they have learned in their own research. I defer to their authority, a practice I learned from my earlier work experience with Roger Bastide, professor at the Sorbonne and director of research at the École des Hautes Études en Sciences Sociales (EPHE/EHESS) in Paris. As you will see as I progress from one chapter to the next of this book, I also apply this methodological rule when analyzing more recent paintings or sculptures, which are evidently and primarily the subject of art-history studies.

An oblique approach

However, this methodological prudence has its limits. At a certain point, my questions and analytical perspective take over. My discoveries and hypotheses are then discussed by fellow analysts, whether Freudian or Jungian, or from traditions other than psychoanalysis.

I explore this somewhat unfamiliar terrain from a viewpoint that is not the product of my best-honed skills. I am well aware of the temptation to aim at some universal theory. Instead, I can only hope to shed an oblique, and therefore partial light on the questions raised and the enigmas encountered.[6] At best, I will only sidle up to these issues from an angle, rather than confronting them head-on, in my effort to contribute to the discussions.

Surprise and amazement

I have just mentioned questions and enigmas. This is because, as an analyst, amazement and surprise are truly the leavening grace of my daily attention.

In my consulting room and in my life, what I am dealing with often is that which usually escapes our attention even as it drives our actions without our knowledge; haunts and even obsesses us; structures us; contains and possesses us, while we remain oblivious to it, especially if we are careful to avoid discovering what it is.

I am speaking of the unconscious. Surprise is a good indicator that we are dealing with the unconscious. That is, we have encountered an entity with a life of its own, its own ebb and flow, an entire enterprise with a specific means of expression—which is usually rather enigmatic. In any case, it can be disconcerting.

What then do I find so striking, so riveting, when I discover a prehistoric rock shelter or cave? What arouses my curiosity, almost physically captivating me?

To bring this feeling to life, let's walk into the cave at Lascaux, caves that are perceived as rather familiar. I am amazed, spellbound, and arrested by the incredible beauty of these surroundings. The vision is at once close to me and almost familiar, and yet it causes my eyes to widen in astonishment and wonder. I ask myself what is being presented and represented: something that I know yet do not truly recognize.

I am at home here, as an analyst, but I am also surprised and even slightly anxious. Although I am a true Jungian, Freud's term, das *Unheimliche* (the uncanny), is a good description of how I feel.[7] I sense a strangeness that is a bit disturbing, and yet familiar to me at the same time. Why?

The animals so frequently seen in rock shelters or caves are admirable. They are admirably realistic, and yet simultaneously literally extraordinary. For example, this beast with two horns, visible at Las-

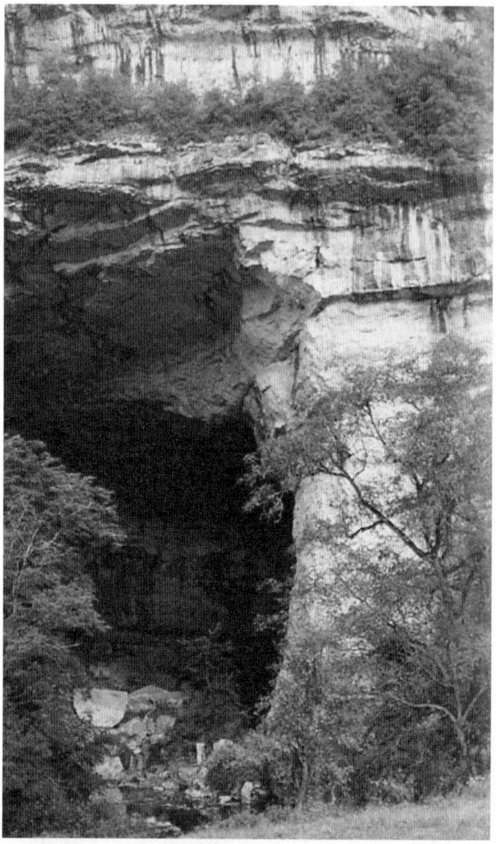

Entrance to the cave at Mas d'Azil, in France

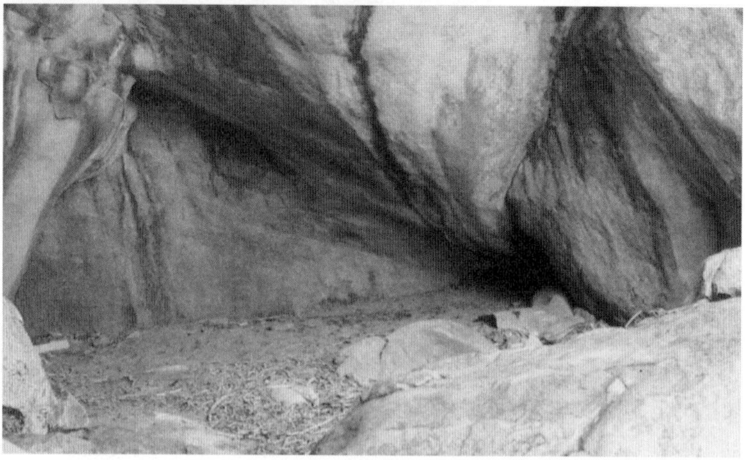

Entrance to Candle Cave in South Africa. Photo by J. Parkington

caux, and usually, for some mysterious reason, called a unicorn, does not exist in reality.

I am well aware that the horn or horns in question might well be a line that escaped from a different drawing, overlapping with or covering the first quadruped, as is often the case with these cave paintings. Nevertheless, to my amazement, what I actually see on the wall is indeed a fabulous beast. And doubtless, at other times, other people's eyes have perceived the same creature as I do—created either deliberately or by accident.

What reality are we dealing with? Lewis-Williams's theory or theories might very well provide an appropriate, stimulating answer to the question.

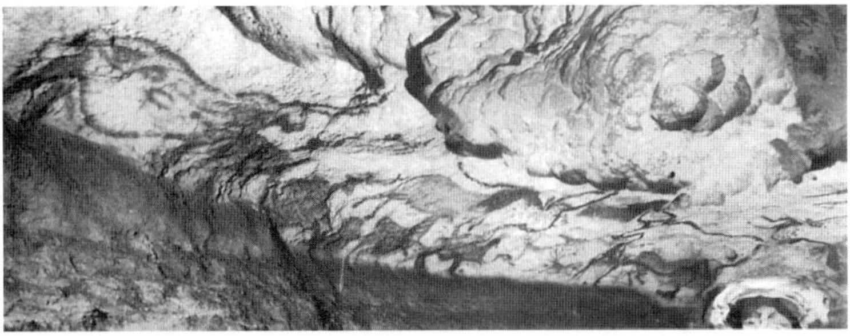

Hall of Bulls, Lascaux. Photo by D. Vialou

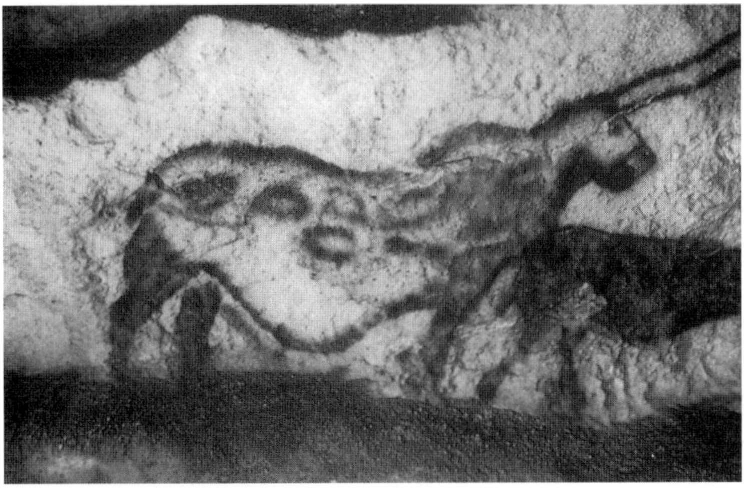

The "unicorn," Lascaux

The theory's strength

The theory derives great strength from its methodology. Because it is a combination of three approaches, it is interdisciplinary in method. Thus, each of these approaches contributes to the discussion with its own assumptions, methods, and conclusions, which delight the researcher, happy to find such parallels and convergences.[8]

It is primarily an ethnographic approach, based on current observations of rock art produced by hunter-gatherer societies in southern Africa in various epochs, and the study of accounts from earlier centuries regarding the natural and social context of this art and the meaning then attributed to it.

A so-called neuropsychological approach is paired with it, to account for the common visual or entoptic effects of "altered states of consciousness." These states have been described in a wide range of times and places, and due to neurophysiological similarities, they are shared by all mankind.

Thirdly, the paleoanthropological approach brings many facts to bear on the question: for example, Upper Paleolithic paintings are often located in hard-to-reach spaces, underground; the viewer's visual perception of what he is seeing may be enhanced or accentuated by the natural shapes in the rock walls, to the point where the effect may be virtually hallucinatory. Lastly, mysterious geometric signs, either by themselves or associated with recurring representations of figures, have also been found.

These three approaches, woven into Lewis-Williams's theory, give it strength and power. Lewis-Williams then calls upon a more generally anthropological explanatory theory, according to which shamanic practices, institutionalized and theorized to varying degrees, observable in many hunter-gatherer societies as well, including those of the Upper Paleolithic, create altered states of consciousness. They are gateways to a different reality.

These assertions caused a great stir among paleoanthropologists, and more generally, in every community of scholars interested in shamanism, anthropology, and prehistory. The discussion immediately spread widely. It also elicited criticism, which, although sometimes subtle concerning methodology, was also frequently sharp, and sometimes even violent, from certain specialists in the field.[9]

Lewis-Williams further reinforced his hypothesis by confronting this criticism, not only by immediately accepting our invitation to Cape Town, but by adding a long afterword to the latest edition of the book he wrote with his distinguished colleague, the French paleoanthropologist Jean Clottes. This afterword contains an accurate survey and detailed critical discussion of the objections his work has raised.[10]

Is the Lewis-Williams thesis or hypothesis really necessary?

Perhaps. Or, it may be one of the best possible approaches to interpreting the curious geometric figures, such as dots, lines, circles, embellishing so many otherwise figurative cave paintings. It is important to note that according to other experts in the field, this type of "sign" may indicate the identity of a human community or a place.[11] These scholars argue that the markings refer to a well-encoded, systematic means of collective identification, instead of to the trance experience.

I will return to my first impression, which remains central to my quest: the feeling of awed surprise, mixed with disturbing strangeness, aroused by the experience of seeing prehistoric cave paintings.

This unsettling and unsettled amazement is accentuated by the fact that, curiously enough, the exquisitely drawn and painted animals so frequently encountered in prehistoric art are almost never accompanied by representations of the landscape. Neither the media the painters used, nor the esthetic of the animal images provides any explanation for this absence. For some unknown reason, the natural surroundings are omitted.

Rocks, mountains, trees, and forests are ignored. These animals are represented outside the context that is natural to them. They live a life of their own, on the wall of the cave. What life is that?

Our first steps

We can only be impressed by this life, reaching us from so far back in the past. They are still powerful enough to enliven us, sparking our curiosity about what was happening to us, in the earliest years of our history. These events may also have befallen other people, in other times. The life in these drawings arouses our intellectual response, in thought and research.

Must one then theorize that rites of some sort—shamanic, perhaps—are required to produce such an experience? Or is it that a certain social and ideological structure is necessary, including "shamans" who specialize in trances, with knowledge of drugs that can induce hallucinations or altered states of consciousness? Or does it entail a fully developed cosmology, transmitted using long-elaborated initiation rites? As an analyst, I am not convinced.

From my readings and experience as a Jungian analyst, I recall the beautiful German term Jung uses to speak of psychic reality: *Wirklichkeit der Seele*, literally the living, active reality of the soul.[12]

One can postulate that what we see on the walls of Paleolithic or even more recent shelters or caves attests to what this particular living creature, the human being, discovered and experienced to his greater surprise, in the prehistoric past, and our amazement and astonishment today.

This is my first hypothesis. Naturally, it is an analyst's hypothesis. Like an analyst's consulting room, a shelter, and, doubtless to an even greater degree, a cave, is a protected and protective container. Inside, a human being, a creature like ourselves, discovers with amazement the living experience of what dwells very deep within every human being, the inner life sustaining him or her and driving his or her representations and his or her actions.

For our distant forebears, the first humans, caves and shelters were the first opportunity to discover an experience that we seek and sometimes find today: the proof that a psychic reality does exist and is just as powerful and real as material, outer reality. It lives its own life, moves of its own volition. It even insists on ruling all else, as soon as it engages one's attention, or when one's psychic condition causes it to prevail.

Amazement is first—at the dawn of humanity, from the time we took our first steps as bipeds, and now, as well.

We are always dreaming, explicitly or surreptitiously, of some Beyond. Lewis-Williams adopts a cautious, differentiated approach to this phenomenon.

He carefully points out the spatial and temporal diversities that have been factors in the evolution of ritual practices and the more or less elaborate cosmological systems associated with them in the past.

Moreover, he is constantly drawing our attention to the "hallucinations" caused or facilitated by these rituals, and the "beliefs" that might thereby have developed.[13] This point of view seems to prove that he considers these thought systems with the detachment of a researcher.

However, the distance between the researcher and his subject tends to fluctuate. For example, it is difficult to determine whether he is describing the beliefs he is studying or his own, when he speaks of making "contact with spirits and supernatural entities," and "supernatural potency of power," or of "spiritual experiences."[14]

Lewis-Williams makes it clear that cave topography and the sensory experiences it induces would tend to foster a relationship with the subterranean or "chthonic" world, rather than a belief in an ideally sublimated, celestial reality. However, I sense that there is only a narrow gap between probable local beliefs and the thinly veiled convictions of the researcher, carried away with enthusiasm about his "shamanic" hypothesis. Lewis-Williams writes of "a realm inhabited by spirit animals behind the rocks," and that "people touched, respected, painted, and otherwise ritually treated the cave walls because of what existed behind their surfaces."

Such assertions arouse my suspicions as an analyst. I find it more prudent to observe, listen, and closely follow what the listener believes, and perhaps wants me to believe, but I always avoid espousing the belief myself.

It would be jumping to conclusions, and smugly reductionist, for us to apply the term "projection." Simply note that any talk of an "inner world" engages the thinker to take an "other" into account. This other may be impressive, powerful, and awe-inspiring. However, it is not necessarily true that the other will be thought of as coming from elsewhere or beyond, be it on high or down below. Mainly, there is no reason why the other will be deemed supernatural. It is an effect of man's unique, complex, and difficult relationship with himself.

Differentiation, humanization, individuation

Now, a second amazement revivifies and deepens the first: Why are there so few human figures in prehistoric art? Moreover, oddly enough, the few pictures and statuettes that exist are quite abstract and schematic. They contrast significantly with the fine, highly differentiated depictions of animals.[15]

Take the so-called "well scene" at Lascaux, for example. The bison is powerfully and realistically drawn, whereas the sort of human figure opposite the animal is represented in a much more abstract style. It is little more than a stick figure, and with the head of a bird.

Actually, the representations of human figures, when they are not reduced to an abstract representation, are still a long way from being entirely human. Often, as in the "well scene" at Lascaux, they contain animal features. They are as theriomorphic as they are anthropomorphic.

This double observation prompts my second hypothesis, which is Jungian to boot. The prehistoric era was the early time of individuation. Mankind had just emerged from the shadows of unconsciousness, or the half-light of preconsciousness. *Homo sapiens* was discovering that he was a human being—a unique, lone species, somehow different from the other animals. But was he really? He was wondering. For the discovery that one is different, and unique, cannot be taken for granted.

The first humans, *Homo sapiens*, who are so much like us, hesitated. They were even hesitant to draw or represent, to draw themselves realistically. They could only barely, dimly recognize their uniqueness, what made them different, their own being.

In his earliest writings, Jung remarks upon the necessity of the individual to learn to live as a unique, separate, and lone creature.[16] In German, he speaks of *einzelsein*. This is the source of his ideas about "individuation."[17]

"Well scene," Lascaux. Photo by N. Ajoulat, CNP-Ministère de la Culture

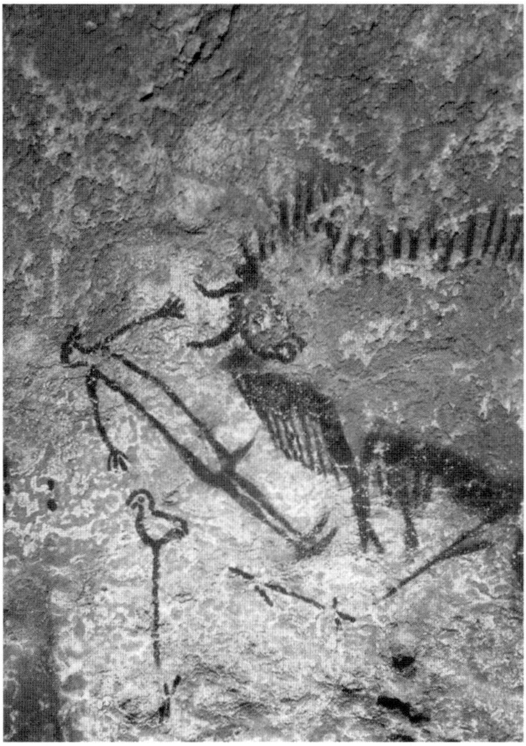

Individuation is a complex process, requiring thought and time. It evolves as a work in progress, developing at its own pace. It involves two dimensions, at least two movements.

The first movement consists of distancing and detaching oneself from the collectivity and from an impersonal collective unconscious, from which one is trying to emerge, or has already emerged.

The second movement is quite the opposite. It consists of dreaming of attachment, or the wish for attachment; an attempt to connect to what one has been familiar with in the past, a familiarity one senses one is liable to lose. A person may even cling tightly—desperately—to what he has lost, a past that is gone forever. This movement is diametrically opposed to the first movement, involving detachment, separation, a will to venture forth and be differentiated.[18]

The process of individuation is truly a work in progress, but it cannot occur in the absence of tension, confrontation, and debate, as well as ambivalence and ambiguity.

A number of rock walls in southern Africa bear magnificent depictions of antelopes. There is also a figure standing on two legs, like you and me, but oddly enough, with an antelope's head. In other southern African paintings, our biped is walking—as well as he can, with his animal head. Another fabulous biped, half-man, half-animal, adorns the wall of Trois-Frères Cave (the Three Brothers Cave) in France.

Surprise and amazement serve as my guide when I am in front of this art. I am astonished and perhaps somewhat disturbed by the unusual appearance of these creatures. But, as I explained earlier and must emphasize again, this feeling of surprise comes directly from the art. And it originates in the past, with the first human beings. They, too, must initially have been surprised and amazed by their difference—an obvious difference they could not ignore, a gulf widening between them and the other animals. It was difficult for them to acknowledge it and become fully aware of themselves and their separate identity, in relation to the beasts.

For it is not easy to be oneself, to discover one's personality. It has

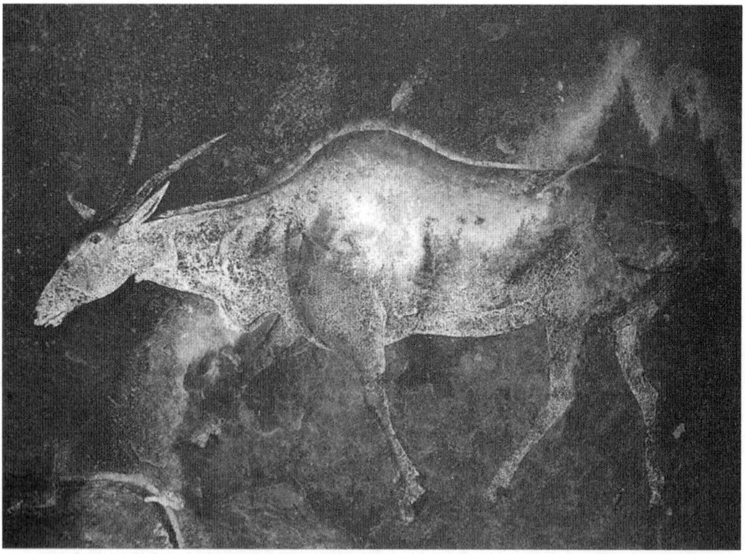

A Cape eland. Photo by Alix Dermigny

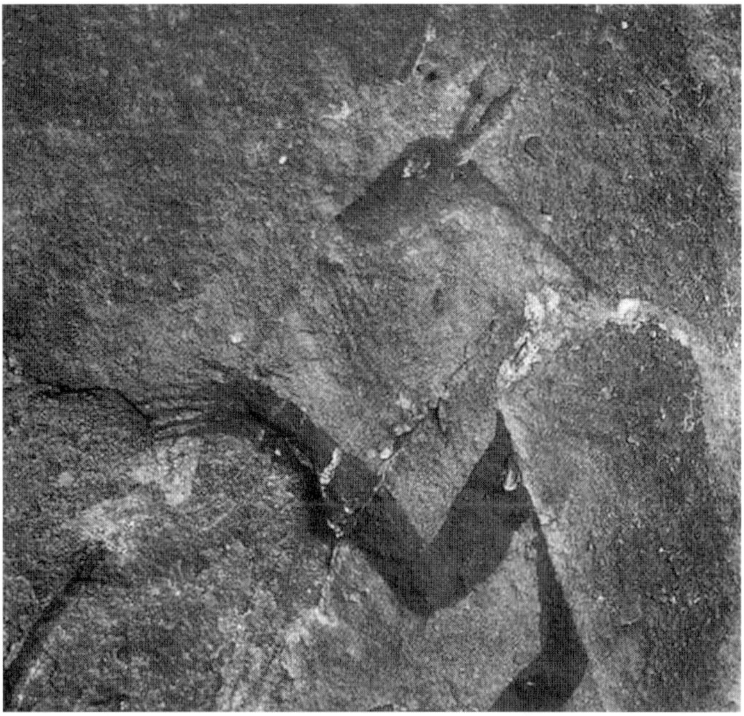

Standing figure with antelope head. Photo by D. Lewis-Williams

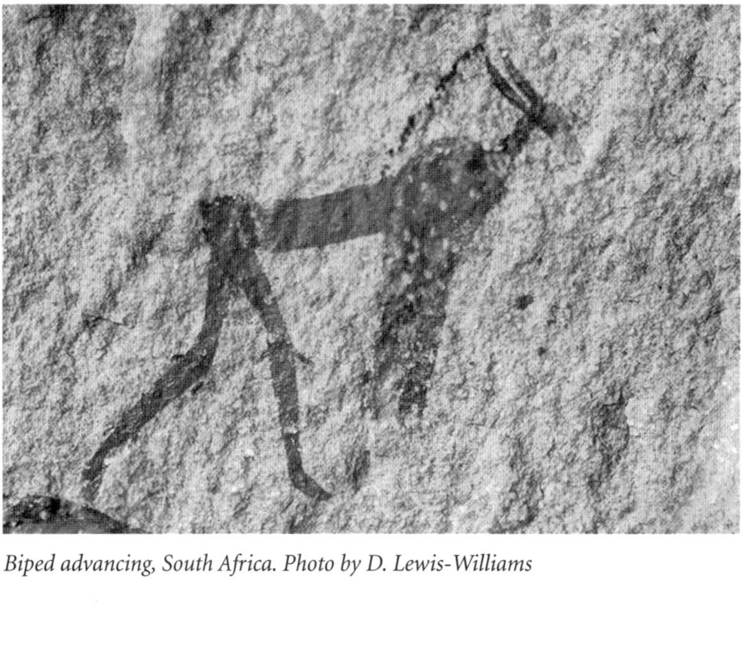

Biped advancing, South Africa. Photo by D. Lewis-Williams

"The Sorcerer" of Trois-Frères

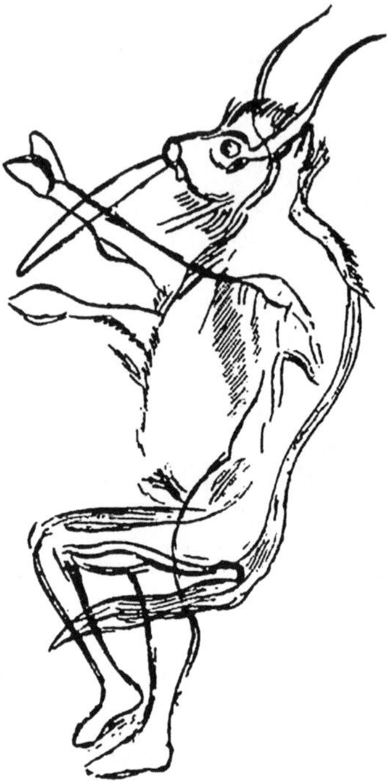

always been a challenge. Whether it occurs in the past, in a cave or rock shelter, or in the present, in an analyst's consulting room, self-discovery is an unsettling experience.

I am assuming that an animal does not wonder who he is. Most of the time, he is part of a herd—which is quite the opposite of individuation, and a good way not to discover oneself alone.

Sexual differences

Humanity discovers it differs fundamentally from the animals, and also that there is a difference between humans themselves.

My third hypothesis is that the first steps toward individuation, at the dawn of mankind, were marked not only by the amazement of uniqueness and solitude, but also by the experience of sexual difference.

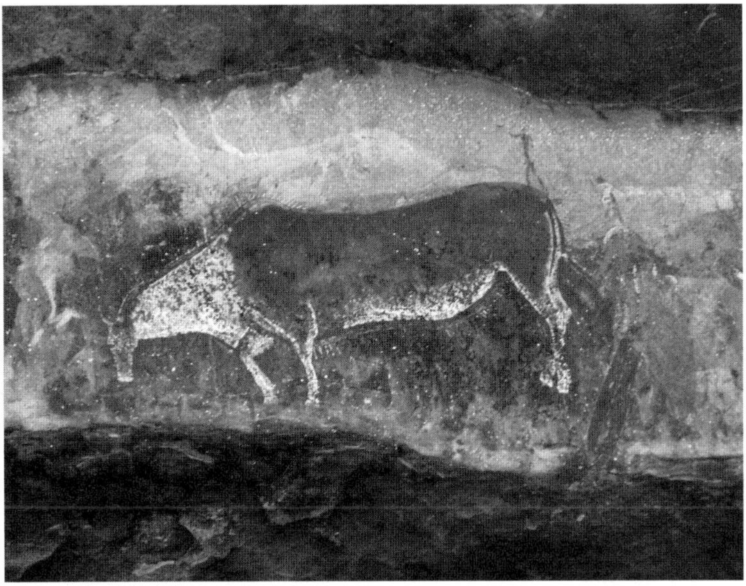

The Game Pass eland with his human. Photo by Alix Dermigny

Let's look more closely at the series of human figures, which have survived since prehistory among the San of South Africa. First, we'll consider the male figures.

At Game Pass, South Africa, a person can still see and recognize the antelopes we discussed earlier. They are accompanied by human beings, although the latter have antelope hooves, and heads that are difficult to identify.

We saw that human figures are rarely represented in prehistoric rock art. When they do appear, they are often stick figures, and/or theriomorphic. Moreover, let's note that they are rarely drawn with faces.

We will now consider representations of women—as seen and experienced by men, no doubt: the "Venus" found in Grimaldi, Italy, now in the collection of the Musée d'Archéologie Nationale at Saint-Germain-en-Laye, in France, or the one uncovered in Austria, at Willendorf. Yet another Venus was also found in Grimaldi. The body—belly and breasts—are powerfully present, and even quite impressive. But the face is absent. Faces are extremely rare in prehistoric

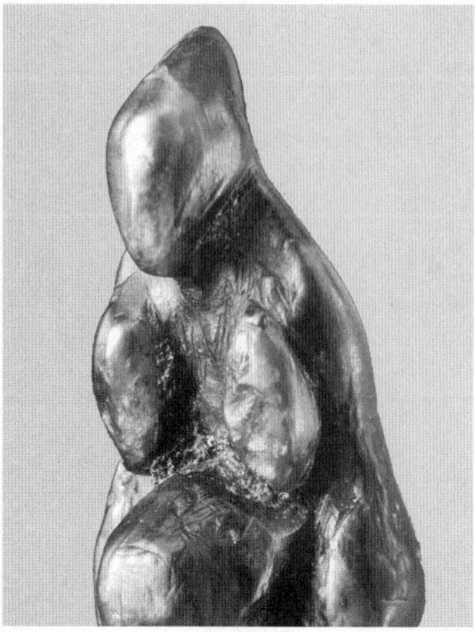

"Venus" of Balzi Rossi in Grimaldi (Italy). Musée de Saint-Germain-en-Laye

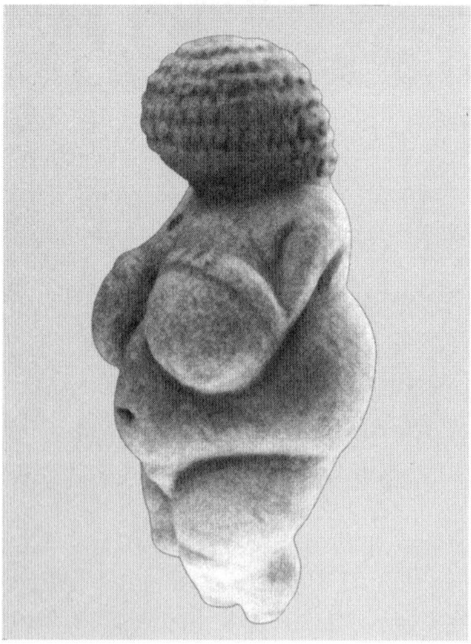

"Venus" of Willendorf. Naturhistorisches Museum, Vienna

art (although you may be acquainted with that of the Brassempouy, "Venus;" it is practically the only one).

There are no technical or esthetic barriers to the representation of the human face, as a glance at the precision and quality of the representations of animals clearly attests. So why are human faces so rarely depicted?

It is almost as though looking at the face, the face of the other, required some boldness. Individuation is more than just separation

Other "Venus," from Grimaldi. Musée de Saint-Germain-en-Laye

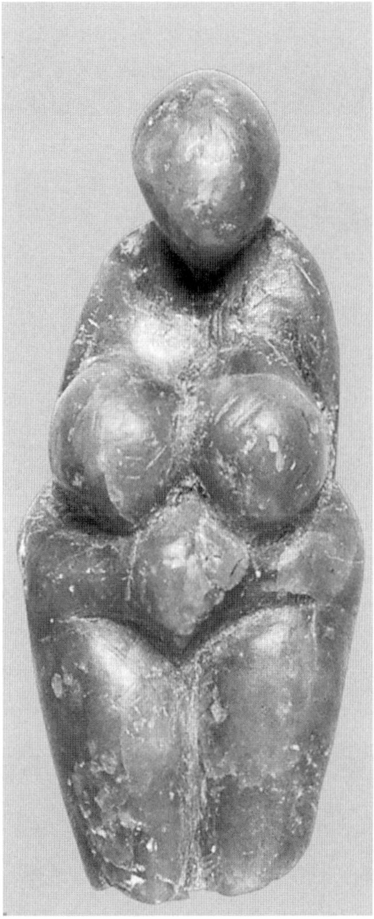

from the herd, the amazing and perhaps frightening experience of finding oneself alone. It is also a confrontation with the proof that one's closest other is different: What is a man? What is a woman? Who is he? Who is she? Who am I?

As matters stand, you are probably curious about representations of sexual organs. There are a few in prehistoric art. But they are relatively rare, and usually quite schematic and abstract. Why?

The sexual organs, like the face, are a difficult question. They involve a number of issues: becoming aware of who the other is; who oneself is; and, in addition, what sort of relationship is possible with him or with her.

Must we assume that the sexuation of the other is only a matter of outer, material reality? Or could it be psychic reality? Both. For the closest other really does physically exist. And he or she is also the object of a deep inner investment, hence the strange, often disturbing and so impressive character of the representations of him and, above all, of her—and the almost supernatural power one is driven to attribute to this other.

Using the hand to think

The fact that prehistoric "artists" made abstract representations of women and men is an expression of a difficulty: the difficulty involved in recognizing oneself, different from other creatures, and alone. There is also the difficulty in clearly seeing and recognizing that the other is different, even though he or she is so close to oneself.

Yet, the creation of abstract shapes, which are not simply and merely natural, can also open the gateway to another experience that is specific to humans: that of symbolic life.

A cave painting in Laussel, France, shows a female figure holding a

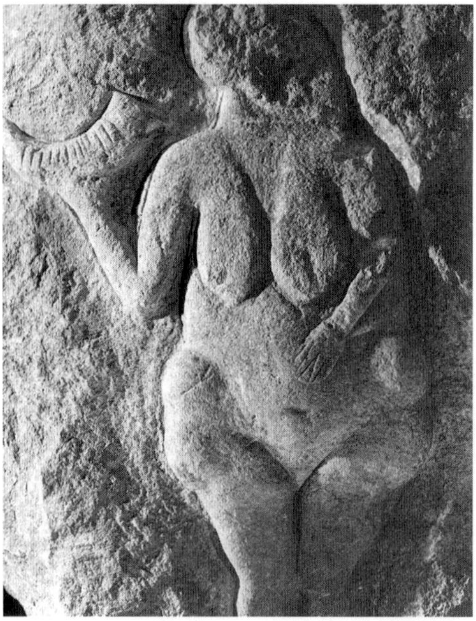

La femme à la corne de Laussel, en France. Courtesy Musée d'Aquitaine, Bordeaux

horn in her right hand. There is some chance that the horn is simply a horn. But specialists in prehistoric art wonder about that. And I wonder about it, too.

There is also some probability—actually a fairly strong probability—that the horn stands for something more than we see at first glance. Considering the way she is brandishing it, in an upraised hand, and the fact that the woman is carved in stone in this position, the horn may be more than a utilitarian, material object.

We are missing the context for this work. What we lack above all is a written text or tale that we could decipher in order to find out what possible ritual, and what myth, surrounds the gesture, and the use of this object, which might play a role as part of a story. It remains that the evidence, the emphasis on this object in this scene, perplexes us all the more because it so happens that it was carved, actually, in order to show it twice. In its very silence, accompanied by this gesture, it arouses our curiosity even more.

Perhaps an object that is grasped and used for purposes beyond its ordinary purpose induces us to wonder. Perhaps the gesture of a hand that portends something more than sheer usefulness, like a carving, made by a human hand to be shown, to be seen, is bound to arouse human amazement—not just our own, but the amazement of the first human beings, discovering their uniqueness among all other living things. We wonder about the existence or creation of a meaning that goes beyond the material and immediately utilitarian; a meaning that today we call "symbolic," something that can also be described as spiritual.[19]

The human hand creates another world, which makes us think.

Self-awareness, regression, and individuation

Another observation we have made about human hands is that handprints are quite frequently found on walls, both in Paleolithic caves and Southern African rock shelters. We are also aware of the scholarly interest elicited by this phenomenon. In particular, John Parkington, another South African paleoanthropologist and anthropologist, has hypothesized that these handprints were made during initiatory rituals for young men.[20] The discussion remains open among the specialists in the field.

Let's again return to the simplest, most obvious interpretation: that these handprints must have amazed the beholder.

The first person to see and be amazed by a handprint was indeed the prehistoric human who made it. How could he have avoided wondering: Is that me? And who am I?

In 1916, Jung wrote, "Often, the hands will solve a mystery the intellect has struggled with in vain."[21] The hand is instrumental in thinking. It takes a creative approach to exploring and also, concretely, "handling" our most intimate questions. The hand works: it gives shape to sensations, feelings, intuitions, or even ideas, making them visible, potentially understandable, and thinkable.

In its creative endeavor, the hand can even attempt to reconcile opposites, to unite what has been sundered, broken, differentiated. For example, the prehistoric ivory sculpture found at Dolni Vestonice, Czech Republic, clearly attempts to reunite the male and the female, to combine the masculine and feminine in a single reality.

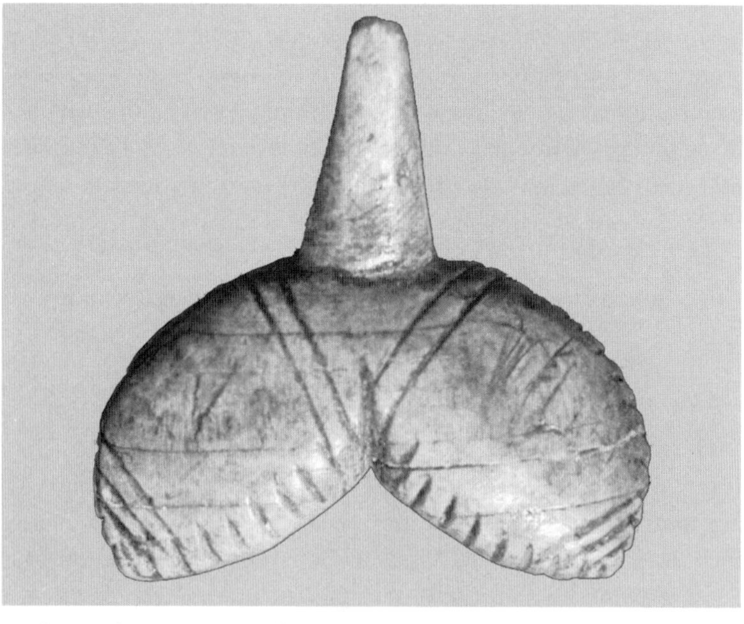

Pendant, Dolni Vestonice, Czech Republic. Photo by D. Vialou

This work of art is a beautiful and creative approach to the chief difficulties in individuation. It certainly seems to be a bid to solve one of the big questions: the recognition and proper use of sexual difference.

Art can attempt to solve this question by sublimation. Sublimation can be an effect or even a function of the art. Freud gave the matter a lot of thought, and following him, Freudian psychoanalysis developed significantly in this direction.[22]

However—and here, Jung is the one to think differently—the processes of creation may also take a different course, the opposite course. Instead of moving forward to solve the enigmas and contradictions by sublimation, they may proceed by regression. Regressing in order to progress toward self-realization has been one of the paradoxes of the creation process, since the beginnings of humanity, and it is a constant in our clinical practice today.[23]

This alternative creative path asks that we recognize, explore, and experience our closeness to and kinship with animals. It involves a sort of turning back, leading to an inner reacquaintance with and reconsideration of animality.

This is how I understand the ambiguity, and especially the ambivalence, we see in the representations of human figures in prehistoric or South African rock art. As we have pointed out, they are amazingly rare, schematic, and/or stubbornly theriomorphic, and, in most cases, faceless.

A debate with animality arises and is played out. It is an adventure, in fact. The outcome is uncertain. Art enables and encourages us to participate, to see, to experiment. It is a lively and interactive game, as we will see when the book delves into other artistic expressions, at other moments in our history.

I recall one evening around the campfire in South Africa after a long, thrilling day of touring a wildlife reserve, escorted by an attentive, remarkably skillful, and careful guide. Late at night, gradually and quite unexpectedly, our guide began to dance. The cooks, waiters, and drivers started accompanying him, improvising music, clapping their hands and singing, and soon we as guests joined in, too. The guide laughed, exaggerating a pantomime of the movements of the animals we had sought out and glimpsed, and in this drama, he was apparently acting out and thwarting the bestiality so familiar to him, which lived within him, and us with him.

This brings us back to ritual and dance, and to the trance states on which Lewis-Williams bases his "shamanic hypothesis," concerning the San of Southern Africa and our Upper Paleolithic ancestors.

Quite possibly, in the early days of humanity, such a religious and social organization arose. Likewise, it is possible that an entire cosmology, and hence a whole system of myths and beliefs, developed. In any case, we have no way of reaching back that far today. It is up to specialists in the field to establish the fact, if it is true, and to keep us informed of their research and findings.

My intention is to offer the observations and questions that occur to me, as a Jungian analyst. The reader will have understood they are not as bold as the hypotheses developed by Lewis-Williams.

I am simply attempting to get closer to the psychic reality of the early days of humanity, drawing upon my experience as a practicing psychoanalyst, and avoiding any unilateral or all-encompassing theories. I am interested in approaching the first discoveries and first experiences, the first steps, doubtless disturbing, taken by our distant ancestors on the journey to individuation. I have noticed the creative and exploratory role of the hand, and I am sizing up the debate, which always engages us, regarding animality. Apparently, it continues to live an active life within us, even today. We must certainly distance ourselves from animality but at the risk of denying it.

The French poet Aragon was indeed a visionary when he said, "Man can take nothing for granted."

An Encounter in Herculaneum

Not long ago, we were at the beginning of our collective history. Now, let's jump forward to the first century BC, to the times of the Roman Empire, more specifically to the region of Pompeii, of Stabiae and Herculaneum, just before the eruption of Mount Vesuvius.

The painting we will address can be found currently in the National Archaeological Museum in Naples, Italy (see next page).

I should know it quite well, since I have already published an essay or two on it,[1] but this painting never ceases to amaze and surprise me. It causes me to question, demanding my attention. In this book, I hope to reconsider and somehow develop these very questions.

This work was hidden from view for nearly nineteen centuries, buried under the lava and ashes of Vesuvius. It was discovered in the 1700s, during the archaeological dig in the Basilica of Herculaneum. In Roman culture, a Basilica is not, strictly speaking, a religious edifice, as in Christian culture. Instead, the word designates the most public space in any town, where people meet to discuss town affairs or politics.

The work dates from the first century BC and was painted under the reign of the Emperor Vespasian. When Goethe discovered it during his travels in Italy, he was amazed by it.[2]

The scene

It is a fresco painting, measuring 1.71 meters by 2.02 meters. The size is significant, because it determines our initial physical relationship to the work.

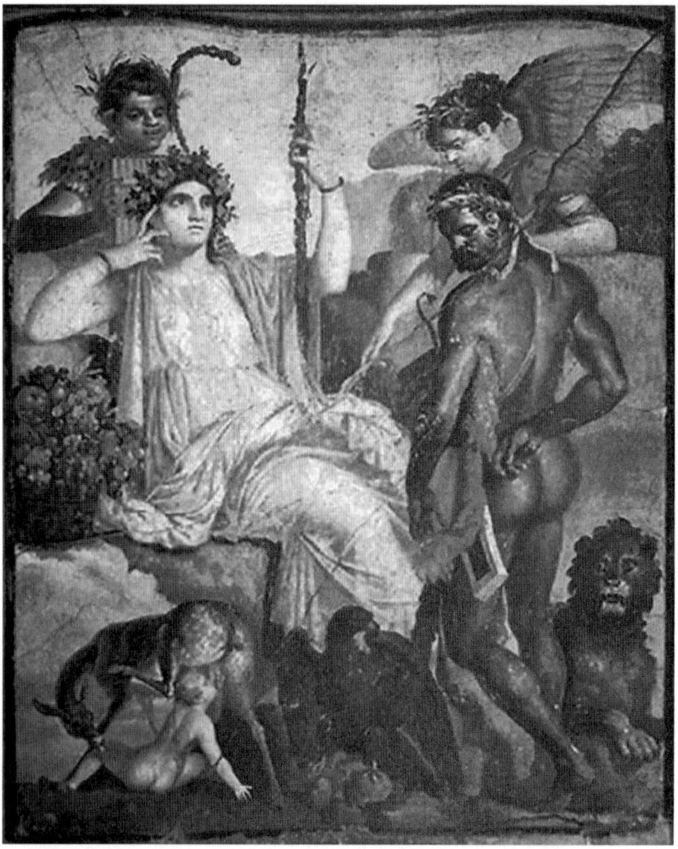

Hercules recognizing his son Telephus in Arcadia, National Museum of Naples. Photo by Alix Dermigny

A woman is reclining. Supporting her head with her arm, she is almost lying down. Her body, draped in white, creates the diagonal line of the painting, a diagonal line barred by the staff she is holding in her left hand.

A man is walking toward her, or is stopped in front of her, his right hand behind his back. He wears an ivy crown; a fur cloak is slung over his left arm; and a quiver and arrows dangle from his shoulder. Figures also frame the scene: a young boy, laughing and playing pipes; a human child suckling at a doe; an eagle; a lion; and, amid all of these animals, a bowl of fruit. A winged young woman hovers over the male figure's right shoulder, pointing with an outstretched arm to the doe suckling the child.

We ask what is going on, or what is about to happen. The scene is highly enigmatic.

At first glance, through mythology

As I mentioned earlier, when a psychoanalyst approaches a work of art, he or she does not work alone. We need the help of specialists in the field, especially art historians. Their knowledge yields essential clues, and we work on the riddle, largely under their supervision. But eventually we must go on alone, as analysts, and that moment has arrived with this curious fresco. We bring our own hypotheses and interpretations; our observations venture beyond the bounds of conventional art history.

Experts in the history of Ancient Roman art classify this fresco as a "megalograph"—the scholarly word for a large painting that illustrates a myth. The hero figures they depict are more or less life-size, like fellow humans.[3]

Who are the figures in this particular fresco? The hunter, with his quiver of arrows and fur cloak, is the Hercules, the half-god, half-mortal.

He is gazing into the child's eyes, and the child intently returns the gaze. Art historians know that the child is Telephus, son of Hercules. Hercules is recognizing his fatherhood, greeting Telephus as his son.

Art historians who are knowledgeable about mythology will note that according to legend, little Telephus was abandoned as an infant in the mountains of Arcadia, in Greece. A doe saved his life by suckling him with her own milk. He survived to be found by Hercules, who rescued him at last.

So the man facing the woman would be the half-god Hercules. But what about the woman? Who is she, this lady with so much poise and restraint, majestically posed and draped, half reclining across the painting?

It's perplexing to art historians. This woman, such an important figure in the scene, is much more difficult for them to identify. After much consultation and discussion, most art historians concur that the female figure would be an allegorical representation of Arcadia, a happy country of early myths. It was in Arcadia that the little Telephus was adopted by a doe, who rescued him from starvation, so that he lived to be found by his father, Hercules.

The basket of fruit, a symbol of plenty, is another clue art historians seize upon to convince themselves the lady is Arcadia. In the tales about this mythical land, Nature always showers her bounty on the fields and orchards.

So we have an initial interpretation—or rather an initial reading—of this work, according to classical mythology. The fresco illustrates the myth of Hercules recognizing his son Telephus in Arcadia. This, moreover, is the title that is generally given to this painting.

A second, more socio-political approach

But what was this painting doing in Herculaneum? What meaning could it have there? This brings us to a second approach, a second attempt at interpreting the work. It takes the myths less at face value, examining them in the sociological and political context of the first century BC.

According to this approach, we are to note that this mural was in a prominent place in the Basilica in Herculaneum. It is the sort of monument that would suit celebrations of the cult of the Roman emperor, in this case, Vespasian.

Like many rulers, Vespasian was eager to shore up his popularity and his power over people by propagating a legend about himself: that he was of the most noble breeding, descended from the Etruscan kings. The Etruscan royalty themselves were said to be the spawn of Telephus, the natural son of Hercules. The blood of the half-god Hercules flowed in Vespasian's veins!

According to this socio-political interpretation, taking into account the period in which the fresco was painted, the fresco Hercules, recognizing his son Telephus in Arcadia, in addition to illustrating well-known episode from Greek and Roman myth, would also, and, more importantly, be a means of celebrating the cult of the Roman emperor.

This is an interesting, instructive approach. But can we be satisfied with these mythological, sociological, and political interpretations? Our attention is still drawn to this woman, this lady, with her body heavily reclining across the painting. She seems very sure of herself and her pose, but curiously defensive. She is withdrawn, protecting herself with the staff, firmly held in her left hand, as she looks with wide open eyes at the man in front of her.

How can we see this woman, this lady, as simply an allegory representing a place, Arcadia? And how can we see this work, this scene, as simply a celebration of the emperor and his noble descent?

What is more, the male figure we see from behind may well be the half-god Hercules. But his presence is too human, too fleshly, too carnal, too true, for us to accept the idea that he is solely a mythological figure, painted for the purposes of flattering the emperor.

We are surprised. And we protest. In fact, the painting protests. It can hardly be reduced to a simple illustration of a myth, or a political instrument.

Reading, and even seeing, differently

When we see in this way, we are surprised, and we even protest. We are moving away from readymade interpretations that are too sure of themselves. This way of seeing is open. It questions received wisdom. Most importantly, it is a way of seeing that is learning to be overawed.

So let us recapitulate—*da capo.* This woman, this "Arcadia," is seated, half reclining, in front of the man we call "Hercules," who is moving toward her. The diagonal line of her body overawes the onlooker.

We are also astonished by another diagonal line that crosses that of the woman's body, created by the arm and hand of the winged young woman. From the upper right, she gazes and gestures across the painting to the scene of the doe and child in the lower left corner.

Our way of seeing has changed. We no longer seek what we know already—the myth of Hercules recognizing his son Telephus in Arcadia, or the cult of the emperor at Herculaneum. Now that we let ourselves be overawed, we can perceive and feel the tension created by the composition of this work, by the diagonal lines intersecting at the

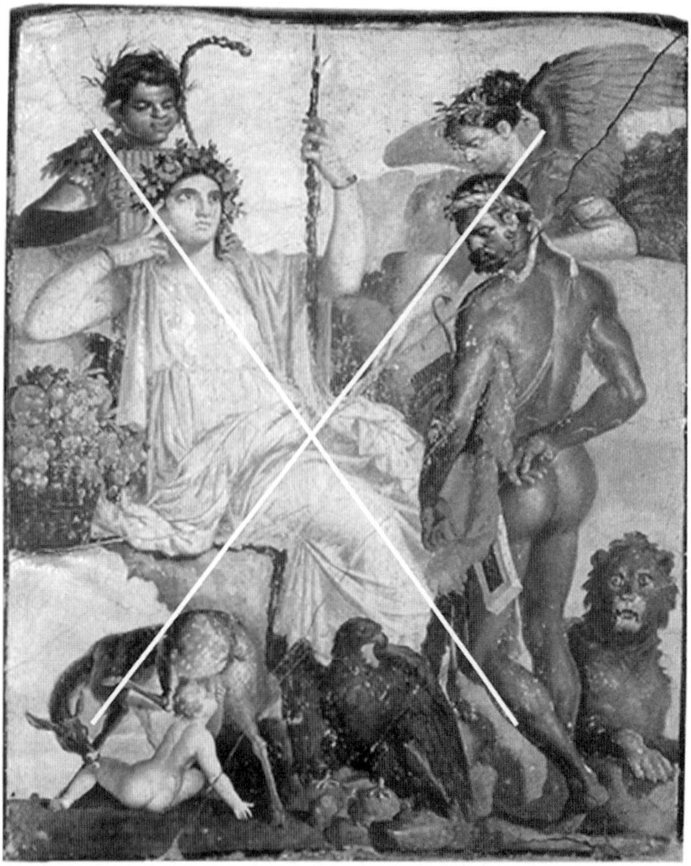

Note the lines of Hercules and Telephus. Photo by Alix Dermigny

very center of the painting, at the very center of the woman's body, held immobile while a man walks toward her, or stops before her, his weapons under his arm.

We can now better perceive and feel the tension, the suspense, created in us by this work that was supposedly a banal allegory or political propaganda: we perceive and feel the suspense of an expected and imminent encounter, manifestly very centered, but suspended—an encounter that is about to occur.

What kind of encounter? What is about to happen?

Hercules and Augé, in S. Reinach 1970

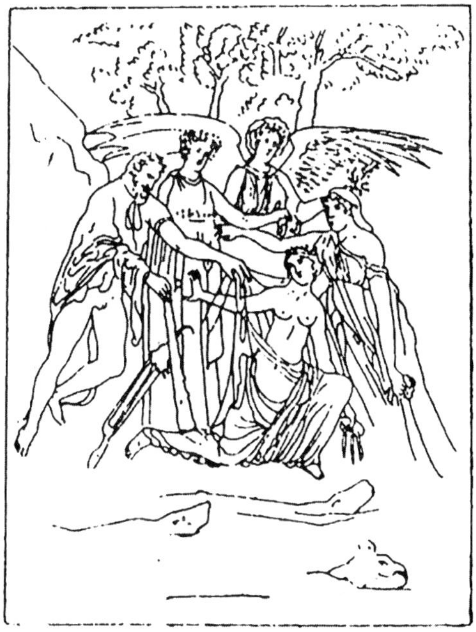

To see is to recall

As we open our way of seeing, letting ourselves be overawed, we recall other poses, other compositions, other analogous structures in the art of the same era, just as the men and women of the time could recall them or at least those who allowed themselves to go beyond the literal meaning of such a scene: an illustration from myth or its immediate political meaning. In all times, there must have been people aware of how agreeable and intriguing it is, to welcome the associations and amplifications that come to us when we are overawed by an encounter with a work of art.[4]

We might recall this scene in the house of the Vettii in Pompeii. Here, we recognize Hercules. Again, the subject is an encounter with a young woman, whose body again lies across the painting.

The encounter is dramatic. The woman's attitude is quite different, though. While in the Basilica in Herculaneum, "Arcadia" was sitting as still as a landscape, here, in the Vettii house, the woman is in motion, frantically struggling to escape. She has lost her balance and is falling. One knee is already on the ground. Like the first, this fresco depicts an episode from the adventures of Hercules, but it is quite another story. It, too, piques our curiosity.

Contemporaries of this work, in the first century BC, knew the story well. It is the encounter between Hercules and a young woman, or rather a girl, named Auge.

The painting in the Vettii house in Pompeii illustrates a misadventure that befalls Hercules while he is journeying around the world, proving his strength. In Arcadia, the king of the land invites him to the court. It so happens the king has a daughter, young Auge. He loves and adores her so much that he wants her to remain forever a virgin. And the best way he finds to preserve her maidenhood is to dedicate her to Athena. Marriage is out of the question.

But Hercules is Hercules. A guest at the king's table, he feasts and drinks excessively. He becomes drunk. And the story would have it that in his drunkenness, he throws himself upon Auge and rapes her.

This is the scene we see. Hercules throwing himself upon Auge to rape her. The story ends in tragedy. Not only is poor Auge raped by Hercules, but she becomes pregnant as a result. She is banished, exiled from her father's court. She bears the baby in the wilderness, and names him Telephus. Exposed as an infant, Telephus survives thanks only to a doe who, as we know, saves him from starvation by suckling him with her own milk.

At Herculaneum, we find ourselves before the enigma of a suspended encounter. Here, in the house of the Vettii in Pompeii, we are right in the middle of the tragedy of a girl, a young woman, savagely raped, then rejected and exiled, and the tragedy, too, of an abandoned child.

Our way of seeing the painting at Herculaneum becomes more complicated, more troubled and worried.

Yet another affair

But again, supported by our attention to composition and therefore to the structural dynamics of this painting, our way of seeing is open to more complexity. For yet another scene is associated with the encounter on the fresco in Herculaneum.

Here, like the Hercules in Herculaneum, the male figure is standing. A woman lies on the floor in front of him. We can see that she is asleep. But the woman, here, is neither Arcadia nor Auge. This woman is another well-known figure from first-century Roman mythology: Ariadne.

Ariadne, you will recall, is also the daughter of a king, and her fate is also unusual. Her father was King Minos, who had asked Dedalus to build that famous labyrinth, to be entered by none, under pain of death. But the hero Theseus came along, and Ariadne fell in love with him. She betrayed her father for him—like poor Auge—and gave him a thread, so that he could safely find his way through the forbidden maze. How did Theseus thank her for risking her father's rage to save

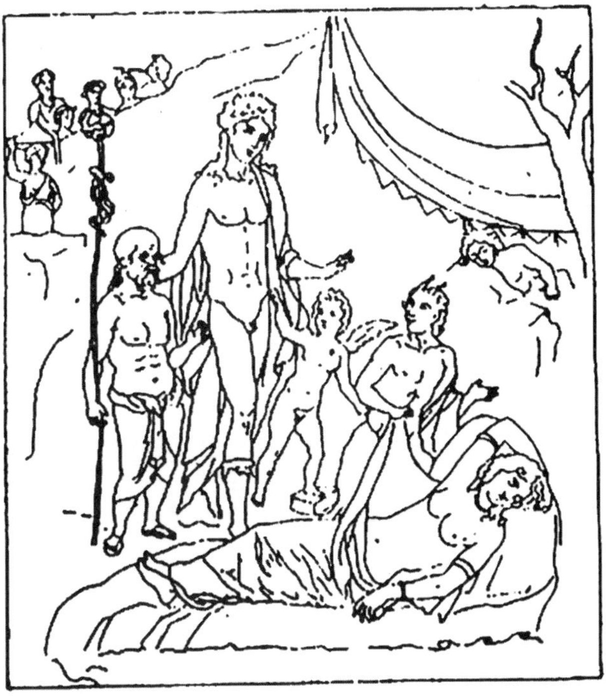

Dionysus and his retinue discovering Ariadne sleeping, in S. Reinach 1970

her lover's life? He abandoned her. You know about the tears of Ariadne and her despair.[5]

Here we see Ariadne, abandoned on the banks of the Naxos, where she has finally fallen asleep, having cried all her tears. The subject is again an encounter between a man and a woman. And again it is a tragedy, the tragedy of an abused and then abandoned woman.

Except that here, the man approaching the girl is not Hercules, as in Herculaneum or in the Vettii house. This is not a warrior thirsty for wine and victory. It is Dionysus, a totally different character from Greek and Latin mythology. We recognize this beardless, handsome youth, rather feminine in attitude, accompanied by a retinue of Pans, more or less youthful, playful and bestial. One of them is holding the thyrsus, the fennel staff associated with Dionysus.

This Dionysus is not going to force himself upon the woman, the way Hercules did. We know—as did all the contemporaries of these paintings—that quite on the contrary, the sight of the beautiful sleeping woman will arouse his love. He will take her to Olympus, the home of the gods and, according to the myth, will marry her in due form. So the story of Ariadne, abandoned by the traitor Theseus, ends happily. It is even said that she and Dionysus had three children.

In this way, the brutality of Auge's rape by Hercules, leading to the exposure of the infant Telephus on the mountainside is answered by the ideally restoring story of Ariadne, found by Dionysus, who then married her on Olympus.

Poor Auge with her terrified eyes and divided gesture—with one hand she defends herself against Hercules, yet she is already on the ground—is hurried into tragedy by the violence of the almost parallel diagonal lines we can see in this painting. Whereas Ariadne, who has also been abused and abandoned, has wept bitterly and is now sleeping, dreaming of the ideal happiness that awaits her, a dream that will finally be fulfilled by gentle Dionysus.

Now we can see what the fresco in Herculaneum contains, in suspension. We can see, or perceive, what creates its suspense: the composition and structural dynamic of this painting contain, in an enigmatic but pressing way, two scenes at the same time: the rape of Auge and the rescue of Ariadne by Dionysus.

Now we can see "Arcadia," the woman who we call "Arcadia," also becoming Auge and Ariadne. This Arcadia, reclining with her eyes wide open, gazing at the man approaching her, and at the same time drawn into herself, her body barred by the staff that cuts off this encounter, knows, or at least shows us, through the painting, that she is both Auge and Ariadne. Auge faces a tragic fate: rape, banishment, exile. But as Ariadne, she dreams of the ideal fulfillment of her dream on Olympus. This Arcadia is also Auge. And she is also Ariadne through the painting.

The strength of the painting in Herculaneum, its creative strength, is that it both covers and encloses the Pompeian scenes; yes, it contains them. Freud would say that it condenses them—here Freud uses the evocative German word "*Verdichtung*," which means that we are confronted by a complex, composite, layered reality, each layer of which covers and includes the others.[6]

The creative strength of this work is to remain enigmatic, to remain in suspension, to keep us in suspense so that at first glance we do not know all that it has to show us. But now we can perceive it. And more importantly we experience it. We experience the terribly dramatic and equally ideal eroticism of this scene.

The two other interpretations of the painting, that it illustrated a well-known myth, or that it served to support the cult of the emperor, did not explain it fully. This painting evidently has a quite different strength, a quite different quality, and a different range. Here we are not dealing with anecdotes, with what has been said and known before. I have just mentioned "condensation." We must go one step further. I would call this work symbolic. On many levels, its strength and uncanny composition make us see, perceive, and most importantly experience, both what we want and do not want to know about relationships between a man and a woman, between a woman and a man.

We live the tragedy and the dream of this woman who is at the same time Arcadia, Auge, and Ariadne—an Arcadia-Auge-Ariadne who is no longer only made up of distant characters, cast in mythological narrative space, but close to us, ourselves as we are today, strangely close to us, to the scenes, tragedies, and dreams of our everyday lives.

For such is the strength of symbolic life. This strength, which touches us, is a questioning force—and first, an enigmatic questioning.

From Freud to Jung

Our approach to this work has gradually progressed from Freudian psychoanalysis, with the idea of "condensation," to Jungian psychoanalysis, with the concept of "symbolic life."

We passed from observing the work of condensation brought about by this painting, to the live perception of a scene, at first enigmatic, but actually highly charged with emotion.

Freud showed us the way, and led us to Jung—as is often the case in the clinical practice of psychoanalysis as well.[7] Let's move forward in this direction, because this work begs for more understanding. Other decisive elements of composition and effect deserve analysis.

First, this surprising figure of Hercules, usually, in Pompeii, Stabiae, and Herculaneum, is depicted in his role as a conqueror, often violent, always hurried, rushing from one victory to another with the ardor of a gladiator.

Yet here he is, with a woman in front of him, and he is not tackling her. Quite the opposite, amazingly, we see him stop in his tracks. What could have made the hero Hercules pause, immersed in thought?

The painting answers this question: the winged young woman, pointing to Telephus, is what brings Hercules to a halt. She is the one who intervenes in the encounter between the man and the woman, an encounter that may turn out badly, as it did between Hercules and poor Auge.

So who is this winged young woman? Scholars of Greek and Roman mythology claim they can identify her. The Greeks call her Parthenos, and the Romans call her Virgo. In other words, she is the Virgin. A figure, a character that was so revered at the time that they made a kind of angel of her, and cast her up into the heavens, so that she became a constellation of stars known today as Virgo, the constellation of the Virgin.

The Virgin of Greek and Roman mythology is a strong presence in this painting. Her features and skin are lovely, and the spray of grain in the crook of her arm is promising. But she is still above the others. What is this "virgin" doing here?

Not only does she stay Hercules from an act of violence like rape, but with her diagonal gesture, insistent and gently authoritarian, it is she who leads his, and our, attention to the doe and child.

This scene of the doe and child is an event in the art of the era. It is no doubt the most successful and accomplished, and the happiest scene in this painting. This is the scene that so enthralled Goethe during his travels in Italy. It is like a painting within the painting. Have you ever seen a picture that represents sensation and emotion so accurately, the happiness of the perfectly confident, mutual, circular bond between child and doe, or doe and child?[8]

We have been told that Hercules recognized his son Telephus in Arcadia. That was rather abstract. Here, truly, he looks at, and discovers this child, his own son. In recognizing the boy, perhaps he recognizes himself, as a child. Possibly—who knows?—now that he is touched by this shared tenderness, this reciprocal attention made manifest by the painting, Hercules goes so far as to remember what he experienced as a child.[9]

Could this doe be something other than prey for this hunter? For this man, this hero, could a woman be something other than an Auge he wants to rape? Is it possible to experience an encounter in such a relationship to the other, in such a confident and tenderly reciprocal relationship as that manifested here between the child and the doe?

It is the young woman behind his head who leads him this far—this Virgo, this Virgin. She causes him to pause; she speaks to him, and he listens. Her power transforms him, so thoroughly that he comes to forget to behave like a hunter, warrior, or gladiator. He not only leaves his weapons slung over his shoulder, but what is more, he forgets the eagle and the lion—the insignia of his strength. They sit at his feet, rather frightened and useless. The quality of the artistic rendering of this part of the scene, with the animals, is noticeably inferior to that of the other figures and objects in the painting.

We may even wonder if this figure, this feminine presence, this girl or young woman, might not be a beautiful representation, a beautiful discovery in the painting of what Jung will call *the anima*—this presence, this voice of the feminine inside us, who would like to reach us from our own childhood, and to whom we often fail to listen.[10]

In its own way, does this painting not make us see, perceive, understand, and, ultimately, experience what Jung will teach us, two thousand years later?

But who is that behind the lady's head?

Look once again at the painting. There is something else for us to see and perceive in this work. What on Earth is that behind Arcadia's head? A funny, fuzzy, half-wild creature is playing the pipes, apparently enjoying himself and mocking the whole scene.

The mythologists will tell us that this half-human, half-wild creature is a young Pan. Pan, as we know, is a peculiar god, or demon. In Latin he is often called *niger* (black), *rusticus* (rustic, crude), *lubricus* (lustful), *nocturnus* (nocturnal). They say he is always ready to poke any girl, or even a goat. Here we cannot see them, but we know that he has cloven hooves.[11]

Arcadia-Auge-Ariadne is consorting with this devil of a Pan, just behind her head. She may even be lending him an indulgent ear. Who knows what the demonic creature is whispering! She is pretending she does not know him. But we can see that she is nonetheless very close to him.

This painting shows us that Arcadia-Auge-Ariadne is close to this Pan—this *animus*, we might say, with Jung. Here, we find a clue to the hidden, intimate complicity this woman has with the man she seemingly defends herself against.[12] As if despite her shy grand lady air, secretly, deep down, this woman had been awaiting the man in front of her—even though he might show himself to be a bit brutal, a bit wild, and, who knows, even a bit bestial. Possibly, this Arcadia-Auge-Ariadne is not as innocent as she likes to appear. At least, her dreams are perhaps less than innocent.

Decidedly, our amplification of this painting has taught us a lot, long before Freud and Jung, about what can go on in the background of an encounter between a woman and a man, between a man and a woman.

From prehistory to this story

Savage life and animality are ever-present in this scene. As we know, Hercules had a history of deliberate brutality. As for Pan of the cloven hooves, his presence is discreet but curiously insistent. Indeed, he seems to be pulling the strings of the drama as it unfolds.

But the violence remains in the background. It emerges only by association and amplification, as if kept at a distance, as if held in respect—at least apparently. Since the times of the hunters-gatherers of the prehistory, the question has therefore changed significantly. The relationship, the encounter with the woman, with the women, and more precisely the relationship between a woman and a man, a man and a woman, is now in the foreground.

We humans have come a long way. Now the question is considerably closer. It has been considerably humanized. Under cover of mythological figures—"Arcadia" and "Hercules"—creatures who are really human, really a woman and a man, are directly and clearly being made to act out a story.

Nevertheless, violence lurks here, more or less contained. Violence is a key presence in this scene, this story from Roman times. The composition of the painting tries to make us aware that now, there is really a debate between the undercurrent of violence, on the one hand, and, on the other, the ideal dream of a perfect and celestial gentleness and virginity that one might wish to cultivate, the dream of the innocence of a child.

Just for fun

Let's now play a little game. It consists of asking yourself a simple question. If you were one of the figures in this scene, who would you be? Dream a little. Where do you stand? What do you see?

Are you the woman, Arcadia-Auge-Ariadne, being approached by the man? Or are you the man, Hercules, the armed hunter advancing, but brought to a halt? Or are you Virgo, above it all, in the sky? Perhaps you are the touching child, tiny, fragile, vulnerable, and yet confident, protected by the maternal doe?

Maybe you see yourself as Pan, this odd, unsettling devil, the trickster whispering God-knows-what to Ariadne.

Or perhaps, like many art historians, you believe that this work is simply a painting glorifying the city of Herculaneum and the Emperor Vespasian?

Play a little. You may find the game worthwhile. Your answer may surprise you—if it is spontaneous and immediate enough, unplanned, uncontrolled, uncensored. Your intellect will only interfere with your discovery of yourself. You may find something you never expected.

The male reader might not necessarily identify with Hercules. You may see yourself as an entirely different character in the scene. Women, if you recognize yourself as "Arcadia," ask yourself if you are sure you accept that playful rascal Pan, perched right behind you, almost touching your hair. The questions demand that our considerations about the painting account for the differentiation we make today between sex and gender. In its own way, the painting demonstrably differentiates between the two. We would have to review our approach to the "anima" and "animus."

From one chapter to the next in this book, we may be led closer to ourselves, closer to the most faraway and yet most intimate parts of our nature. Gaining this insight is one of the purposes of this research.

3

Whatever Happened to Paradise?

This essay will explore the painting that hangs in the Städelsches Kunstinstitut in Frankfurt, Germany. Created in the southern part of Germany, the painting is attributed to an "Upper Rhinish Master" whose name has been forgotten. It dates from around 1410–20; that is, the "international gothic" period in European art history of European art.[1]

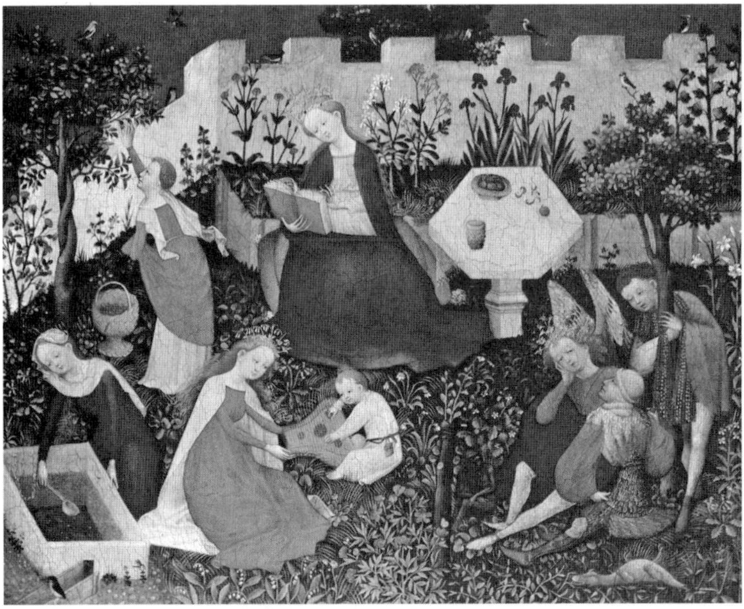

Paradiesgärtlein (Garden of Paradise)

The painting is a small tempera on wood, only slightly wider than two hands, measuring approximately 10 by 13 inches (26.3 × 33.4 cm). If you are strolling through the Frankfurt museum and can allow yourself to be drawn to a particular painting, your attention will surely be riveted by this particular one. The liveliness and richness of its colors and the precise harmony of its composition cause it to stand out from the surrounding masterpieces.

An initial approach: the scene

The painting's scene appears to be happy, ideal, and soothing. To all appearances, it promises every simple pleasure. What gives the painting strength and makes us pause before it, is that despite this apparent innocence, it is stubbornly enigmatic, and thus becomes strangely disturbing to anyone who lingers before it very long.

The painter has depicted the corner of a garden, apparently protected by walls, inhabited by various human figures, flowers, and birds. The scene is provided for the viewer's contemplation, as if he or she were looking down upon it. If our eye wanders at a leisurely pace, it will gradually make the round of the human figures contained by the garden wall, one by one. Each figure is exactly where she or he belongs, so absorbed in the appropriate pose as to be quite tangibly present. Yet each of these people is curiously absent as well.

A woman dressed in red is picking cherries, which she collects in a fold of her robe before transferring them to the wicker basket at her feet. A second woman, in blue, is drawing water from a fountain. Meanwhile, a third, also in red, is seated on the grass with her back to the other two. She is playing with a baby, who sits on the grass facing her. A Renaissance string instrument, a psaltery, is between them.

Only after surveying all three women does the viewer's eye likely reach the central figure, draped in an ample blue robe and cape. Her crowned head is bent, reading a book, in the heart of this garden. Could it be Mary? This, we are told, is a *Garden of Paradise*, according to the title. In such a setting, this is indeed Mary; it is a representation of her in her eternal beatitude.

But why should she be holding a book? Is there in this heavenly

Eden a library available to the saintly, from which they can borrow books and read about their tribulations in the world below? Moreover, the garden is so inherently earthly that one begins to wonder if the female figure might not be Eve in Paradise before the Fall, instead of Mary in her eternal glory. But whoever heard of an Eve clothed in robes and a crown, in the company of other women, reading? Perhaps it is the Virgin Mary, after all, depicted at that special moment when she is awaiting the fate the angels are about to announce, a fate which is already inscribed—that Mary is going to be pregnant?

Maybe Eve or Mary? But why choose one or the other? Instead, allow the gaze to float. Assume the enigma. In clinical practice, before searching for answers, analysts must learn to accept the enigmatic pressure of a representation, its mystery, in order to grasp the slippery, living reality hidden in the questions it raises. The surprise effect, the astonishment aroused by unexpected ambiguities, is also a valuable guide. Whether we are looking at a painting or listening to a story, attention to the surprise effect and cultivating a taste for the unexpected remain our best ways of noticing a singular event. In this case when, as in analysis, we make the Jungian turn toward amplification, the feature will be easier to grasp if we proceed by comparison. We will begin, then, by associating this painting with others that are assumed to be similar to it.[2]

The closest Garden

What flowered, fenced-in garden most closely resembles our painting by virtue of its structure and place in history? To my knowledge, it would be a work found in the Castelvecchio Museum of Verona, attributed to Stefano di Verona.

This *Madonna of the Rose Garden* is thought to have been painted in 1410; that is, either at the same time as or immediately before the painting that hangs in Frankfurt. In Verona, as in Frankfurt, the viewer's gaze looks down on a scene where a woman in a great blue cloak occupies a place of honor amid a profusion of flowers and birds. And, again as in Frankfurt, our eye travels around the center of the composition and then returns to that center, feeling contained by the fence of the garden, on which various species of birds are perched.

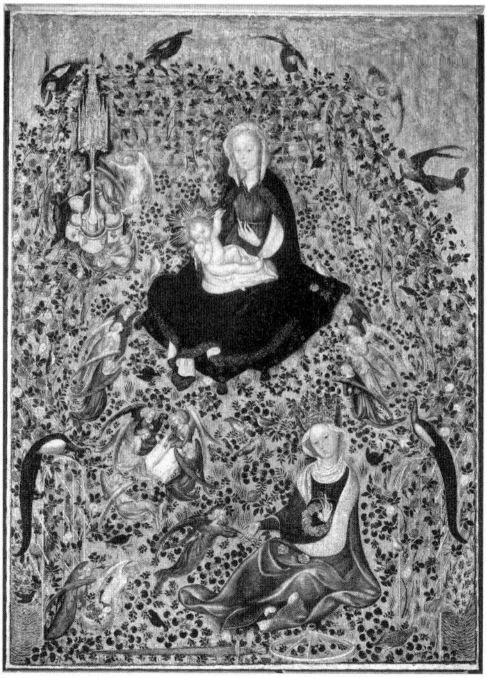

Madonna of the Rose Garden

As in Frankfurt, the viewer of the Verona masterpiece wonders about the contrast of blue and red in the clothing of the female figures: blue over red for the central figure; red over blue for the smaller female figure that mirrors her attitude from a lower part of the picture. Here, too, a fountain is an important element in the background.

Yet the difference between the two paintings is striking. Both are painted according to the same structural organization and obey, in appearance, the same representational pattern: that is, a *hortus conclusus*, a closed garden in which a worldly Virgin is the central figure. But the lives of these two Virgins are quite different.

Our move from Frankfurt to Verona, from Germany to Italy, is quite a change of milieu, and it suggests a change of protagonist. In Verona, the woman ruling over the painting is undeniably the Virgin-Madonna of Christian myth, reigning over the golden trappings of eternity and surrounded by angels. Her "worldliness" is her instinctive understanding of her authority, which is really not of this world. In Frankfurt, however, this woman is a crowned noblewoman, who, although still dressed in blue, may simply be strolling in the garden adjoining her castle, reading a book. As a result, her relationship with the flowers, fruits, and music, and especially with the women surrounding her in multiple mirror images of herself, is quite different—more immediately fleshly and animated by another spirit.

A single detail conveys the degree of the change, as contained in the transformation of an important structural motive. Look at the fountain. In Verona, the fountain is shown as a golden piece of liturgical jewelry, borne up by angels. In Frankfurt, it is concretely located on the ground, within reach, like a well, with a ladle conveniently chained to it.

A fountain recurs in so much medieval art as the Fountain of Youth or the Fountain of Mercury. Here it is depicted as functional; it can be used. The viewer thinks, even I myself, standing at the edge of the painting, might be able to see myself in its waters. Instead of transcendence supported by faith, and therefore the uplift of heavenward religious transport, there is another type of communication entirely—a woman beckoning from the lower part of the painting, at my eye level: this is an invitation that might even be addressed to me as I am.

From farther away

If we now step back and place a little more distance between us and the two paintings we are comparing, our eye will note of a distinctive change in the dominant hue between one painting and the other. Between Verona and Frankfurt, it changes from gold to green. In Verona, we are still quite close to the art of Ravenna, and, therefore, to the icons and frescoes of Byzantine art, which are always on a golden ground. From early Christian times, these gold-authorized role models have gazed down on us from their position high on the altar, and high in the dogmatic, gold-standard teachings of the Church. Despite the modem concept of "projection" to explain the authority we invest in such images, the pictorial evidence insists that, quite to the contrary, the figures represented there held and maintained us beneath the authorized power of their gaze for centuries.[3]

In 1410–20, however, both in the painting from Verona, and even more so in the one from Frankfurt, the viewpoints have been reversed. Now the scene is at eye level, so that we are viewing it from just slightly above. What do we discover? An open, animated scene, inhabited by multiple figures, making it so human that it almost seems as if we could walk into it; a field that, in passing from gold to green, transports us from a transcendent, eternal Beyond, existing outside time, to a garden space of immanent, available spirit.

From the sacred to the profane

Already in the Verona Madonna, the Virgin Mary of Christian myth, wrapped in the traditional great blue cloak covering her red robes, and strangely pensive and sad, the way a Pietà might be, has acquired a twin in the lower part of the painting. Closer to us, a more human figure, this twin is garbed in red over blue, and we recognize her according to her traditional attributes, the wheel and the sword. She is Catherine of Alexandria, a young woman known to have been martyred as a virgin in the first centuries of the Christian era, who was later made the patron saint of unmarried girls.

Both Virgins are represented in all their glory and celebrated in accordance with tradition. They appear fated to meet with a Passion that is nearing, with pain that is exemplary and still from afar, but which now better approximates human experience. In Frankfurt, the central subject of this new experience-near-fate for the feminine is even closer to us than she is in Verona, and visible in even greater detail. Certainly the noblewoman in blue is still in the center of the scene, but now who can say with certainty whether this so humanized Mary is really Mary, or the original Eve of Christian myth?

Who are the women surrounding her? What is their purpose in this garden, which is no longer what it was in Verona, where it was so clearly a mystical Rose Garden? A Catholic viewer can easily recognize Saint Dorothy on Eve-Mary's right, picking cherries, since Dorothy is the patron saint of gardeners. The woman drawing water from the well would be Martha, known throughout Catholic iconography for the role she plays in the New Testament, in the life of another Mary other than the Savior's mother. Meanwhile, Saint Cecilia, the patron saint of musicians, is in accord with this tradition presenting the psaltery to a babe who might be the Infant Jesus.

Such a conventional reading of the painting can be a comfort. In fact, I do not doubt that most of the artist's contemporaries were content to see it in this way. But why, if we allow ourselves the gloss of the Verona painting, should Catherine of Alexandria proliferate as a Dorothy, a Martha, and a Cecilia sometimes in red, sometimes in blue? What has led the painter to incorporate such a marked alternation of red and blue?

It is not possible for me, with my Catholic background, to be unaware that although Martha, who is an ordinary girl, may be clothed in blue the way the Virgin Mary is traditionally shown, Dorothy, who is in red here, is a martyr, and Cecilia, who is also in red, was decapitated, as was Catherine of Alexandria. The tragic history of these virgin-martyrs, as a counter-point to the traditional celebration of Mary's virginity, is meant to tinge our sojourn in this supposedly paradisiacal garden with a note of the world's sorrow.

The garden, in fact, deserves to be looked at a little more closely. As if in analogy to the now markedly halo-less heads of Dorothy, Martha, and Cecilia, another detail that brings them closer to the most familiar, most secular human universe, the garden itself is such a far cry from a mystical, allegorical Rose Garden that it could almost be taken for a botanical garden, that is, a scholastic Aristotelian display of the genera of Flora.

I have asked myself what flowers and what fruits were represented here. It was possible to make a horticulturally accurate inventory of them, to identify each species. As might be expected, each of these species has its own particular function in the allegorical celebration of the Virginity of Mary. Amid this inventory, there is one rather singular plant worthy of note.

If one peruses the circle of female figures that extends to the child playing the psaltery and begins again with the woman in blue I have suggested we call Eve-Mary, we find, at the foot of the table lain at her side, a green plant with fuzzy leaves, presenting the following particularity: it is bearing fruit while still in blossom.

Incarnation as a flower

Flower and fruit at the same time is a concise and eloquent symbol for the difficult concept of the promise that is simultaneously its fulfillment, a fulfillment that certainly seems to be offered for consumption.

This Christian prospect is certainly an attractive one, a dream still powerful enough to inspire faith in dreams. It is also a wish that is as consummately ideal, and as counter to natural expectation, as that of an Immaculate Conception, or a Virgin Birth. What is more, the fulfillment of the dream is not located in some timeless and transcendent Beyond, or reserved only for a select group of exceptional people. It is within our reach, in close proximity to the senses, arousing appetite and desire.

The painter's paradise has become so earthly, the dream so arable, and the flowers and fruits so ripe for ready enjoyment, that even though this particular strawberry plant may have been intended as a traditional celebration of the Virgin Mary, its presence here surpasses any role it might be playing as an allegorical symbol. Here it is a real living symbol offered up to the delectation and astonished questioning of a fifteenth-century humanism still in its early years.

The taste for symbol

As soon as one takes note of the discreet, nearly hidden presence of the strawberry plant in the heart of the scene, and as soon as one has made oneself attentive to this conjunction of flower and fruit, so seemingly innocent and botanically correct, yet so seductively appetizing, we perceive the painting in a new way.

Now the painting arouses our fantasy-senses and our vision is enhanced. We experience—rather than simply see—Dorothy reaching for the cherries, the taste of the water Martha is drawing from the fountain, the sound of the music from the psaltery that Cecilia is holding, and the fragrance of the flowers and the fruits in the garden as a whole, all without any clear knowledge of what we are experiencing. A symbol is alive inasmuch as it convinces the person who experiences it to live, in a way that previously had escaped him or her. It is then up to the subject of a symbolic experience, like the viewer of this painting, to recognize and explain what is going on with that symbol.[4]

The newcomers

What about the presence and purpose of the group of male figures? The men form a group of three, apparently a trio working toward a shared goal. Although one of them may be wearing a halo of flowers, like Cecilia, and a pair of wings even more brilliant than those of the angels of Verona, it is difficult to see them as seraphim, or members of the chorus in some celestial Hosannah.

With my understanding of Catholic iconography, I can recognize the figure on the left as Saint Michael, with Saint George facing him and Saint Lawrence standing near the tree—the latter especially recognizable because of the checkered pattern on his scarf.

As in many paintings, the Satan-defeating Archangel is flanked by two Holy Martyrs. Here, however, this trio is dressed in the latest fashion of the day. This detail, arriving on the scene in 1410 or 1420, obviously is meant to make the scene contemporary, and perhaps that might be the artist's indication that the Christian message should be seen as relevant to his time.

But the mood is so contemporary that their saintly histories have faded into oblivion. Saint George's terrifying dragon has been reduced to a lizard basking, belly up in the sun, while Satan is present in the form of a dark monkey lurking under the flowers and fruits of the strawberry plant.

It is also a shock to see George, Michael, and Lawrence included, or at least waiting to be included, in this "*Garden of Paradise*." Never until now had men entered such a *hortus conclusus*, literally "enclosed garden," or the garden of the body of feminine integrity, which must be kept closed to celebrate Mary's Virginity.

What are these men doing here? What sort of relationship, or non-relationship, links them to Dorothy, Martha, and Cecilia?

The answer to this gendered spiritual question lies in the composition of the scene. The two groups—the group of three women and the group of three men—are placed on either side of a table.

This is another previously unfamiliar compositional element in the usual closed-garden motif; the mystical *Rose Garden* of Verona certainly did not contain a table. This table is clearly an invitation to enjoy.

Its vertical line leads the eye to the flowering and fruiting strawberry plant and Satan depicted as a dark monkey lurking underneath. The table mediates a relationship between the group of women and the group of men, while simultaneously keeping them chastely apart.

Moreover, the vertical line consisting of the table, strawberry plant, and Satan is reinforced by a second vertical line, the one formed by the woman in blue and the infant who are busy making music in the grass.

These two vertical lines serve to separate the women and the men. The first, on the men's side, is about enjoyment, conveyed by the table and the strawberry plant, but it is also about sin, symbolized by the dark presence of the monkey Satan. The second line, which is central, associated with the women, represents the virgin birth of a child, which takes place miraculously, without any need for a man to participate in the conception.

How will these men and women ever overcome these barriers and meet?

The scene thus remains in suspense, heightened by the fact that nothing seems to trouble the women's serenity: each is as perfectly whole and sufficient unto herself as the fruit tree whose interlacing limbs seem to form a self-containing embrace.

Could this be the key to the perplexity of the warrior George, the Archangel Michael, and Lawrence, the newcomers waiting on the edge of the painting?

Michael, in particular, seems to be affected. Sitting with his head resting on his hand, his expression thoughtful, gazing out at us—almost as though he were trying to come up with answers to our own questions—his pose is so striking, so expressive to us today, that one is tempted to describe it as melancholy.[5]

We are definitely no longer in the happy period when Mary's Virginity could innocently be celebrated. The mystical *Rose Garden* of still medieval Verona is far removed from the strange and troubling tension of this supposedly paradisiacal tableau.

Michael, who was an Angel for so long—even an Archangel—may have very good reasons to be pensive, if he is reflecting mournfully on the happy time of Christian myth, which is now past. It is as if we can hear his thoughts at this pivotal moment in history.

What can be done? How does one go on from here? The question is rendered all the more insistent by the fact that the strongest line of tension in this scene consists of the gaze George the dragon-slayer is directing at Eve-Mary still in blue, who, absorbed in her book, seems to be impervious to it.

From one story to another

In the same way that we compared the Verona *Rose Garden* to the garden of Frankfurt, we will now consider another painting, from a period markedly later. It dates from 1483, nearly seventy-five years later, when the fateful fifteenth century was ending.

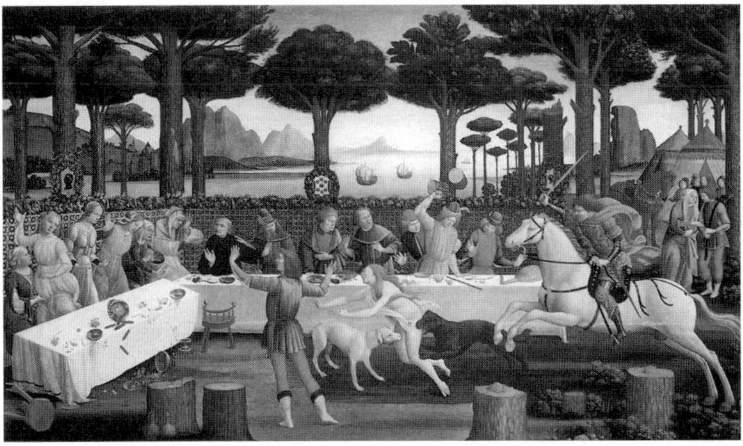

The Story of Nastagio Degli Dnesti (The Banquet in the Pine Forest)

This painting is in tempera on wood, measuring 83 × 138 cm (32 by 54 inches), and it currently hangs in Madrid's El Prado museum. Part of a series of four paintings, it decorated a Florentine room from the time of the Medicis.[6]

This work is yet another closed garden, emphasized by the wall of green in the background of the scene, and the table placement, which forms an angle.

But it is impossible to mistake this garden for the traditional Christian Paradise, or even the doomed Garden of Eden. The background is the only thing in common.

In this case, the scene exposed to us in this garden is unexpected, violent, and raw: a hunting scene, where the quarry is a woman.

Consider the question this sequence of paintings invites: which of the three men, George, Michael, or Lawrence, has risen, mounted a horse, and is now engaged in a chase, sword held high and cape flying in the wind?[7]

The quarry of the hunt is unmistakably a woman, for she is nude, and cries out in pain as she is bitten by two furious dogs, one black and one white, while the horseman pursuing her is about to attack her and stab her with his hateful weapon.

This is a notion that would have left the "Rhinish Master" who painted the *Garden of Paradise* in Frankfurt aghast, and would have seemed worse yet to Stefano di Verona, painter of the *Madonna of the Rose Garden.* The scene had been laid out for a genteel Renaissance celebration, the women on one side and the men on the other, with a priest in the middle, all dressed in their Quattrocento party finery.

The story represented here is a wedding party, and the painting itself was commissioned as a wedding gift from Lorenzo de Medici to a young Florentine noblewoman.

But the musical harmony of the group has abruptly been broken. The men have been frightened out of their poise, and the women are rising hurriedly, jostling one another and upsetting the table that had been placed in front of them, spilling the dishes and platters of food. The musicians have dropped their instruments, the flute, lute, and tambourine, or flung them away. The delightful music of the psaltery in the garden in Frankfurt is now irretrievably gone.

Assuming that the savage horseman is related in some way to George, Michael, and Lawrence of Frankfurt, where does the naked woman come from, devoid of any resemblance to a Virgin in blue? What could possibly have led to such a revolution, to such a subversion of Paradise?

This painting is the product of a tradition preceding the Christian one. The artist is Sandro Botticelli, the Botticelli, who though well acquainted with Christian Madonnas, is better known to us for exalting the Venus and Flora of Greek and Roman tradition. Indeed, his bride-to-be rising behind the banquet table could almost be related to the Venus he painted that same year, gazing insistently at a sleeping Mars.

The nude woman being pursued could be a cousin of the Flora who in his painting of the preceding year, 1482, greets the goddess Venus Anadyomene, or the nearly nude Venus being pursued by Zephyr, the West Wind, in the famous painting *Spring* of 1477.

In the sequence of "garden" paintings we have quickly compared here, we can see that the Virgin Mary of Christian myth has entered a setting in which Flora and Venus are at liberty to gambol, and the change in her surroundings certainly suggests other attitudes toward the male–female encounter than the separation imposed by the notion of virgin birth and sinless redemption.

The frame and the organizing motive of the three works we have seen up until now is still that of the closed garden built around a woman. What, then, is the source of the brutal and inherently bestial lust unleashed here in the final painting of our arbitrary series? The scene must certainly have been a surprise to the young newlyweds

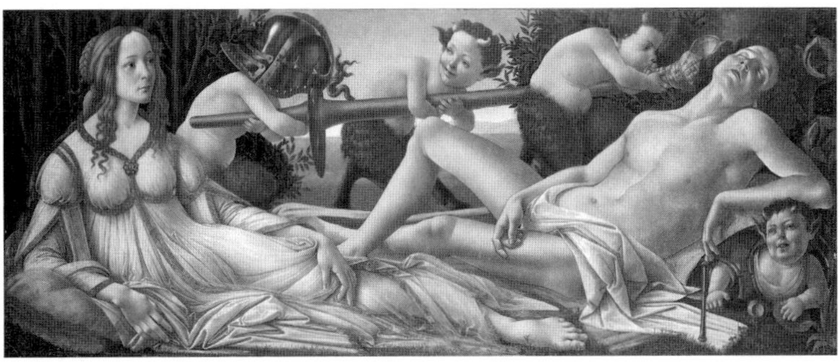

Venus and Mars

who received the painting as a wedding gift, and it may also have surprised Sandro Botticelli himself, when he realized he would have to paint it.

A similar context, but an altogether different story

To get a better understanding of what is happening in Botticelli's painting, it is important to know that the story illustrated in it is a very old Italian story. In 1483, it had been circulating for at least 130 years. Our Eve/Mary in the Frankfurt garden painting might even have been reading it, given her cosmopolitanism, for it was set down by Boccaccio in about 1352, in his *Decameron.* In that book, a noblewoman tells the story to a group of her peers, in the comfortable, worldly context of free exchanges.

In the narrated story, a noble heiress is so proud of herself and her high birth that she wishes to have absolutely nothing to do with the men around her. Naturally, one of these men falls in love with her and tries to seduce her, but she remains impervious to his advances. So disturbed is he by the beauty's disdain that he soon loses himself in melancholy wandering and ends up committing suicide.

As punishment for his act of violence against himself, he is condemned to a Hell where he must perpetuate the hunt for the woman. This is an infernal hunt to which the narcissistic beauty must also submit her own body, her punishment for haughtiness.

This terrible, ironic tale had already been circulating for seventy years before the *Garden of Paradise* of Frankfurt was painted, and it was often told in Italy, playfully, to incite women to be looser and more open to men.

It was this story that Botticelli, at the request of Lorenzo de Medici, turned into the visionary painting that was presented as a gift to a pair of young Tuscan newlyweds.[8]

With this work from 1483, are we not as far as possible from a Christian paradise? Are we not looking at the most violent compensation that can be imagined, at the most violent and savage counterpart to the Northern Christian ideal of the eternal, unassailable Virginity of Mary?

And yet, is this not the revelation on the brink of erupting in their own garden that Dorothy, Mary, and Cecilia are trying to keep to themselves as they sat at Eve-Mary's side in view of the men?

And is this dreadful possibility not the same thing that is holding Michael, George, and Lawrence immobile in melancholy perplexity?

It would seem that a hellish confrontation between the sexes is what these women and these men, who have been saints for so long, are poised to keep in suspense as long as possible, to preserve their paradisiacal harmony.

The crux of this tension might be the inability to find a smooth transition from absolute, whole, undivided love, ideal love whose enjoyment leads to martyrdom or suicide, to the bodily consummation, or incarnation, of love.

For a long time, Christianized Europeans believed, or were taught to believe, that such an incarnation had occurred in the early decades of the Christian era, which were mythical times.

The evidence of our eyes, however, suggests it happened between 1410 and 1420 and the end of the fifteenth century, when Christian iconography made the passage from gold to green and the relationship between blue and red was inverted.

At this time a viewpoint inversion also occurred. Our position changed from one beneath the gaze of the Holy Figures to one at eye level or above, which meant we had to confront the scene of increasingly diverse and increasingly profane contradictory urges animating and agitating each and every one of us, man and woman alike.

With particular eloquence, and in a nearly visionary way, *Quattrocento* painting expressed these contradictory urges and tensions, which are still present in us. Even before we learned to recognize them in closer proximity to us, it showed them as permanent inner realities.

I would like to thank John Beebe for the valuable advice as I was writing this essay, originally published in the San Francisco Jung Institute Library Journal.

⟨ 4 ⟩

From Dürer to Cranach

MELANCHOLY IN BLACK AND RED

Approaching another era in our collective history, the *Garden of Paradise* hanging in Frankfurt and the *Story of Nastagio degli Onesti*, from the Decameron, painted by Botticelli, drew our attention to the transformations under way in the late Middle Ages and at the dawn of the Italian Renaissance. The works we are now going to discuss—an engraving by Dürer and a painting by Cranach—date from the first decades of the sixteenth century, times that were also a period of decisive scientific, social, and cultural transformation, perhaps more radical than any transformation we have experienced since.

The twentieth and twenty-first centuries have brought, and continue to bring, enormous changes in our relationships to the world and ourselves. As yet, it is still too early to measure their scope and impact.

We will consider these works from the early sixteenth century alongside some of the transformations under way in light of those we have experienced ourselves, since the first decades of the twentieth century.

This reflection begins with an initial observation. It is somewhat melancholic: psychoanalysis isn't the way it used to be.

In 1911 psychoanalysis was still brand new. This is the Third International Congress of Psychoanalysis. We are all fairly familiar with this family portrait.

Nearly everyone is in his or her place. Sigmund Freud, the found-

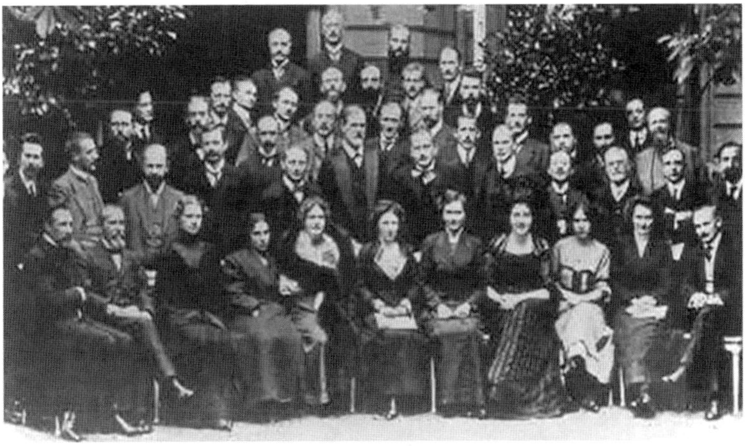

The congress at Weimar

ing father of psychoanalysis, is in the center. Because he is a short man, he stands on a stool for the picture. To his right, slightly beneath him, we can see Sándor Ferenczi. Otto Rank and Ludwig Binswanger are in the same row, on the far left. On the far right, Ernest Jones stands next to Wilhelm Steckel. The ladies are seated in the front row: Lou Andreas Salomé is the one with the boa. Emma Jung is two seats to her right, and Toni Wolff another two seats over. Sabina Spielrein is absent.[1]

Carl Gustav Jung flanks Freud to the left. But, oddly enough, he is leaning forward, as if eager to get out of the frame.

The first decade of the twentieth century was a time of hope and lively creativity, especially in the arts.[2] It was also the time of the first discoveries and early development of psychoanalysis, its most lively, productive, and promising debates.

Then, it was possible to think that psychoanalysis would provide reasons, perspectives, a method, or at least modern reference points, a specific, certain and agreed-upon matrix to help each of us in our relationships. Religions had largely lost their credibility in this domain. In their task of helping us to know ourselves better through our relationships with ourselves, with that which is beyond us, and with others, it seems they were even largely disqualified.

For quite some time, these expectations and hopes placed in psychoanalysis had been dashed, or at the very least muddled. When and why?

As early as 1911–12, precisely when the Congress in Weimar was organized—the congress that gave rise to the historical family photo we just saw.

Jung discovered the writings of a nineteen-year-old American woman called Miss Miller. She was torn between her amorous emotions, a desire to plunge headlong into life, and her attachment to her mother, her family, her past, and her childhood. The writings consisted of a few poems accompanied by dreamy reflections, a few fantasies, and a visionary drama that she had compiled in a state of altered consciousness, between sleep and wakefulness.

Here we see Jung up close. Everyone expected this young man to follow the path that Freud had noted in his *Three Essays on the Theory of Sexuality,* written in Vienna five years earlier. Jung could have embarked on an exploration of Miss Miller's childhood in an effort to understand her difficulties, and her dilemma in adulthood.

Rather than trying to gather information on this young woman's childhood and thus know her better, Jung, on the contrary, threw

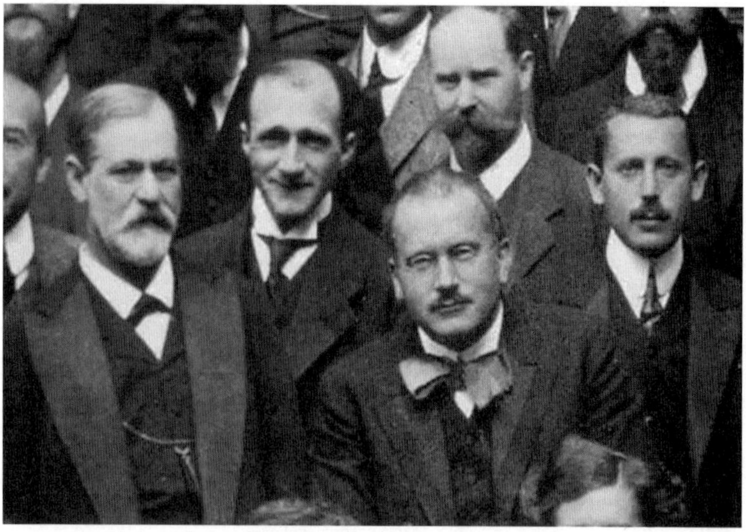

Sigmund Freud, Carl Jung, and Alfred Adler

himself into an abundant and passionate investigation into all sorts of myths, rituals, and works of art: Greek, Roman, Hindu, Christian, and even Scandinavian. However, the material Jung studied shared one common characteristic: its subject was incest, sacrifice, and returning to the mother.

This was a complete change of scale. It involved going from the reflection on an individual's singular story, to largely multi- and cross-disciplinary research into various expressions from all of humanity. The arts have notably responded to some of the problems and solutions faced by an individual dealing with separation and the task of mourning. A tension arises, between our aspirations to return to a protective past and our forward movement. Jung was aware that growth seeks to leave this past, to disengage us from it. It propels us toward becoming ourselves, a process for which he will later coin a term: "individuation."

The photograph below shows Jung, much later, in the study of his house in Küsnacht. He is surrounded by some of the works of art that

Carl Jung

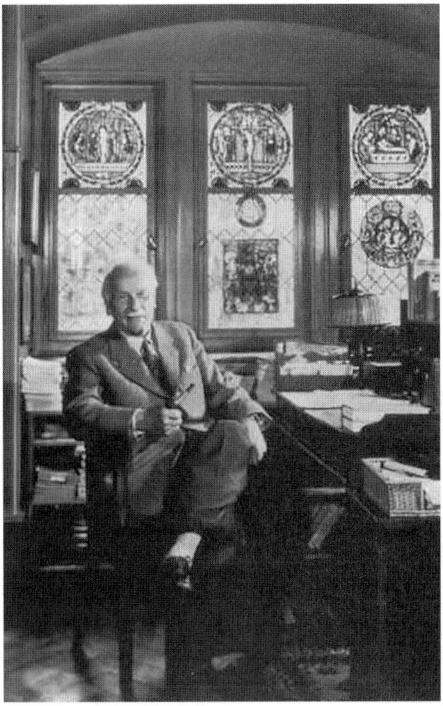

accompany him in his work as a clinician and in his writing. Here, they are Christian works of art.[3]

On Jung's part, the step he took was not only from the most individual, the most singular, to the most collective. It was also a leap from a theory that had already been conceptualized by Freud—based on oral, anal, and genital sexuality—to an adventurous, dramatic, visualized reflection, borne by the works of art that punctuate the history of humanity, and also by the myths and rituals of the religions that have preceded us.

And Jung's departure also implied a change in the relationship to time, to timescales. It was a leap from the timescale and the rhythm of an individual's history to the great rhythms of our cultures, of a history that advances and thinks collectively, with its own means of expression.[4]

Freud did not really appreciate this change of scale in psychoanalytical research and thought, leading him to protest.[5]

The psychoanalytical edifice was wobbling on its foundations. By 1913, the two minds who were the pillars of psychoanalysis, Freud and Jung, parted ways. Ever since, psychoanalytical unity has been lost.

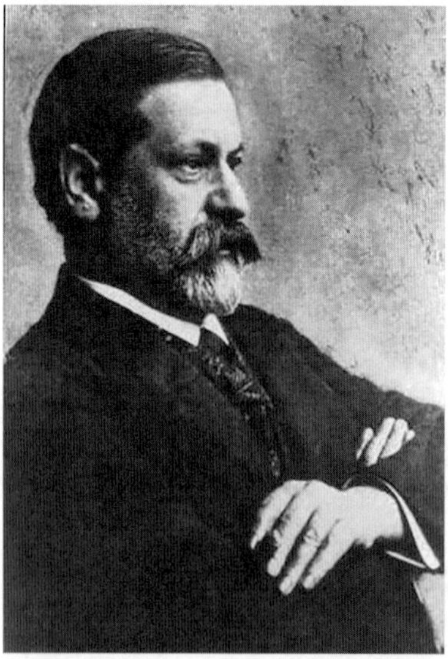

Freud, in 1906

Freud, Jacques Lacan, Melanie Klein, and Jung

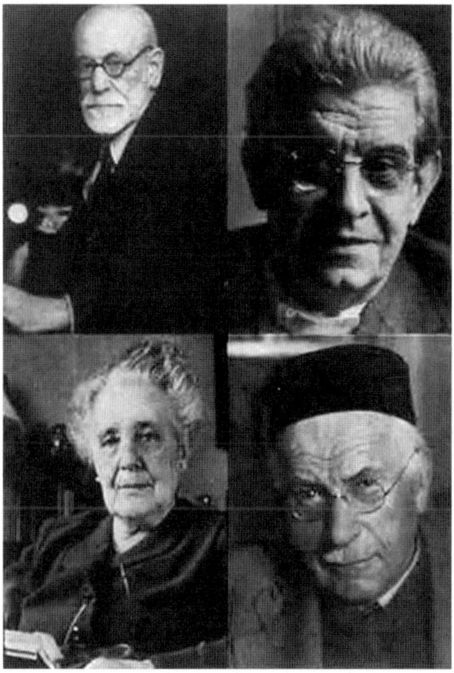

Here we can see Sigmund Freud, at the top left. To the right, Jacques Lacan. On the bottom left, Melanie Klein. On the bottom right, Carl Gustav Jung. The unity of psychoanalysis is shattered.

It dates back to at least June 17, 1910. On that day, Jung had just received Freud's essay entitled *Leonardo da Vinci and a Memory of his Childhood.*

The book, as it has long been presented in France, contains an essay by Freud that was the starting point of a new area of research into the psychoanalysis of art—called "psychobiography." Psychobiography consists of trying to understand a work of art through the artist's life, his experiences in childhood, and, if possible, from as early as the cradle.[6]

Jung's reaction to Freud's psychobiographical essay on Leonardo da Vinci was enthusiastic. "[Your] Leonardo is marvelous," he wrote to Freud immediately afterward. "I read it in its entirety, and soon, I will reread it again." And he added, "This is the first of your writings in which the inner guidelines are such that I feel, a priori, in full agreement with them."[7] The two masters found themselves in near-

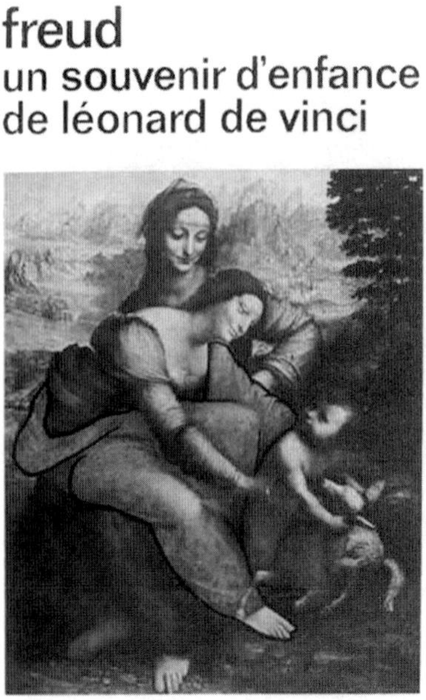

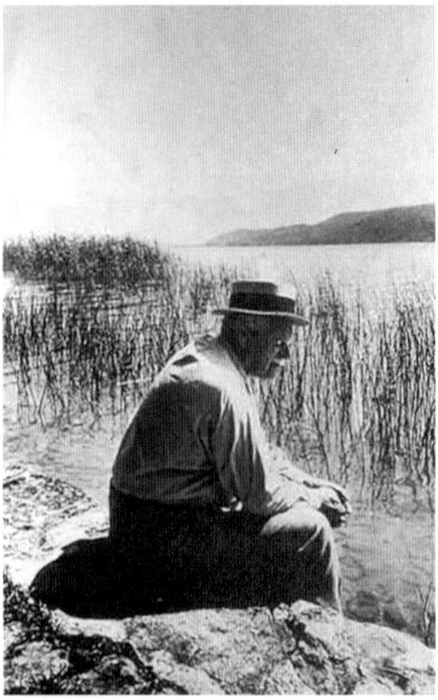

Jung

total agreement. Jung continued, "I would like to spend more time with these impressions—and peacefully pursue the long chains of thought that develop."

Here we see Jung, deep in thought, beside Lake Zurich. I discovered this photo of Jung only recently. One of my daughters brought it over from Switzerland for me—and I discovered that in this photo, Jung bears a curious resemblance to my paternal grandfather. This detail may seem merely to be a simple biographical anecdote. Yet it seems that it is a question of my relationship to Jung, and, more specifically, of his relationship and our own relationship to time. Our relationship to time and history is marked by the experiences, experiments, expressions, thoughts, and productions of those who preceded us, under the conditions and with the resources available to them, and by what they have transmitted to us, a heritage we in turn consider and reconsider, to push it further forward, in our own way.[8]

Jung, discovering Freud's essay on Leonardo da Vinci, mentioned a wish to pursue "long chains of thought." How are we to understand such a dreamy remark? It leaves a strange suspense, keeping up waiting for what comes next. In 1910, such "long chains of thought" could rock the ship of psychoanalysis and disturb the good order captained by Freud. And they have the power to disturb us, too.

However, we may remind ourselves that some thoughts, still seemingly largely unconscious, may come to us from afar, and then emerge, or threaten to emerge. The unconscious indeed thinks in its own way at its own rhythm and through images as well. It does so without us knowing where it will take us.

Let's think visually about two major questions at the heart of the debates that have occupied us since the beginning of psychoanalysis.

Where are we at with the unconscious? Is it only the effect of repression, of repression of sexuality and notably of infantile sexuality, as Freud taught? Or is it the initial thing, always already there, always restarted, always living? Could it be like a primal matter from which we distinguish ourselves, for better or worse, as conscious and speaking beings—but which never stops holding us, playing with us, and calling us, expressing itself in its own way?

Where are we at with our relationship to time, to history, on its different scales, from the most individual to the most collective?

In order to reflect upon these questions visually, let us examine two familiar works from the history of art. I note their familiarity because it is one of the first difficulties to avoid when we approach a work of art. Often, we recognize a painting, an engraving, a poem, a sculpture, a piece of music, or an architectural work having seen, heard, or visited it before. The work calls on us to look at it anew, to review it and rediscover it with as much spontaneity and surprise as possible.

Works of art we shall consider

On the following page is the first of two works we will consider.

If you know this engraving, you also know its title: *Melencolia.* This is, incidentally, the only legible word in the picture, written on the banderole in the top left quadrant of the scene.

Otherwise, a heavy silence prevails. There is no other word, nor is there breath, or movement. You can feel the weight of the figure's body, on itself and on the floor. It is settled on the right side of a jumble of objects.

No breath, no movement. The bell's clapper hangs, immobile. The scales are in balance. No flight despite the wings that one sees on the back of the main figure and on the child, bent over, almost prostrate on his writing block.

Here, rather than feeling any flight, we are clearly witnessing falling. Gravity weighs down the already leaden wings of the figure resting its head on its left hand and arm. Is this a woman? A man? A fallen angel? We hesitate and question. Faced with the scene, we start doubting and we are puzzled.

This landscape has no opening. Our eye travels to the space at the top left, seeking a way out. The glance in this direction collides with the banner reading *Melencolia*, and this word decisively stops us. It is gripping, because it addresses us like the deaf cry of a bat—or rather a terrible regressive hybrid, part bird, part mammal, part saurian.[9]

Why *Melencolia*, then? Let us look closer to understand. Be sure

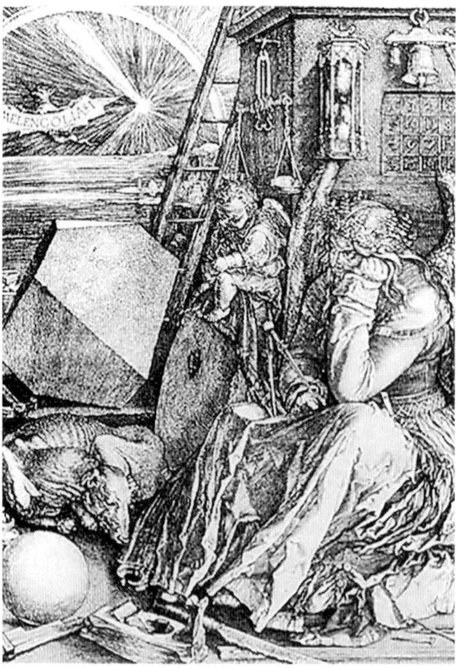

Dürer, Melencolia I, 1534

to note the type of objects accumulated in this scene. They are the instruments of knowledge and technical progress: a ruler, a compass, a plane, scales, an hourglass, a globe, a polyhedron...all instruments that man invents to advance and prove his understanding of the world, relying on his own resources and genius, rather than the illumination of some revealed truth or teaching from a higher authority.[10]

In 1514, times had changed a lot over the last two or three decades, notably since 1480, the decade when Sandro Botticelli painted the *Story of Nastaggio degli Onesti.*

Scientific and technical discoveries were being made at a dizzying pace. In all areas, means of communications had been improved. Printing had been invented. The New World had recently been discovered. New wealth was at hand. Globalization had arrived, though its advent was creating some disorder. In any case, the fact that the Earth is round is now widely accepted.

The world had changed so much that an entire concept of how to live in the world was threatened with obsolescence, extinction. The happy age of shared myths had past. The Christian myth was certainly still powerful and respected, but it no longer served as the only standard by which everyone's thoughts, feelings, values, and actions were measured.

With all of the instruments of knowledge shown here, the question of measure, of weight and measure, is posed everywhere. Thus, the main figure in the engraving holds a compass. This instrument had long been in other hands.

Dürer's *Creation of the World* impacted me so much that I chose it for the front cover of one of my books.[11] It can be found in a thirteenth-century pharmacopoeia, currently preserved in Vienna at the Austrian National Library. In it we see the paternal, searching, and passionate attention God gives to the universe's creation, gestation, and movement of transformation.

This God is not an all-powerful Zeus on Olympus, nor a sacrificed Christ—even though here He seems to be Son just as much as Father. He observes the world, following it with His eyes, and at the same time, He takes, or gives the measure of what is being produced. An experiment in order is under way, and this God contributes, with

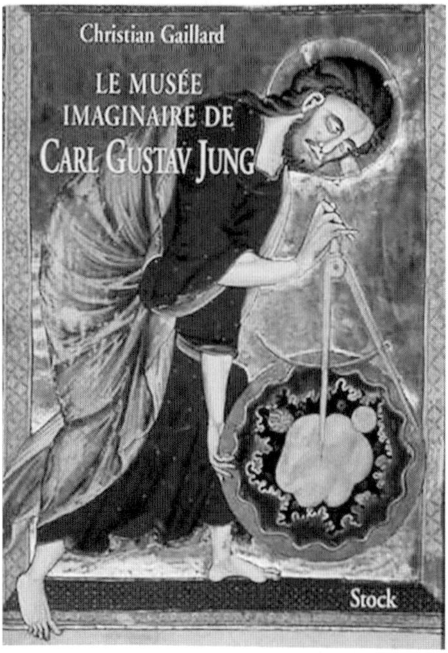

The creation of the world, 1226

an internal dynamic, still uncertain and still almost formless. Yet it is already in movement. And He accompanies this movement with a gesture that supports and guides it—a gesture that is even more perceptible in His foot, pressing on the painted frame of this page for support as He and His world take a step forward.

Here, everything is in movement and constantly evolving. Creation is in action. It is on the move. It is a current affair—a work in process, or rather, a world in progress, whereas in Dürer's engraving, even the movement of the compass is at a standstill. We have fallen from above. Despondency threatens, along with disorder and disarray.

In order to understand, let's proceed through association and amplification. Dürer himself incites this approach. In the same year, 1514, he created another engraving, dedicated to *Saint Jerome in his Cell.*

This engraving is exactly the same format as *Melencolia,* and we know that Dürer often presented them together, as if in his eyes they were complementary; or as if for him, they should reply to one another.[12]

Saint Jerome is writing, with a lion and a dog at his feet.[13] A skull sits on the windowsill, watching perhaps. Although the saint is far from cheerful, he is nevertheless part of a story, a tradition: the Christian tradition that he, in turn, will advance through his own works.

And, according to the evidence, he has a future ahead of him, at least in the short term. The engraving shows us the cardinal's galero hat hanging on the wall behind him. Saint Jerome will become a cardinal.

But does he suspect that in a little more than a century, he will find himself in another position? He will become a simple "philosopher in meditation," instead of the Saint and Father of the Church of earlier times. I am referring to Rembrandt's oil painting on an oak panel, now in the Louvre, entitled *The Philosopher in Meditation.*

This philosopher can no longer rely on illumination coming from above. We see no sky above him, and neither does he. Yet, if it were there, it would shed some light on him, and he, in turn, could implore

Albrecht Dürer, Saint Jerome in his cell, 1514

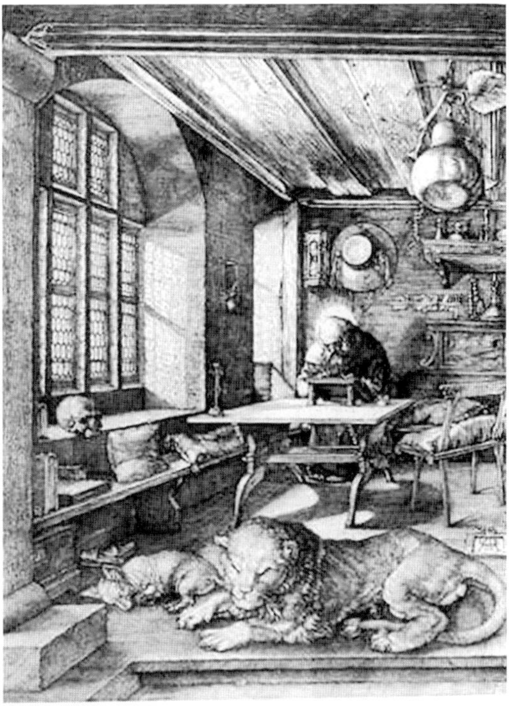

it or invoke it. In the absence of sunlight, the scene is quite dark. This philosopher, in his somber cell, is centered on himself and concentrating at the foot of a staircase that shows the spiral gravity of his meditation on himself.[14]

But in returning to Dürer's engraving, does the enigmatic character in *Melencolia* know that he could be, and perhaps has been, a Saint Jerome? Probably not. No more than he knows how to live like the meditating philosopher in Rembrandt's picture. He knows neither where he came from, nor where he is going. With him, we find ourselves in a sort of construction site, open for who knows what type of edifice—the foundations have yet to be laid—for who knows what end. Even Nature is almost absent from the scene.

And the prospects for the future are also blank. What will become of the child hunched over his writing board? Perhaps he will be a scholar, or more likely an engineer. In any case, despite his wings, he seems unable to remember that he was once an angel.

Time is suspended without past or future. Eyes wide open onto a present on the brink of chaos. Is this not melancholy? Not the medieval melancholy familiar to us, of days gone by.

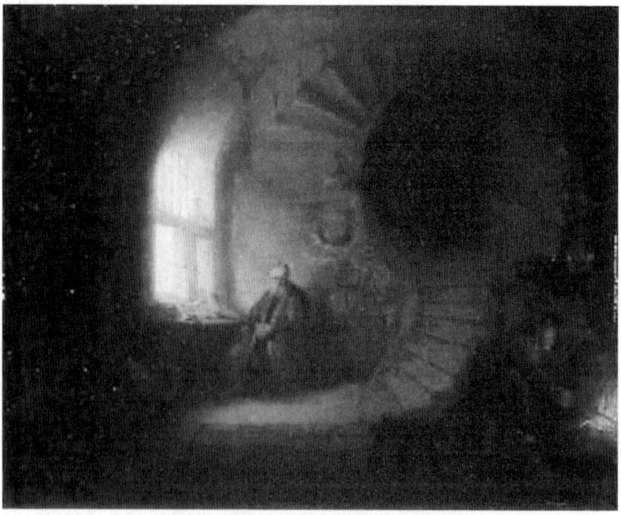

Rembrandt, The Philosopher in Meditation, 1632, Louvre

The engraving below dates from circa 1480, and was reproduced in the Augsburg Calendar. That *typus melancholicus*, his face lowered and concealed in folded arms as if to sleep better, was *a blind despondency*. It was a hiding away or withdrawal comparable to laziness, extensively represented and commented upon during the Middle Ages.[15]

The modern melancholy as Panofsky identified and analyzed it is different. Again, the individual suffers both from feeling and from thinking, but this time he is clearly open-eyed.

The modern form of melancholy is the opposite of the earlier apathy, where the figure hides his head, caring for nothing and no one. Instead, lucidity wrenches one away from the refusal to see and to live. This melancholy is a struggle that could seem hopeless, if it weren't so tense in the present, between sense and nonsense. The past is not only lost, but lost from sight. History is merely a construction site, on the brink of chaos. There are no landmarks, natural or manmade, to guide the traveler on his journey.

Try to imagine yourself as the central figure in Dürer's scene. Immediately, you confront feelings of confusion that are extremely disturbing, and even painful. Your very identity vacillates. Who am I? Am I a man? A woman? Human or angel? Struggling with the uncer-

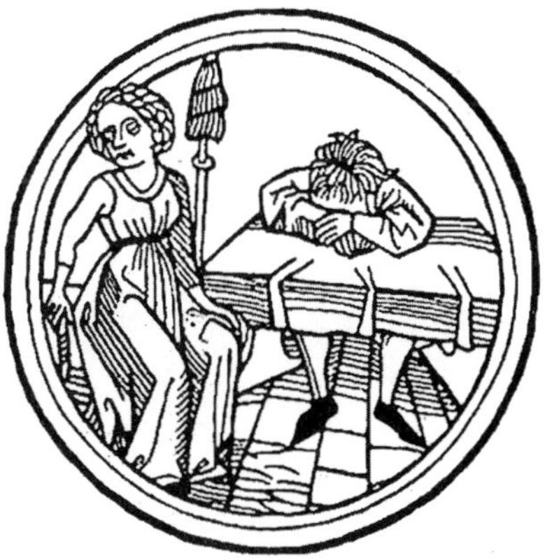

¶ Melencolicus·
¶ Vnsercomplexion ist von erden weÿch
Darūb seÿ wir schwärmütigkeyt gleich

tainty of identity, we are truly at a loss. We do not know which way to turn. That we are so utterly confused compounds our suffering.

It is cold in this melancholy, in the terror of this lucidity experienced entirely in the present. We are so lost that even the past is confusion. We lack any known or knowable perspective, surrounded by the debris of a bygone world where a hostile and menacing disorder cannot find how to reorganize itself.

We are hanging, in suspense, between one world and another, divided, distraught, where feeling or thinking no longer bring the weights and measures that allow us to orientate ourselves and gain some perspective. Here we are, with eyes wide open, at risk of becoming world-weary.

I am rather impressed by this dark lucidity, by the dark quality of this pessimism, eyes open to the present. It is a sustained disillusionment, in which I recognize Freud's position.

Freud, as we saw earlier, knows how to keep his eyes open, observing the world, others, and himself. And yet this is a posture in which one incurs the risk of rigidity. One is liable to freeze, to remain immobile, and to close oneself off from life's unexpected encounters and discoveries.

And I can recognize part of myself as well, in this type of somber lucidity—but only sometimes, and only a part of myself. As a Jungian analyst, I cannot say that this attitude is an accurate reflection of my relationship to the unconscious, to time, and to history.

Another work, another life

Cranach's painting, currently in the collection of the Musée Unterlinden in Colmar, France, is constructed on the same iconographic theme as Dürer's engraving, as its title also indicates: *Melancholy*. However, the experience is completely different.

It's 1532 and eighteen years have passed since Dürer's engraving. The no-illusions angel of this engraving has changed a lot. He—or rather she—breathes differently.

In fact, this angel is no longer asexual. It is a woman, and in red. And this woman is looking at us. It is truly a woman that Lucas Cran-

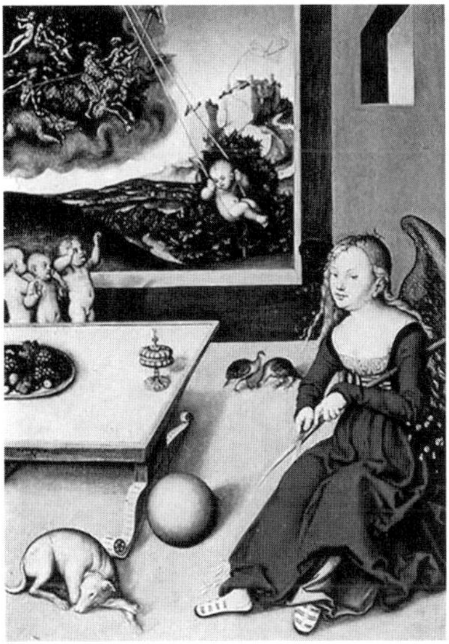

Cranach, Melancholy, Colmar

ach presents here, facing us. Manifestly not an angel or a virgin, Virgin Mother or martyr like the ones we saw earlier in the gardens of the Middle Ages we reviewed in the previous chapter, but rather a courtesan, or demimondaine.

Moreover, with her plunging neckline and seductive look, she is not only an angel so incarnate that she has become profane, but by the thorny crown she wears askew on her undone hair, she is so brazenly tantalizing that she is frankly blasphemous.

Above all, she is summoning us, perhaps even making an appeal to us. We are no longer stupefied by the desolation, loss, and disorder that Dürer's engraving conveyed. Cranach's painting has created a wholly different relationship to the event, to what and to whom is presented and intervening now—a vivid relationship, a troubling one, but that, instead of leaving us perplexed, summons and mobilizes us, soliciting desire, the desire for life.

With Dürer, we were in the dark abyss of an admirably lucid but immobile melancholy. Now, with Cranach, we have gone from this dark, heavy melancholy to the colors and animation of desire.[16]

And yet, we are not beholding a work that obeys Renaissance perspective as Brunelleschi established it—a type of perspective the purpose and effect of which is to enable us to control the world by placing everything where it belongs, and effectively dominated by us, in the order thus created. The view we are given on this scene is, by technical definition, a "bird's-eye view." Rather than engaging in controlling and dominating the outer world, the scene opens up and presents itself as an invitation to come closer to a world that is opening to me. I can enter, I am even invited to enter into the field. The scene that invites me in, the encounter offered, looks at me and concerns me quite directly and personally.

I find myself taken in, surprised, solicited, and aware of myself, at the same time as I find myself invited, incited to react by this woman who is there watching me, who holds my eye, part angel, part sorceress, I don't really know which.

The painting of the *Garden of Paradise* was already organized according to this perspective, and that it already attracted us, as if by surprise, drawing us in the same way, with the same attentive, exploratory, wondering motion. It is quite possible that with these works, painting found a way to invite us to go forward toward a world, toward encounters, discoveries, and experiences that today, drawing upon the first advancements and more recent developments in psychoanalysis regarding the relationship with the unconscious, we might describe as inner encounters, discoveries, and experiences.

Since our relationship to time and how it organizes our approach to the arts is one of the questions we are considering, let us note that this work presents us with a relationship to history and time that differs from what we were able to observe in the earlier engraving.

In Dürer's engraving, our gaze collided with some sort of flying mammal, screaming at melancholy to the point of pushing back the rainbow. Here, in the painting by Cranach, a window opens, like a painting within the painting.

This window gives us a view of a hubbub of fantastical cavalcades, a knight at arms riding a goat at full gallop, and naked sorceresses riding mounts that are even stranger: boars, horned cows, or serpent-dragons. The whole parade is afloat on a huge dark cloud, about to burst. This is a phantasmagorical, fantastical, supernatural pandemonium of fears, chimeras, and temptations that one could call medi-

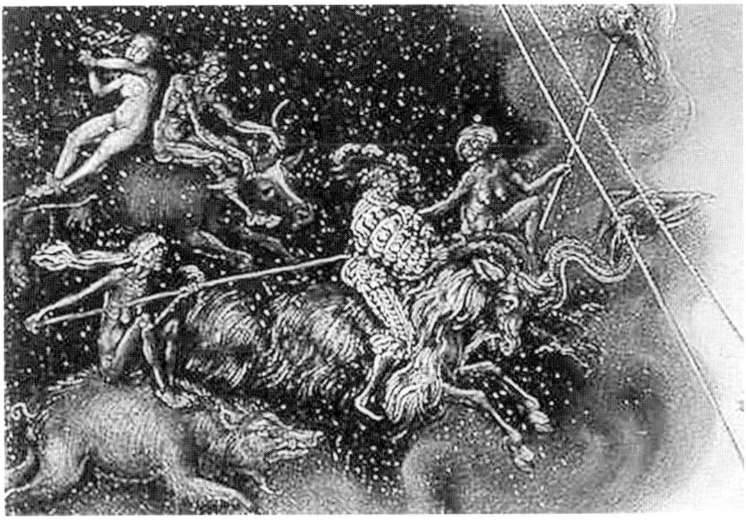

Detail of the window in Cranach's Melancholy

eval. Though presumably kept at a distance, in the background, the Middle Ages are still very present. The room in this picture acknowledges time.

The past, evoked and recognized, is evidently in the picture and opens the encounter with the woman in red, who might almost wink at us, playfully or mockingly. This interior space is an animated space that opens itself to encounters.

Likewise, the children have changed a lot since Dürer's engraving. Here they are fully fleshed putti, whereas the infant in Dürer's engraving seemed to be a future scholar poring over his studies, as dark and joyless as the heavy Melancholy by his side.

Let us also note that Cranach's playing children pose a curious problem of perspective. At first sight, the one on the swing seems to be outside the room, on the other side of the window. But the cherubs pushing the swing are in the room with the woman in red. So it is possible for the baby on the swing to go back and forth, from the outdoors to inside the room, his to-and-fro movement linking the outside return to the past and the indoor space, the present, where the woman in red awaits us.

These children are a way of opening up the space to time, opening onto the consciousness of the history. This woman is indeed no longer a child. Her game is not like theirs. But the children are still there. They come and go. They are, manifestly, the link between the outside and the inside, between days gone by and now.

In another version of this same scene, also painted by Cranach in 1532, and currently in the Staten Museum for Kunst in Copenhagen, the children use a lever to play at trying to roll the globe through a hoop—a globe that is also in the Colmar Cranach, as well as Dürer's engraving.

It is a game, but a very serious one, at times physical and quasi theoretical, of surveyors or engineers applying their ingenuity, strength, skill, and creativity to solve a particularly arduous problem.

These children are not only the link between the outside and the inside, between the various ages of life, between our collective past and today. They are also the link—in the vocabulary we use today, we might say they are transitional—between play and knowledge, showing the association between the liberty of playful rough-and-tumble and the applied, experimental, and exploratory exercise of knowledge.

The immobile perplexity of Dürer's engraving, the despondency threatened from within by world-weariness, is far away indeed. On the contrary, these children express the impetus of life, the impor-

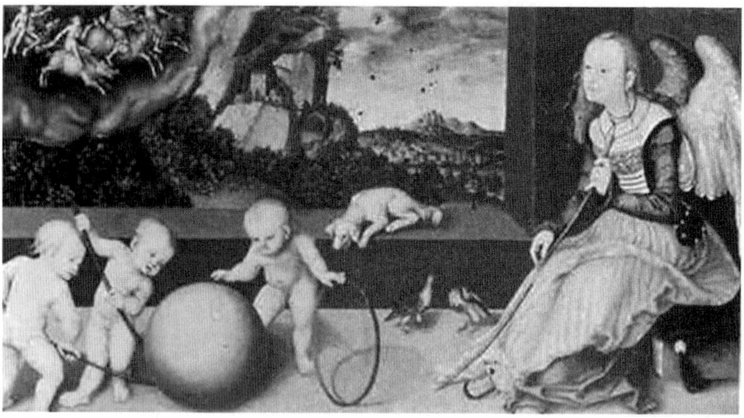

Cranach, Melancholy, Copenhagen

tance of play, and a taste for knowledge—an impetus, interest, and taste that I experience through this painting—even if the painting's reminders of Dürer's engraving also remind me that I am still obscurely menaced by melancholy.

When I encounter these works by Cranach, particularly the more expressive and completed *Melancholia* from the Musée Unterlinden, I feel at home as a Jungian analyst.

This painting offers me the experience of an inner space that opens and becomes animated. I see and experience it, encountering the presences that inhabit and animate such a space. They can move me. Sometimes, insidiously, they even impose themselves on me. At those times, my ego is disrupted, wobbling, suffering, protesting, defending itself, often fighting back as best it can.

Also, I often see that these intimate inner presences, surprising and nonetheless familiar can easily turn out to be iconoclastic and heretical—like the children, who will discover who knows what, and especially the woman in red. Once manifestly an angel, she now watches us from the corner of her eye, almost daring us, with her crown of thorns askew on her undone hair.

Undeniably, the Judeo-Christian God is more distant from us than He used to be. A whole world order—a Paradise perhaps—has been lost. We have to get over it, get used to it. Mourn, and move on.

The Holy Church no longer leads the way to the customary progress through study to spiritual realization the way it did in Saint Jerome's times.

Meditation has become philosophical at the risk of all perspective being lost, as we saw with Rembrandt. New weights and measures must be found, and with our eyes open, we must continue to seek, even when disillusionment and confusion threaten and even when chaos threatens.[17]

There, we have recognized the quality and somber strength of Freud's position regarding the relationships to the unconscious and to the present and the past, once we have given up the ideals and promises of a past that is gone, never to return. This position, when it was newly discovered, also contained the ambition to last forever, unanimous, universal.

Except that Cranach, who was well versed in the dreams and phantasmagoria of the Middle Ages, and who manifestly remembered Dürer's engraving well, opens another path, far more lively, animated, and inviting. The fallen angel becomes a woman, a woman in red, and the children at play are discovering the laws of the physical world and experimenting with them.

And so, life replies to the weight of melancholy through the taste for encounters and research. The painting gives us the tangible experience of the erotic, of an encounter, and of the games of knowledge.

Now, it is clearer to us how Cranach's young woman in red responds to Dürer's black melancholy, just as, thanks to these works of art, it is clearer how Jung responds to Freud.[18]

Like Jung, I could call this young woman in red, introduced to me by Cranach, my *anima.* I recognize my soul in her. But the image is so much more eloquent than my words. The painting shows me that this soul also has a body, that she also is a body. She could be someone to discover, although getting to know her might be fraught with difficulty and even disillusionment.

5

Narcissus Crouching

FROM OVID TO CARAVAGGIO

The next work of art we will study is decisive, not only in the history of forms, but also in the history of man's relationship to himself, and our understanding and practice of this relationship.

Moreover, it is decisive in the way it stealthily creeps up on an old story that has been told thousands of times for centuries. In taking the tale by surprise, it reverses the old meanings and gives a new turn, another meaning, and a broader range to the myth.

This work is also crucial for those of us who are curious about the differences in approach among the various traditions contributing to the psychoanalytic movement today.

The painting on the next page is Caravaggio's *Narcissus at the Source.* It currently hangs in the Galleria d'Arte Antica at the Palazzo Barberini, in Rome—when it is not traveling the world, representing baroque art.[1]

The canvas dates from the very end of the sixteenth century and was probably painted between 1597 and 1599.[2] It is a medium-sized oil painting, which appears to be square, although it actually measures 110 × 92 cm (43 × 36 inches).

It is ordinarily attributed to Michelangelo Merisi, better known as *Il Caravaggio.* We will return to its attribution later, as it gives us a clue as to the work's importance.

The title illuminates the story illustrated by the painting. The tale of Narcissus exists in many elaborate versions, the best known being the one from the Roman poet Ovid. Around the time of Christ's birth,

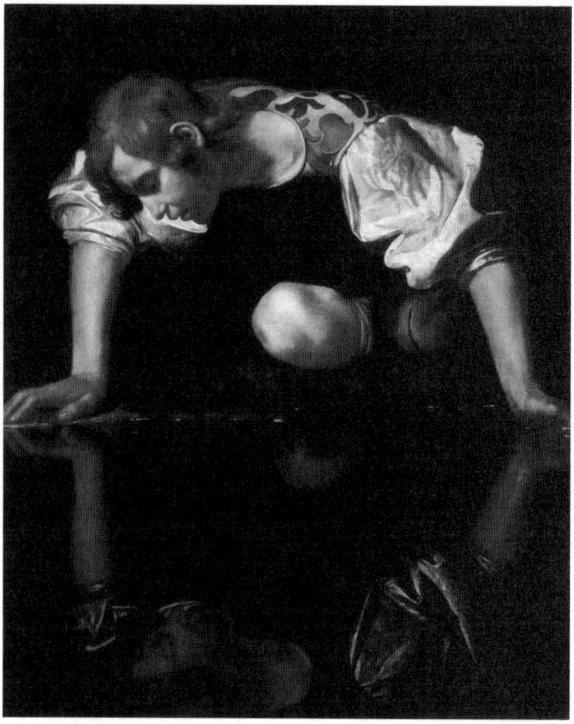

Caravaggio, Narcissus

before the Greek navigator and storyteller Pausanias, Ovid included Narcissus in his *Metamorphoses.* However, the story is likely to be even older than its ancient Roman and Greek sources. It might even be one that has been told since the dawn of storytelling itself, ever since human beings began to represent themselves, or to try to represent themselves, and recognize who they are—ever since humans have been able to speak and say about themselves. As we saw in the chapter on cave paintings, the first human representations arose in the earliest times when we were able to recognize ourselves in our differences and singularity.[3]

The painting's muteness and frontality

Caravaggio's representation of the story strikes us with its brutally silent frontality.

We thought we were familiar with the story of Narcissus, that we had understood it thoroughly. But now it is emblemized in a way that is radically devoid of any discourse or narrative. It simply presents itself frontally, as if the painting had performed an almost surgical cross-section of the account it is supposed to illustrate.

In motion picture terms, it looks like a freeze frame: an instant in the unfolding of a narrative. The picture says nothing about what came before or what ensued or might ensue.

This silent, instantaneous freeze frame, lacking any echo, is more striking in that it includes no reference to the nymph Echo, a figure any reader of Ovid would expect to find in the picture. Nor is there any depiction of the narcissus flower, which was always the emblem of the central character in the story and expressed the story's ending.

As a result, the work is presented to the viewer like an object out of context, a sort of UFO come from who-knows-where. It sits still, unrelated to anything that might come to the rescue of the observer, who is certainly discountenanced.[4]

This surgical cross-section is all the more effective, fearsome, and inescapable because it shows water—an element that, like time, is ordinarily characterized by a movement or flow.[5] However, here, the water is immobile, and as a result, the course of time is also arrested in its flow—which does not fail to stop us if we do not immediately take refuge in the story we expected to see illustrated here.

The painting has hushed the verses it was supposed to represent, verses that are supposed to be familiar to all of us. We are dumbstruck, voiceless.

However, the gap, the tension, and especially the contrasts between the classical story of Narcissus and this painting by Caravaggio might give birth to the very sense of the story, just as they produce the immediate effect of this work.

The poem's ambiguities

Ovid was a subtle, mobile poet. He reworked the old story of Narcissus in his own period, that of Augustus (63 BC–14 AD). Telling of the birth of Narcissus, son of the river god Cephissus and the nymph

Liriope, thereby establishing the story's setting in the mythical world,[6] he charmed the reader by evoking the sylvan pleasures of the hunt, young people basking in the sun, and the freshness of the brook.

The poet was especially eloquent in describing the young man's grace, playing upon the reader's sympathy and identification to lure him closer to a charm that is seemingly timeless, almost eternal, yet also ambiguous.

He told of the passion that young men and women had for Narcissus, of this character's self-satisfaction, his impossible dialogue with the nymph Echo, his fascination, upon discovering his reflection in the water, for his own image, his passionate and desperate attraction for this image, his attempts to embrace it, even on the edge of the Styx, his death, and, finally, the flower—the narcissus—that bloomed in place of his body.

Is this story a tragedy or a drama? One hesitates, reading the poem. We certainly grieve, we weep over the unhappy fate of the young man, but we remain filled with the ideal bliss induced in us by the way the story comes full circle. Ovid enjoyed celebrating the pleasures and delights of nature. He enchanted us with the picture of an almost ideal, nearly perfect young man, whose very ambiguity is enchanting. And his poem concluded with a flower. The reader is satisfied. The celebration of the beauties of nature, ending with the blossoming of a flower, leaves us in a reverie, and it is tempting to remain there.

Yet Ovid did mention the words of the soothsayer Tiresias, who foretold that Narcissus "would live a better life if he did not look at himself." He even appealed to Narcissus, reprimanding him, when he wrote, "Credule, quid frustra simulacra fugacia captas?" / "Why try to catch an always fleeing image, / poor, credulous youngster? What you seek is nowhere, / and if you turn away, you will take with you the boy you love. The vision is only shadow, only reflection, lacking any substance."[7]

Clearly, this was an admonition. But how should it be understood? Should we take the poet at his word, literally? Perhaps, in addressing his unfortunate hero this way, he is simply disguising a warning to the reader, not to be overly enchanted by the story. Like Narcissus, we are liable to get lost in a reverie that may last until death ensues.

Or might something else account for Ovid's warning? The poets, writers, and especially storytellers of the time often gave lip service to an official morality, smug and supercilious. By tricking the censors in this way, these authors could surreptitiously convey the real message or lesson of the story they were telling, a lesson liable to be subversive or dangerously disruptive.[8]

But as soon as I voice this question, I can see my Jungian colleagues smile knowingly, too happy to intervene. They want to point out that even if the Roman poet is probably playing a trick on the decorous here, he has nevertheless hinted at a word, an idea, or rather an intuition that might help us gain a better understanding of the message contained in this Latin poem from 2,000 years ago.

Didn't you say something about the shadow?

Indeed, referring to the image Narcissus discovers in the pool, didn't Ovid say that he was dealing with a shadow? Let us reread the admonition Ovid addresses to the young man and to the reader as well. Does he not speak explicitly in Latin of the *umbra*?[9] He may have uttered the word even without knowing exactly what he meant by it.[10]

And perhaps that meaning is precisely what Caravaggio understood better, after Ovid. Unlike the poet, the painter feels no need to play with the luminous pleasures of nature and youth. He has immersed the scene in browns and blacks so heavy that they invade the whole landscape.

In this painting, the shadow is indeed present. There are many shadows, a great deal of shadow, and darkness overwhelms the scene. And, as opposed to what we read in Ovid, flowers, clear water, and the amorous nymph are not part of the story. Even the forest and rocks the poet sang of so pleasantly have disappeared from this painting.

Moreover, the young man as painted by Caravaggio, although still just as handsome, well-groomed, and well-dressed, in the most becoming white shirt, seems to be somewhat frightened as he peers at the vision. He clings to the edge, arching his back and resisting. Both arms are tense as he peers at the vision rising up and arousing his dread. At the same time, we see that the reflection is blurry, tending to be swallowed up and vanishing in the darkness of the waters.

Caravaggio's painting seems to confirm the keen, scholarly observation of my fellow Jungian psychologists, as anachronistic as it might seem, when they speak of an "encounter with the shadow."

Yet this observation might lead to a serious misunderstanding; the statement may be somewhat approximate. We would do better to look more closely and explore this particular painter's relationship to shadows.

Indeed, Caravaggio was never shy about venturing onto paths that transgressed the ideal rules and lights promoted by the social and religious order of his time. He enjoyed seeking out models in objectionable places, such as cabarets and houses of ill repute, where he joined a bawdy crowd of drinkers, carousers, brawlers, and brazen wenches, apt to burst into lusty laughter under the influence of cheap, coarse wines.

Simply take another look at the joyously brutal drinking scenes and the figures Caravaggio depicted in their physical pleasure or their suffering. The ideal representations, or the good manners and models of the Roman ruling classes, are notably absent from the paintings. Consider *The Cardsharps*, painted in 1594, around the same time as *Narcissus.* Two conspirators are breaking the rules of the game: exchanging signals, plotting to rob the unsuspecting gentleman. In the *Musicians*, from 1595, the figures gaze seductively at the observer, barely managing to keep their skin draped and decent. The *Boy Bitten by a Lizard*, painted in 1594, is rendered so sensuously and sensually present by the painter that he becomes almost provocative, as if he were wearing makeup on his contorted face; the rosiness of his lips seemingly artificial. He bears an odd family resemblance to the *Young Sick Bacchus* of 1593.

Even when Caravaggio paints the most conventional religious themes, they take such a daring turn that we find ourselves at or beyond the limits of decency and decorum. His *Saint John the Baptist*, from 1598, is treated as if he, too, might be a Bacchus.[11] Likewise, the *Rest During the Flight into Egypt*, painted in 1597, becomes an opportunity for Caravaggio to feature, front and center, a tantalizingly draped angel. His body, seen from behind, is the focus of all of the painter's attention, and ours.

As for the Madonnas, Caravaggio enjoys lowering them from their pedestal. They are quite down-to-earth women, even if it might offend and shock the artist's most valuable patrons. Although painted later, in 1606, the *Madonna dei Palafrenieri* is a typical Caravaggio Madonna, in a low-cut robe that reveals her voluptuous bosom. Moreover, although He is at least 5 or 6 years old, the Holy Infant wears not a thread of clothing. For all of these reasons, the canvas was rejected by the cardinals in charge of the *Fabbrica di San Pietro.*[12]

A few years earlier, in 1599 or 1600, another prelate, Cardinal Matthieu Contarelli, had commissioned a painting on a classically edifying subject, the conversion of Saint Matthew, dedicated to the cardinal's patron saint. But in *The Calling of Saint Matthew*, currently displayed in the church of *Saint Louis des Français*, Caravaggio took the liberty of painting a room in which the light of heaven is at great pains to shine. It is a shadowy and probably smelly inn or tavern where Church dignitaries, priests, and upper middle classes of the time would never deign to set foot, at least if there was some risk they would be seen and recognized. Yet it was Caravaggio's first public commission—in fact, we see the money being counted, in the center of the scene.[13]

What was the painter seeking, by treating such lofty, sacred themes in this unorthodox way, setting them in such unholy places? Undoubtedly, he sought the expression of life, real life—the burst of pleasure. This is particularly evident in the *Amor Vincit Omnia*, dating from 1601 or 1602, in which a stark naked little boy leaps out of a tumble of draperies—perhaps an unmade bed.[14] At the same time, Caravaggio was striving to revivify the art of painting, to restore the power that, in his eyes, had been lost in the overly formal interpretations of mythological or religious subjects that were fashionable at the time. Actually, Caravaggio brought Heaven back to Earth.[15]

This unholy artist was so reluctant to celebrate the pious beauty and ideals of the moment that he was soon labeled with a host of epithets referring to his profanity. Despite his outstanding renown, he was in a dangerous position. At the risk of being called anachronistic myself, I am tempted to compare Caravaggio to Pier Paolo Pasolini.[16]

Like our contemporary Pasolini, Caravaggio paid dearly for his free-spirited nature, with exile and even perhaps his life. He died at the age of 38, in circumstances that were dramatic enough even before they were romanticized, of his brawling, his excesses, and his attraction to uncouth, brutish friends.[17] And with the poet and filmmaker from Friuli, Caravaggio also shared a passion for an unorthodox Jesus figure.

Baroque exuberance, in Caravaggio's time, was already being toned down by an esthetic intended to be a return to the classical. Caravaggio's paintings stood in great contrast to fashionable tastes. Many of his contemporaries were enthusiastic about his work, but many more were shocked by it at the time and for centuries to come.

The French painter Nicolas Poussin, who was born around the time when Caravaggio was painting his Narcissus, and therefore was more than a generation younger, was a master of light and color. He found the older artist's work so unbearable that he once exploded, "Caravaggio was born to destroy painting."[18]

Coming from a painter, a statement like that is uncharacteristically violent. But not undeserved, considering both the fate to which Caravaggio consigned the themes cultivated by the ruling classes of his time, and what one can expect from painting.[19] Today, the painters called "Caravagesques" are honored by museums.[20] It is obvious to us that Caravaggio's art influenced Vélasquez, Rubens, and Rembrandt. However, for centuries after Poussin, the Italian master's work was out of favor, and sometimes even rejected.

His art did not emerge from its long "purgatory" until the mid-twentieth century, when we again acquired a taste for emotional expressiveness and engagements—for "the affects"—of the baroque period in the arts, especially in music.[21]

The fact that Caravaggio's work was ignored for so long would seem to confirm the hypothesis of our Jungian colleagues, when they see pictures that reflect the socially inappropriate and personally troubling drama of what we, with and after Jung, call "the shadow."

But in examining more closely some more paintings by Caravaggio, and especially his *Narcissus*, we may arrive at a keener awareness of what is at play.

When we are attentive to how we look at this Narcissus, a question arises with increasing insistence.

We wonder where and how to look at the painting. We may focus on the upper part, the young man at the water's edge, whose story Ovid has told. As soon as we attempt to do so, our eyes are drawn in the opposite direction, to the lower part of the canvas, toward the depths of the waters where the darkened reflection of the young man wavers between appearing and disappearing.

Our gaze is divided—just as the composition itself is divided, by the horizontal line in the middle, marking the separation between the water and the land.

This line dividing the image in half is all the more crucial to the effect of the work, and perhaps also to its meaning, insofar as the composition as a whole forms a circle, or tries to. This circle is created by the curve of the young man's position, as he bends his back and bows his head, meeting the inverse arc of his reflection in the water.

This circle happens to be divided almost exactly in half by the horizontal line, forming two semi-circles. The squarish shape of the canvas on which Narcissus is painted gives the circle even greater emphasis. The powerful geometric aspect of the composition is singular and surprising for its time. As we have observed, the attention to geometry contrasts with the content of most of Caravaggio's works, marked by their sensuality and even lustiness, despite the taboos of the time.

The first of Caravaggio's other works we will review is the expressionistic drama of *Death of the Virgin.* It was painted only a few years after *Narcissus,* in 1604 or 1606. Today, this canvas hangs in the Louvre. It was banished from Rome as unfit for the church that had commissioned it.[22]

This is a theater of death, and the massive dimensions of the canvas (it is over nine feet high and about eight feet wide) underline the drama. The heavy red draperies in the background confine us to the central space, closing off all perspectives of an escape, particularly any upward movement.

There is not the slightest light coming from on high, light that might allude to or promise an Assumption. Nor is there any allegorical or symbolic object to elevate the meaning of the harshness and raw violence of the tragedy. Caravaggio merely painted a basin at the foot of the bed, terrible in its ordinariness.

For the heart of this scene, its slightly off-center center, the focus of all of the attention, is the dying, or dead, figure on the bed. Her belly is swollen, beneath the dark red of her wrinkled robe, and she is surrounded by grief-stricken men and women, who are careful to stand well away from the prone body.[23]

The *Narcissus* of 1597–99 is totally different. It is immobile, frozen, in terms of both soul and form. The young man's position is fixed. And the middle line dividing the composition almost precisely into two halves is practically straight.

What is happening with this Narcissus? It contrasts so strikingly with the rest of Caravaggio's oeuvre that experts sometimes doubt that it was he who painted it.[24]

Centration, decentering, and disaggregation

The work is frontal, as we observed. When we look at it, our gaze is divided. This effect is much more brutal, more difficult to bear, than one that would give the viewer a perspective to follow, or invite him to engage in some movement of the soul, even if it is painful.

The young man's knee, in the center of the picture, might soothe and reassure our gaze, for it might serve as an axis or hub, anchoring the rest and providing some structure and unity.

Look closer: even the knee has a double.[25] As a result, the entire composition is a story of partition and division between top and bottom halves. Our attention will be drawn to the lower half. It compels us, just as it is compelling the young man in the image, try as he may to tear himself away physically, his arms flexed. It is the center of gravity of the whole.[26]

Actually, the threat comes from below. It is the area ruled by shadows that are liable to swallow up the young man's face, or at least the image he has of himself. The reflection is dark, disturbing, and rather horrifyingly indistinct, as if it were about to vanish into the darkness of the depths, or to linger there, emerging only slightly.

The threat is such that in this painting, the young man himself, in the upper half, the young man Ovid praised so much, is simultaneously terrified and fascinated. It is as if the shadows in the lower part had begun to attack him. His fancy brocaded shirt, with all the careful embroidery, seems to be ripping, coming apart, slashed to ribbons by the shadow.

Narcissus is discountenanced. The somber image he sees of himself seems to be attacking or harming him so violently that his own body and his own garment are getting the worst of it.[27]

This painting by Caravaggio certainly removes us from the indulgent self-satisfaction of a young man on a sunny day, quite content with what he is in his own eyes and in the eyes of others, the way Ovid depicted him. Nor are we in the mutual admiration game, where the other is always merely the idealized reflection of oneself.[28]

As a result, it is not entirely irrelevant to speak in Jungian terms of the "shadow" here. However, to do so would be to psychologize the work: to ignore the historical context and make this drama fit into the personal psychology of a young man, called Narcissus here. He is not really contemporary to the way we think today, the way we experience this type of relationship to ourselves.

The "shadow" explanation is blind to, or denies, the dark fragmentation the painting shows us. This shattering attacks not only the image of the young man—the image he treasures of himself—but also, his own countenance, his integrity itself.

More recent interpretations

When trying to understand works dating back several centuries ago, created in contexts totally different from our own, it is definitely challenging to refrain from imposing an interpretation that confines its frame of reference to modern theories and conceptions of art.

We tend to be especially fascinated by the theorizations derived from psychoanalytic tradition—whereas what we should seek is an accurate evaluation of the work in the context, time, and place of our collective history.[29]

Take the knee of Narcissus in the painting by Caravaggio. Some of my fellow scholars, neo-Freudians from the Lacanian school, have focused upon this knee as the element that leverages the work by Caravaggio to fit into their theoretical expectations.

Here, I am referring to the essays on this work by Hubert Damisch (1976) and Gérard Wajeman (1984, 1985). Damisch and Wajeman, who are typically French, take similar approaches in that they both explicitly refer to the teachings of Jacques Lacan. As we all know, Lacan devoted a good part of his psychoanalysis to identifying and denouncing the illusions of what he has called "the Imaginary."

Damisch and Wajeman see this Imaginary, which Lacan differentiates from the Real and Symbolic,[30] in the circular organization of the painting around the young man's knee. Based on the placement of the knee on the lower part of the young man's body, they interpret it as a Phallus—a term that should be written with a capital P, according to their way of thinking, for it is the expression, or hope, for a wholeness that is in fact impossible.

In sum, their approaches are quite similar to Ovid's. For the Latin poet, Narcissus's motion consists in an effort to embrace himself, even though the wish proves to be impossible to fulfill. We can follow them up to that point, as long as we confine ourselves to Ovid's text.

But their theories fail to apply to Caravaggio's painting. How can they not see that the knee in this painting is actually doubled? As a result, here, it shatters the One it was supposed to represent, promise, and promote. And how can they give such short shrift to the line that so evidently bisects the image, a line that is the focus of the structural and dynamic tension of the upper and lower halves of this scene? Hence, they fail to account for the part of this composition that bears the weight. Its center of gravity is undeniably the lower half, so dark and disturbed: the source of the upper Narcissus's contamination.

Straightforward observation of the painting gives rise to our divergence in approach from analyst colleagues. We are aware that their concern is to denounce any totalizing illusion. We might share this concern with them in any number of other contexts, particularly in clinical practice. But not on the subject of this painting, which actually defies and challenges this interpretation, ultimately responding to it with the structure and tension of its composition.

Therefore, we must be ready to state the theoretical underpinnings required by our observations. They will carry us beyond and deepen the interpretation based on the "shadow," suggested by Jungian colleagues. We must also say something about the dynamic of the "self" in its radical differences from the claims, which are actually intentionally totalizing, of the "ego."

After mentioning the French interpretations that currently prevail in psychoanalysis, do we feel too isolated?[31] Absolutely not. For we have a powerful ally. Although he will probably not accompany us to the end of our exploration, he may help us take some steps forward.

According to Freud, they are wrong

Freud, who forged the concept of narcissism from the myth of Narcissus,[32] undoubtedly sought to identify and condemn the "wholenesses" an individual may dream of, or dream of creating, in the "desire to be One." But his goal was also to show and name that which, on the contrary, works to challenge and undermine the quest for such a wholeness.

This advancement of Freud's research and thinking directs our attention away from the interpretation our Lacanian contemporaries are inclined to develop. For, with regard to narcissism, Freud comes to speak of an injury. This injury is evident in the facial expression and pose of Caravaggio's Narcissus. He is obviously suffering. His pain distances him considerably, practically opposing him to the flower we were expecting, on the basis of Ovid. And from the "Phallus"—"imaginary Phallus," that is—one of the favorite objects in Lacanian psychoanalysis.

The problem of this Narcissus is that the narcissism that fed his ideal ego, where he was able to experience life with others, happens to be severely battered by what he has discovered, or rather by what is emerging, unbidden, about himself.

His narcissism is injured. And, on the subject of narcissistic injuries, in a crucial 1917 essay entitled, *A Difficulty in the Path of Psychoanalysis,*[33] Freud identifies three types, specifying that they may be devastating.

Upward downward

Freud cites the impact of the observations of Copernicus and Galileo. When we finally saw the universe where we and Earth are located, we were forced to admit that we are not the center of the world. The decentering was upward.

Freud draws a parallel with the ways the experience and lessons of psychoanalysis open our eyes to what dwells within us. Many of us are unconscious that whatever animates, haunts, or drives us usually comes from our inner depths, and the rather dark and sometimes savagely instinctive impulses that dwell there. The decentering is downward—a fact illustrated and perhaps even sensed, but only implicitly, in its time, by this Caravaggio canvas.

Since Freud speaks of yet another injury, this could contribute to our comparisons of Caravaggio's Narcissus with Ovid's—a Narcissus created almost sixteen centuries earlier.

Freud writes of an injury we receive when we are obliged to admit that the history of humanity goes back to dark, archaic, primitive times, when we were so similar to the animals around us that we had to struggle to emerge. Hence the enigmas of our earliest history, before writing was invented, times we pondered in the first chapter of this book. Likewise, we are continually haunted by the dream of a blissfully perfect state of nature—a perfection attained by a flower, perhaps. Yes it is merely an alluring dream, a fantasy Ovid tries to warn us about, at the same time as he himself indulges in cultivating its charm, as a poet.

In this regard, Freud speaks of an injury, a narcissistic injury. Such a term is fitting for the somber attitude we generally associate with this father of psychoanalysis. We explored it to some extent earlier, and if we recall the engraving by Dürer, one might describe it as melancholic.

From that point, let us take one more step with Freud, a step that might bring us even closer to the Narcissus by Caravaggio. Starting in

1920, in fact, precisely when Freud resumed his thinking about narcissism, and how it is related to the forces of annihilation and death he had learned to observe at various scales of their expression, from the most personal to the massive brutality and violence of our societies, Freud came to write about forces that seek only destruction, violent disorder, and disaster unto death.[34]

These are powerful and frightening words. Dürer's "angel" must have known how they felt. Is it not clear that Caravaggio's Narcissus is also fearful? His back is arched. He tries to resist. And perhaps he is about to be lost, body and soul.

We know that as an older man, Freud rather uncharacteristically began to "mythologize," calling what he elaborated at that time a "myth." He speaks of a "struggle between Titans," that of "Thanatos" wrestling with "Eros."[35] This was something he tried to think about in more theoretical terms as a very hypothetical "death instinct"—a suggestion that has continued to arouse discussion, to our day. Many analysts, even Freudians, reject it.

Is the death instinct not what we are dealing with here? What reality is this piece of art showing us and allowing us to experience? Is it a matter that Freud attempted to express in his own way?

To see it as the "shadow" described by Jungian psychology is manifestly inadequate. It is too limited, and moreover anachronistic.[36]

Some of our neo-Freudian colleagues are inclined to avoid seeing this reality that is so formless, primitive, and brutally threatening that it becomes inhuman. They tackle only the dreams, illusions, and imaginary constructions used to cover it up. However, we cannot ignore the evidence that this work from the late sixteenth century insists on bringing to our attention.

Like many of our Freudian colleagues, I am somewhat perplexed by the prospect of accepting Freud's "death instinct" hypothesis. It is surrounded with an explanatory metapsychology that hesitates between myth and the requirements of thinking that is both clinical and more generally theoretical.

Perhaps we must think differently and turn our attention toward alchemy. Freud took little interest in the literature and iconography of the alchemists. Jung, however, studied them closely, as a pioneer.

The alchemists emphasize the idea of the *nigredo*—quite different from what we call the "shadow." The *nigredo* is night, sometimes bottomless and endless. The alchemist artisan–philosophers and seekers, often solitary and always a bit heretical, had apparently experienced the nigredo in their own way, in their laboratories and oratories, sometimes to the point where they got lost in it.

And Jung notes that there are references everywhere in their texts to *divisio elementorum*, to *separatio*, to *solutio*, and even to *putrefactio, calcinatio, incineratio.*[37] He points out that to describe their experience of a reality that was so terrifyingly shattered, reduced to such an elementary state, so radically undifferentiated, they used the term "*materia prima.*"

Can we consider that the Narcissus by Caravaggio, and perhaps the earlier one by Ovid—and perhaps the Italian painter and the Latin poet, as well—had knowledge of this reality, if not explicitly, expressis verbis, at least by experience?

In any case, Jung recognized in the nigredo something he had to deal with when, after his rupture with Freud, he spent a long time alone, lost, and struggling with inner encounters and ordeals. For 17 years, he forced himself to draw and paint page after page of these adventures. He worked almost blindly, without really understanding what was happening at first. Then, he began to comment on and discuss them in his *Red Book*. It is the crucible of Jung's own way of being an analyst, and of thinking.[38]

In the iconography and literature of the alchemists, Jung recognized his own experience: sensorial, emotional, and intellectual. He came to speak of "*Zerstückelung*." This forceful, violent word in German literally speaks of a "shattering"—a terrifying event that may crush a person, or at least his ego. The result may be a disorder or even a catastrophic chaos, similar to the one in Dürer's *Melencolia* or in Caravaggio's *Narcissus.*

As I have written earlier, I recognize the Jungian approach better in Cranach's scene of the lady in red, with the scholarly, playful children next to her, than in *Melencolia* by Dürer.

Jung learned, for himself and his patients, that rather than a state, crisis can be a step. It can be a moment in a movement of transformation, a process. True, this process is still uncertain, but we can learn to reconnoiter, navigating as we go along, like explorers, adventurers, or discoverers.

Was there any clue to or expression of such a process in the work by Caravaggio?

This split circle that forms a whole

We observed that a circle is the basis for the composition of this painting. To be more precise, it is based on two semi-circles forming a circle drawn inside a square. As we saw, the partition and tension between these two half-circles is barely perceptible, if we read this painting according to Ovid's poem, or if we identify with this ideal figure of the young man in the upper part of the scene.

It is not that simple to see and perceive this line, which sunders the two halves of the composition. Consider what that difficulty means. The fact that this formal effect is not at all typical of Caravaggio's work makes its meaning even harder for us to grasp. Such a linear, geometrical division is literally extraordinary.[39]

A fact that is too extraordinary can be neglected or ignored. To do so is often proper, or useful—especially for the researcher, but not in psychoanalysis. Especially if one is venturing along the paths Jung opened to psychoanalysis. Jung assumed his singularity enough to be attached to the observation or study of facts, phenomena, and events that are ordinarily held to be so eccentric that they can easily be described as aberrations.

Take UFOs, for example. They are generally considered to be such extraordinary phenomena that they do not even deserve our serious attention.

The reader may recall that earlier I described this work as a UFO. Jung devoted a book to this sort of extraordinary apparition.[40] He did not do so to take any position on the question of the physical existence of unidentified flying objects. The subject of his book is the meaning of what is said about UFOs, and what was trying to be expressed: something that could be good to listen to and ponder.

Jung's approach is largely formal. He engages in a broad investigation of the reports of such objects, including drawings or paintings of them in other times and places.[41] He sees these human manifestations as an attempted response to an excessively threatening state of inner fragmentation, or outer disorder. The assembled shapes are sufficiently contained and containing to be much more livable than the condition or context that might have provoked them. He uses the terms of crisis, distress, call for help. And he speaks of the self.

This takes us far away from the ego, its narcissistic pretension, its dream of wholeness so vividly pointed out by our Lacanian analysts.

Jung suggests that in a context of utter disarray and despair, there is an attempt to form a whole that is only too conscious of its tensions and contradictions, but which nevertheless exists. He sees these objects or shapes as a series of trials or experiments with a wholeness that is in the process of being found or created.

Such is the wholeness shown in the painting by Caravaggio. This wholeness is not presented as an accomplished perfection. Instead, it is an expression of the tension of a quest for completeness, an experiment by trial and error.[42]

The "ideal" is excluded. One may dream of an ideally fulfilled self. Or one may act as though one has attained it. But such a self must then be said to be imaginary. Jung writes of many of our illusory constructions, especially in relation to totalitarianism of every sort, like totalitarian governments. And he demonstrates they are counterfeits or ersatzes. Jung is seeking to grasp the realization of another self, the self that is the subject of this painting, and it is not of this type.

Looking at Caravaggio's Narcissus through Jung's lens, we might venture to say he is related more to Christ—the crucified Christ—than to the young man Ovid introduces to us in the beginning of his poem.[43]

Indeed, the ideal or idealization of reality was not something that interested Caravaggio as an artist. In fact, one might wonder if he was led to paint this dark *Narcissus* by all of his earlier work, and by his very conception of art.

But, as we have also seen, this painting is such an event in his life's work, it is interesting to examine whether it will really remain as singular as it seemed to us at first; if it will be a landmark in his later career, and in the developments in painting after his time, in our history of forms.

The singularity and modernity of such a composition

This painting's frontality and the nearly abstract nature of its composition—a barred circle in a nearly black square—makes it stand out so strikingly from the rest of Caravaggio's oeuvre that, as we mentioned earlier, scholars have hesitated to attribute it to him. But is it really so erratic, so extraordinary, and so unique that it is without parallel in the rest of his painting?

In fact, Caravaggio later painted a canvas that bears a strong relationship to *Narcissus—The Conversion on the Way to Damascus*, painted in 1601. It currently hangs in Rome, to the left of the great altar in the Church of Santa Maria del Popolo.

You will be struck by the flash of lightning ripping through the pictorial space. It is formed by the white light coming down from the sky above the horse, and it has struck Paul. Paul has been thrown to the ground, and we know that when he stands again, he will not be the same man he was before this event. No longer Saul, persecutor of the first Christians, he will become an apostle of Christ—according to the account. What matters here is evidently the pictorial event resulting from the dazzling white light on the animal's shoulder, so bright that it expresses the lightning striking this man.[44]

Truly, this work is a bolt of dazzling lightning, perhaps even more powerful than the Narcissus we have been looking at. Like lightning, it rips through the canvas, through the painter's oeuvre, and through the art of its time.

It certainly supports Poussin's statement that from his point of view, the work of Caravaggio had destroyed painting, or was going to. After these two events, the *Narcissus* and the *Conversion*, painting would cease to be what it had been before; it would undergo a transformation in the centuries that followed, painting would indulge in showing classical narrative, and even strive to show it, all neatly tied up in a whole, as was the case before. But these two works by Caravaggio definitely transform the way we look at painting.[45]

I mentioned abstraction in this regard. Since Caravaggio, we have learned to live with it since Monet and Manet. Monet taught us to see what is created by a painting, rather than what it represents or the story it tells.

Although Monet was a great lover of gardens, streams, ponds, and fields, he put the last touch on his canvases in the studio, not outdoors. His painting strikes us by its own effect, an effect which is an experience in itself, to be discovered, rejoiced in, or rejected—and to be thought about.

As for Manet, if he caused a scandal in his time, it is because his painting is often so frontal that it detaches us even more from any easily navigable perspective, from any opening onto a familiar world, whether this world is mythological or realistic. When the artist applies a layer of paint that makes no effort to disguise the flatness of the canvas, and the frontality of his composition denies us any vanishing point, we find ourselves facing the immediacy, and therefore the enigma, of a silent, new reality. I am thinking of the reality of his *Olympia* (1863), for example.[46] We are forced to look at it without really knowing what to say or do with it. Our reflection must open to the painting itself, to what is happening with it, to the experience it gives us, and no escape is possible.

Twentieth-century abstraction emerged from this simultaneous detachment from the outer object and from any narrativity.[47] Our abstract art gradually traveled so far from the outer world and our taste for stories that it became more and more spiritualist in purpose and sublimated in form.[48]

In their composition and formal expression, both canvases by Caravaggio, *Narcissus* and the *Conversion*, open a path in this direction, and venture to explore it.

However, unlike our abstract arts—and this difference is decisive—these two works also stage the weight of the body, and make us feel it. Narcissus is tensed, with an arched back, and Paul thrown to the ground. The effect is the opposite of the abstract launch into sublime, spiritual flight. Here, all the movement in the composition soberly points downward. That is hardly the direction of sublimation.

We noted that the paintings resembled freeze frames. Besides surprising us by cutting up the well-known story we expected, these instants leave us in suspense, waiting, awaiting what will ensue.

Time is suspended. But history, the history of forms, our history of art, the history of man discovering who he is, discovering himself how he is, in his relationship to himself, must find its path. Where will it lead us?

These works by Caravaggio show us the adventure looming. Doubtless, it has never been this close. It is becoming really human, almost personal. These two canvases engage our attention, a fully emotional attention, with two fellow human beings, our kin and kind. Both are suffering. Through painting, one of them becomes Ovid's hero, and the other Christ's apostle.

We have gone beyond thinking of ourselves by projecting ourselves into such a figure offered by mythologies we have inherited, or created by the dominant ideologies, or preached by the church of the moment. This Narcissus might be an ordinary person like you or me. This Paul, who has fallen from his horse as well as from the convictions that drove or agitated him until then, could be one of your friends, or you or me, navigating some personal difficulties.

The risk these ordinary people are braving, as we see it in these canvases, is awe-striking. It gets deeper. Not only does this danger become quite personal, but especially, he who has the nerve to look will see that it is not only the threat of a fall, of defeat. Here, the risk is disintegration, death, and chaos.[49]

Indeed, the question challenges us: where are we going, where will we go, how will we take another step, on the brink of such an abyss?

Anticipating our collective history, I have made Jung speak. When he wondered about the art of our time, on the subject of the creations of Joyce and Picasso, he thought in terms of process—the creation process, the individuation process.

With Caravaggio, we are at a certain moment and in a certain context of our collective history, situated at the dawn of the seventeenth century, not in the conditions of our twentieth and twenty-first centuries.

If there is a collective adventure under way in our history, in the movements of transformation of our culture, it is evidently playing out under different conditions and circumstances, and we consider that. The time frame is long, the "longue durée," as Fernand Braudel noted.[50]

We know that this adventure that forms and sometimes deforms us often happens to be marked by brutal crises and transitions, by events that bring us from one state or stage of ourselves to another, as was the case with these works by Caravaggio—which remain in suspense.

Suspense becomes waiting. And this waiting is not without fear, or at least not without ambivalence.

6

Who the Heck Is Bluebeard?

THE NINETEENTH CENTURY GRAPPLES WITH AN OGRE

Our next encounter may be even more disturbing than the one with Narcissus in the preceding chapter.

We will look at four engravings by Gustave Doré dating from 1867. Widespread opinion currently dismisses the academicism triumphing in the arts during the second half of the nineteenth century scornfully, as "*pompier.*"[1] Evidently, the word is sometimes fitting. But it is too general to summarize all of what was being presented, represented, and lived at the time. And especially, for what was in preparation.

Likewise, Gustave Doré is sometimes considered a "minor" artist. But it would be unthinkable to relegate this painter, sculptor, and engraver, who took on the illustration of Dante's *Inferno*, to a minor rank.[2]

Observing the first of the engravings, *Bluebeard*, our more intellectual viewers may say that the key is its main subject, exerting an attraction for the hands and almost hypnotic gaze of the young woman, seen here in profile. True, the key is in the center of the scene and, as a result, the entire composition of the picture seems to designate it as the primary subject of the story, imposing it upon our attention. For all of us, the key is a powerful symbol. We are often searching for keys and, if possible, a single, universal key, which would unlock the world's secrets for us, giving us access to boundless knowledge about everything. Were we to possess such a key, we could even open the immaterial doors of the mysteries of the mind.[3]

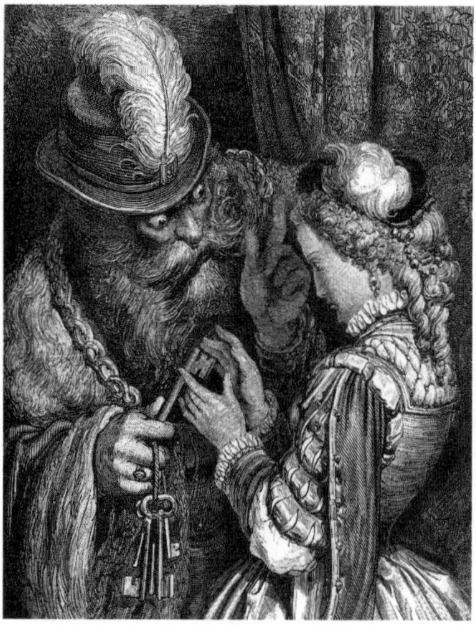

Doré, Bluebeard I

But what if the key were a trick? A red herring? This engraving belongs to a familiar old story, set down in writing by Charles Perrault at the end of the seventeenth century, in 1697. It is entitled *Bluebeard*, and it has been told to generations of listeners for at least three centuries now.[4]

Most people know that the story somehow centers largely on the key—a key that has been given to the young woman we see here, with strict instructions that she refrain from using it under any circumstances. From the outset, we are dealing with well-known, common lore.

But the power of this picture derives from something else. The most obvious element of a composition is sometimes not the essential subject. In fact, it may be there to distract our attention. Perhaps this young woman is about to fall for the same trick. According to the illustration, she is not aware of anything besides the key, and yet she would be wise to look around and take notice, as would we.

As we allow our eyes to roam,[5] there is something we can no longer avoid seeing. It is an enormous, ham-fisted creature, bristling with whiskers and fur, his eyes popping out as if to devour a prey. It's an overpowering presence speaking to or perhaps even scolding the young woman, who is focused only on the key.

This figure is not on the fringes of the scene; on the contrary, physically, he practically overwhelms the picture. But the artist may knowingly and deliberately have placed the key in the center of the composition to trick us—a false clue to distract us from the essential.

The story's moral

Since the story of *Bluebeard* is well known, we are well aware of the lesson or moral it is supposed to teach us. Perrault indulged in putting it in a little rhyme at the end of his story.[6] He writes:

> O curiosity, thou mortal bane!
> Spite of thy charms, thou causest often pain
> And sore regret, of which we daily find
> A thousand instances attend mankind:
> For thou—O may it not displease the fair—
> A fleeting pleasure art, but lasting care.
> And always proves, alas! too dear the prize,
> Which, in the moment of possession, dies.[7]

So curiosity is a wicked flaw. Actually, the fact that this moral is accompanied by a scantily veiled warning not to yield to the temptation to open locked doors makes it all too explicit. No one would dare bother the grownups or the people in charge with inquisitive questions or new ideas that might trouble the established order.

As if one warning were not enough, Perrault adds another rhyming moral to this story:

> This a story is of time long pass'd;
> No husbands now such panic terrors cast;
> Nor weakly, with a vain despotic hand,
> Imperious, what's impossible, command:
> And be they discontented, or the fire
> Of wicked jealousy their hearts inspire,
> They softly sing; and of whatever hue
> Their beards may chance to be, or black, or blue,

Grizeld, or russet, it is hard to say
Which of the two, the man or wife, bears sway.

This moral is much more cheerful—for women, at least. The terrible story simply speaks of bygone customs. Today's men would do well to reckon with the power, authority, and judgment that in most cases have been acquired by modern women.

So it is merely a word to the wise. Or is it? The story from which Perrault drew his fairytale, now a classic that is retold and reread even in the twenty-first century, wrapped in its double moral, has probably been told ever since the remote past. It does not allow itself to be forgotten that easily, and even today, it has the power to scare us.[8]

As we read the text and look at the series of four engravings, take the story at its word. Regarding our first remark about the role of the key in the composition, and that of the figure who now dominates, examine what Doré's engravings do with this text. They may add something that could be helpful in our approach to the story or, on the contrary, they may omit something that we should be a little more curious about.

The beard and the blue

No doubt every reader of Perrault notices that the text is uncanny from the outset. Unusual and quite enigmatic. Why on earth is the beard in this story blue? The color is totally unexpected for a beard, which is ordinarily white, black, or salt-and-pepper. But not blue. The casual mention of the odd color is a glaring beacon. It should attract our attention.

Moreover, in French, the title of the story is not simply "*Barbe Bleue*" or "*Bluebeard*," as we might expect. Such a title would introduce the story of a character nicknamed Bluebeard. Instead, its title is "*La Barbe Bleue*," or "*The Blue Beard*." The use of the article draws our attention to an object—in this case, the beard—rather than to a character.[9]

Just in case the detail of the beard in the text escaped our attention, Gustave Doré's illustration features it quite prominently. The artist even exaggerates the whiskers, extending them luxuriantly. The man is really quite hairy all over. He is even cloaked in animal furs like some inhabitant of the deep wilderness, a sort of primitive, half-savage whose very beastliness makes him all the more frightening—whereas in Perrault's story, the husband was still at least superficially a sort of great lord, or at least a wealthy gentleman, "who had beautiful houses in the city and in the countryside, gold and silver dishes, brocaded furniture, and bright, gilded carriages." All such qualities are left out of the picture, where the artist puts the accent on the disturbing strangeness of the character in question, a weirdness that apparently prevails over the richness of his possessions.

As for the color blue, we cannot look to Doré for any sort of insight, because being an engraver, he works in black and white. In the illustration, the beard is black, so this feature of Perrault's description disappears. Actually, the starkness of the black and white does not make the engraving an especially light-hearted or reassuring vision.[10]

But we do have an excellent clue that may help solve the mysterious question of blue, even in Doré's illustration. As we saw earlier, Jung discovered this clue when he analyzed Picasso's paintings. Briefly, Jung showed how the occurrence and then the predominance of the color blue in the painter's canvases—a "midnight blue," he specifies—is oddly similar to the blue of the Egyptian underworld, the *Duat*. Blue actually signals a sort of descent into hell, a *nekyia* from which one might not return,[11] so perilous are the subterranean, chthonic encounters down below. They are frightening visions, somewhat blurry, as inchoate as they are disastrous. Jung himself had experienced this torment throughout the years when he was toiling over his *Red Book*, without really knowing where he was going. Hence his attention to what Homer might have said about the subject to the glimpses Goethe gives of it in *Faust*, or to Nietzsche's observations on the theme.

Perrault's story and Doré's illustrations of *Bluebeard* point us in this direction. They are connected to it as closely as many of the other works I have mentioned. Their specificity and difference from the Picasso blue-period paintings is that instead of drawing our attention to figures who are somewhat lost, fragile, or broken—alcoholic women or lonely acrobats—the character in this story is a powerful, wealthy man. He is determined to obtain everything he seeks and desires, a fact that changes the deal significantly. It means that the young woman, and us with her, is facing an adversary who is much stronger than she is, and all the more dangerous.

Again, Gustave Doré emphasizes and develops this detail Perrault only hints at. Look at Bluebeard's hands. They convey all of the character's strength and might, dwarfing the young woman's delicate, tiny fingers. His bulging eyes are terrifying, and his physical presence overwhelming and invasive. His violence is more than potential, making this enormous mass of hairy flesh truly an ogre.

What exactly is an ogre?

The term is relatively recent in French—in fact, Perrault was the first writer to popularize it. Among the characters and themes Perrault enjoys directing in his tales, the ogre is unique. The monster plays an especially prominent role in the collection of stories in which Bluebeard was originally published, *Les Contes du temps passé* or *Contes de ma Mère l'Oye.*

Think of the terrifying story of *Tom Thumb*, for example. When the miniature boy's parents decide to get rid of him by abandoning him in the forest, he survives and rescues his brothers owing only to the fact that he is taken in by an ogre and his wife, and tricks the monster into eating his own children.

Actually, the ogres in Perrault's stories are so frightening that they do really intend to devour small children, a serious threat. Life is at stake. When we read Perrault, tale after tale deals with a matter of life or death.

In examining similar tales from other lands, Verena Kast reminds us of some foreign variants in a book she dedicates to victimhood, and how to deliver oneself from it.

The book is entitled *Abschied von der Opferrolle. Das eigene Leben leben* (which could be translated as "How to free oneself from the victim's position. Living one's own life"). In it, Verena Kast discusses *Bluebeard* and tells us that in other versions of the story,[12] this character—if that is the proper word—might be made of different metals,

metals that are totally inhuman. For instance, in the Italian story, the gentleman's nose is made of silver. In a Swedish version, it is made of gold.[13]

So this husband actually is a monster. Our perception and reflection vacillate. We are filled with dread. All the more so when other versions of the story tell us he eats human corpses. He is so inhuman that we sometimes represent him to ourselves as a god of death. As a result, with this particular character, death in person, so to speak, steps into the story.

In his own way, Perrault informs us. When, alongside the young woman in *Bluebeard*, we open the forbidden room, what do we behold? We discover that this great gentleman, a somewhat fatherly husband, with his compelling yet terrifying promise of riches, is really a bloodthirsty murderer. The bodies of his victims are in there. He is a serial killer.

The vision is horrific. The scene is terrible, terrifying, and unbearable. It is almost unspeakable, and, in any case, unlivable. There is blood everywhere, pools glittering with the reflection of the corpses. The young woman recoils. She wants to flee. We understand her terror.[14] But, being readers familiar with the story, we must face the horror and keep going.

We are all the more obligated to go on with the story by the fact that the etymology of the word "ogre" is already a highly explicit signpost. It may contribute to making us attentive to the scope of what we are dealing with—as long as we inspect it more closely.

The word "ogre" is derived from the Latin common noun "orcus," meaning ogre, known in modern Italian as "orco" and in Spanish as "uerco." The Latin noun comes from the name of a somber Roman divinity, often represented as a bearded, hairy giant, who was doubtless an earlier Etruscan figure. This fearsome creature was none other than Orcus, the god of the Underworld, or Hell.

Gustave Doré, dealing with this theme, takes it quite seriously. He exaggerates the illustration, making explicit what has only been suggested by Perrault's text. He specifies the threat, almost violently emphasizing the rough and limitless brutality and power, akin to bestiality, of the ogres Perrault describes. Doré composes his illustration in such a way as to draw our attention with even more precision than Perrault's texts, to the child, to what the child experiences.

In one of the plates he engraved for the story of *Tom Thumb* in 1867, the same year he drew the four illustrations for *Bluebeard*, he depicts a scene entitled *The ogre devouring its own daughters.* We see an enormous creature, hands already about to take the girls' lives, with eyes bulging almost as monstrously as those of Bluebeard. It is important to note that the figure's sex is hard to determine. Is the predator the Ogre or the Ogress? Meanwhile, the little girls, the ogrettes, are still peacefully and innocently asleep, side by side, in the bed where the monster is about to grab them.[15]

The Ogre or Ogress—the figure's sex is hard to make out[16]—is seen from below, at an angle. This point of view would be that of the children, if they opened their eyes. The composition makes us experience the story from the children's viewpoint.

All of us, in the past, were once children, and so we can readily identify with the babes in Doré's illustration. It is not that we have nothing to learn from reading about the ancient Egyptian underworld, or the monsters of folktales of various European countries like Italy or Sweden. This research commits us to making a wiser evaluation of what we read in Perrault and what we see in Doré. As we see, this type of investigation is meaningful only as far as it sustains and really animates our approach to what Perrault has given us to read, in his tales, and what Doré has given us to see.[17]

This investigation, involving a brush with terrifying, deadly beings due to Perrault's tale and especially Doré's illustration may very well make it mandatory for us to return to our own experience as infants: the encounters and dangers and terrors we experienced at the time—and that perhaps we are still experiencing, and to attune all the power of our senses and emotions to this return to our sources.

I am sure that I have aroused the interest of our Freudian colleagues. The ideas and remarks voiced here reflect the most determined aspects of their psychoanalysis. These are the ideas that drove Freud's pioneering research and thinking about childhood and children, about infantile sexuality, and that have provoked a scandalous outcry for over a century now.

I celebrate with them in this reference to Freud's discoveries. In our time, psychoanalysis is a combination of many traditions and schools. But regardless of the tradition in which it develops and is practiced, attention to childhood experiences is something that can have primordial importance. It's evident in my clinical practice.

Yet there are rumors that Jung and the Jungian tradition might have some tendency to ignore this Freudian lesson, or at least to neglect or forget it. These rumors can be disproved simply by reading or rereading Jung, to recall the attention he himself paid to childhood—to his own, in particular.

Saying and showing can be frightening

In the memories, dreams, and reflections the elderly Jung described or dictated to his secretary, there is a memory of childhood that was especially striking for him. It marked him to such a degree that it sustained and oriented his own way of being himself, of becoming an analyst, of thinking.

In the first pages of his autobiography,[18] Jung reports an extremely disturbing scene—actually, a strange and troubling experience, an event that allegedly occurred when he was two or three. It would seem that his parents were momentarily separated; perhaps his mother had been hospitalized briefly.

The child experienced a serious misunderstanding with regard to an evening prayer his mother had taught him. He used to like to repeat it for reassurance, to ward off both the free-floating anxiety of darkness and the menaces of Satan.[19]

Spread out thy wings, Lord Jesus mild,
And take to thee thy chick, thy child.
If Satan would devour it,
No harm shall overpower it,
So let the angels sing!
This child must stay safe and sound.

The image of the great bird with its wings spread may appear protective and comforting, like the verse praying for the child's safety.

But in this case, the words betray the primary impression, the expectation the prayer would be reassuring—unless they are actually revealing a contradiction woven into the very fabric of this invocation.

The "chick" in the story is obviously also the small child who must be kept safe and sound. In the local Basel dialect spoken where Jung grew up, "chick" is called *Kuechli Kuechli.*[20] And, in the same dialect, Kuechli were also little cookies that were a great regional culinary delight. As a result, for young Carl Gustav, praying to Jesus, was asking Him to swallow him—to avoid being devoured by Satan.

No matter how loud the angels sing, in the gathering night, the half-said prospect is indeed terrifying. Whom are you supposed to trust, when the Jesus your minister father is always preaching about, and to whom your mother is always praying, turns out to be, or might very well turn out to be, quite the opposite, a devouring creature within which the little child might disappear? In fact, let us recall that although the first mentions Jung makes of his father in his autobiographical essays are respectful and sober, he also describes his father as a somber, irritable, and really ineffectual man. Jung writes that to him, the word "father" meant trustworthy and... incapable. He says that is the handicap he started with. As for his mother, although she appeared to be quite the opposite—reassuring, physically strong, and imposing—she often blurted out strangely subversive remarks, even on the subject of her husband's sermons.

This is definitely enough to undermine the basic confidence a child might want to place in each of his parents, in the couple they form and, ultimately, in himself. It is also enough to make any faith waver, and to cause the disintegration of all capacity to believe. Doubtless, it is the source of the questioning distance that would characterize Jung throughout his life, especially in matters related to religion and Christianity in particular. It also explains his taste for open research, inclined to challenge any statement claiming to be the truth.

This includes Freudian statements. In the confusion aroused and maintained by the words of the prayer, Jung seems to have experienced something in childhood that fits in with Freud's teachings, at the core of his relationships to himself and his family, at the core of his sexuality in its expressions, discoveries, and most elementary questions. These childhood events do indeed shape, direct, and drive all of an individual's later growth, especially if the child grows up to be a seeker.[21]

But should Jung be said to be a Freudian? A Freudian who was unaware of his Freudianism? Or a Freudian who stubbornly refused to admit he was a Freudian? Not exactly.

Jung's memory is indeed related to a child's experience of the oral, feeding, and therefore potential devouring, and also what is obscurely digestive and anal in the confusing weave of the body's most elementary functions, which are also its most vital. There is an uncertain and threatening intrication between the child's own body and the body of the other—that of his mother, Jesus, or Satan.

But this experience that Jung was able to summon from his childhood memory, an experience he never forgot, throughout his life and work, an experience he spoke of as an old man, when he had been asked to write his memories—places us well beneath the infantile sexuality that is the subject of Freud's theories, in a much more primitive world.

It is the dangerous world he ventured to explore when, after breaking off relations with Freud, he engaged in the solitary, uncharted journey of making his *Red Book*.[22] It is the descent into chaos he watched his patients accomplish, as he learned how to guide them. Jung recognized it as the realm the alchemists risked journeying, in their own way, with their own illusions, for Jung had deciphered their manuscripts and images, to understand their quest. It is a world that many Freudian analysts after Freud have explored: notably Melanie Klein and also Winnicott and then a whole school of contemporary psychoanalysis, especially British.

Why did Jung venture so far? Precisely because from early childhood, he was driven in that direction, and also because he had the wisdom or duty to assume such a position, always exploring and never taking anything for granted, from one step to the next in his life as a practitioner and thinker. It's also because more than likely, he consequently had absolutely no sense of orthodoxy, of obedience, of an untouchable dogma—and therefore, in his time, no concept of a Freudian dogma.[23]

The point is that what is at stake is an archaic reality that it is impossible to reduce to the first childhood experiences. It is the very same archaic reality implemented by Perrault, in his stories, and by Doré in his engravings, and by many other artists in many other forms of expression. By bringing this world to life for us, they enable us to experience the feelings it arouses. We can get back in touch with this world, without taking the risk of getting lost in it, body and soul.

This archaic reality dwells within us, haunting us, sometimes obsessing or overflowing from us, especially when we insist on ignoring it. It lives its own life, more or less independently, often untamed, in the depths, the deepest depths of ourselves. It is ever menacing, of course, and especially radically alien. With all the vigor of its savagery, it fights any measure we might take to assimilate, control, or contain it, and also really to understand it.

We wish to believe that we have left this archaic reality far behind us. But it remains powerfully present, and in sum, it is the raw material of ourselves, largely oblivious to the temporality in which we dwell, the chronology of our days and ages in life. It mocks the very concept we live by, of passing time. For time does not pass. It stubbornly lingers. And it demands our attention, in a variety of ways, including that of the arts.

Freud went rather far in this direction. Speaking of the unconscious, he found the words to say how violent and barbaric it can be, and how insistently repetitive. He even described the way it is "timeless" (*zeitlos*).[24]

In this regard, in the latter part of his life and work, Freud also spoke of a "death instinct," as I noted previously, that would be opposed to the "life instinct." This opposition evidently polarizes the issue. A dichotomous approach is too reductive to account for what we behold here, an archaic reality dwelling beneath polarities, beneath any differentiation between instincts, or drives. It is too cerebral or intellectual to plumb these depths.

Moreover, Freud's discoveries, although powerful and impressive, do not require that we challenge his approach to the unconscious.

Both theoretically and clinically, we are confined to defining it by repression—the repression of sexuality, and more specifically, of infantile sexuality.[25]

However, Jung, in one epistemological and practical stroke that contributed significantly to changing the course of psychoanalysis, reversed the question of the relationship to the unconscious. He postulated that consciousness could be, as we saw earlier when we thought about our prehistory, a relatively recent event in the history of life, and that therefore it would proceed from the unconscious—an unconscious that is alive and always actively present within us. This is really a reversal of, and practically a revolution in, the Freudian approach to the concept.

The reversal makes the Jungian approach one that we can clearly describe today as "emergentist."[26] The most notable result of the approach is that it invites us to receive, experience, and think the unconscious on companionable terms, instead of on the basis of repression alone. It calls on us to observe it prospectively, knowing that there may be something to be gained by venturing into its most archaic expressions, into its most undifferentiated, shattered, chaotic depths. They are what we speak of now, as soon as we set our sights on an awakening, a transformation, or a differentiation.[27]

As we have seen, the arts provide an opening, along with the random events and encounters of life, like the ones that occur with the clinical practice of psychoanalysis.

7

A Contemporary Bluebeard Story

Let's begin with a recent case history from a fellow analyst, which is within the framework of a study group several of us formed to collaborate on clinical and theoretical matters.[1]

This case history may lead us to reconsider what we gleaned from Perrault's fairytale and Doré's engravings. What these productions convey may deserve further investigation, especially when read from the standpoint of our present clinical practice.

This is the story of a woman who, outwardly, seems to be a successful, untroubled person, healthy in body and mind: well-educated, elegant, and well-bred. At least, that's how she appeared to her analyst, who described her as "a very attractive 40-year-old woman, rather austere, with the severe, haughty demeanor certain Germanic women have;" "with a town-and-country style of elegance." "She wears tasteful, practical clothing, in muted colors."[2]

The analyst noted that the woman remembers her father as a wealthy businessman, powerful and imperious. He had inherited his own father's prosperous trade in a provincial town. She remembers her parents as always quarreling. Her father eventually distanced himself from his wife, practically ignoring her, as time went on.[3]

She said that other people had always described her as a model child, and she agreed. She had been a good student: obedient, cheerful, and active. Later, she took an interest in ancient and contemporary art, and had begun studies in philosophy in the provincial town where she still lived. Likewise, she made frequent journeys to Paris to participate in the city's lofty academic circles. When she began her analysis, she was preparing to write a doctoral dissertation with encouragement of her professors.

She had been married for a few years. Her husband was a prominent attorney in their town. Both of them enjoyed giving dinner parties for friends, family, associates, or local dignitaries.

Her analyst noted her perfect punctuality, a sign of her commitment to the analysis. She was so serious about being a good subject that she read Jung carefully and was fluent in the vocabulary—the one used by her Jungian analyst.

At this point in this story of a present-day psychoanalysis, perhaps the reader will recall the Perrault tale: the heroine's mother, "a lady of quality," and her friends, all delighted to be invited to Bluebeard's splendid palace to see his riches, feast, and celebrate. "All was promenading, hunting and fishing parties, dances and gaiety; delicious things to eat. No one slept at all: the night was spent in playing tricks on each other."[4]

The second engraving in Gustave Doré's *Bluebeard* series (below) depicts the party. Unlike most of his other work, it is somewhat anec-

Doré, Bluebeard II

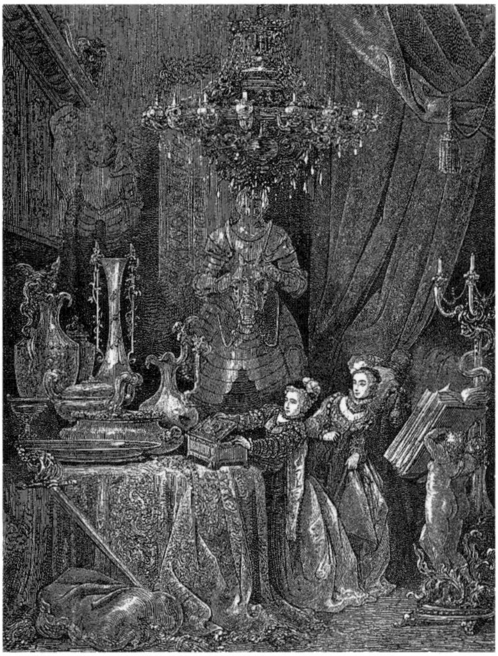

dotal. Doré shows nothing of the mother, despite the fact that, as we noted from the Perrault story, she plays a rather prominent role, having encouraged her daughter to wed this disturbing man. The mother is absent from Doré's scene—unless the knight in armor in the background is a metaphorical stand-in for the mother and the lord of the manor.

The other young women in the story, according to Doré's engraving and Perrault's text, all resemble the heroine—who actually has almost no heroic attributes, being rather two-dimensional, and lacking even a name. All we sense or know about her is that she is about to find herself in a crucial situation, facing an ordeal that may or may not make someone of her.[5]

The female subject of the psychoanalytic story I am sharing might be a modern cousin to these maidens. She, too, is rather bland, according to the descriptions. However, like the young woman in *Bluebeard*, she is actively curious and thirsty for knowledge—about the arts, philosophy, and particularly about psychoanalysis.

Outwardly, she seemed to be fine. That is even how she introduced herself. But she gradually told her analyst something quite different, initially by little hints or scraps, as if speaking from afar, and with some wariness. Beneath this seemingly perfect exterior, her life was traversed, shaken, and tormented by scenes of terrible violence, with her husband, on countless occasions.

At these times, she would assail her husband with barrages of questions and virulent criticism. She would investigate every part of his life, to squeeze his secrets out of him, to crush him, intellectually. At other times, she would abase herself to him, appearing to be servile and absolutely submissive, with inner feelings of total dejection and shame. "Rejected," "persecuted," and "devastated" are the words she used to describe these moods to her analyst, who notes the stark contrast between the aggressiveness of the attacks and the wife's second position, as a lowly victim.

One day, when the young woman was once again recalling one of the terrible marital fights with her analyst, the latter blurted out something so spontaneous that it surprised her. "But when you open your husband's secret doors, you may open Bluebeard's secret chamber."

A misguided missile or a strike that was right on target?

Now Bluebeard, unannounced, enters the field of this analysis. And it isn't entirely clear if the ogre's appearance is the result of one of the analyst's own associations, an observation she might have kept to herself, or even an intervention that might have been a clumsy intrusion. Or could it have been an attempt at interpretation?

The young woman paid absolutely no further attention to the intervention. The analysis seemed to proceed as if nothing had happened, with the same accounts of daily life, of the same dreadfully vicious marital quarrels, and the radical reversals of attitude noted already, the swings from rage at the husband to utter subjugation to him, a self-abnegation so extreme that the woman was practically crushed or annihilated.

Little by little, events from the past, both distant and recent, returned. Initially, in the early analysis sessions, they were described factually, without any show of emotion. Only later did they take on weight. The erratic discourse about them subsided. But the memories came back, growing more specific, imposing themselves on the young woman, who stopped to consider them. Amazed, she began to explore and connect these events. She returned to them and pondered them.

Disaster and death in her life

The story written by Perrault and illustrated by Doré is a terrifying story of violent, bloodthirsty murder, of serial killing. The story of this young woman soon proved to be almost as striking.

We gradually learned that her life had been disrupted by violence and death several times—brutal deaths and murderous gestures.

First she recalled the story of falling in love with a boy at school when she was 16 years old. This beautiful love story ended two years later with the death of her boyfriend, after months of cancer treatment that served to reduce him to an emaciated shadow of himself. She said the event caused her to lose her memory, which had been excellent.

Much later in her analysis, she added that after this death, she felt cut off from the world for years, feeling nothing, as if she were "functioning behind a pane of safety glass," she says—a feeling, or rather a numbness, a drastic absence of feeling, that is the same thing she experiences when her clashes with her husband reach their most violent intensity.

In the account she gradually gives of her life, the bodies accumulate. To list them briefly, there is the death of her old female cat, blind and deaf, whom she loved dearly, but who could no longer recognize her (cats and kitties, in various conditions, often lamentable, emerge often in the description, or rather the reconnection, the reliving of her life story and of her inner life). She associates this death with that of her grandmother—both the grandmother and the cat died the same year, when she was still very young.

Very early in her analysis, she mentioned her other grandmother in a matter-of-fact tone, devoid of any particular emotion, without paying her any particular attention. The story about this other grandmother, who lived in the country and came from a strong rural Catholic tradition, was that in the 1920s, learning she was pregnant with a fourth baby, she decided that it was hard enough raising the three children she already had. Alone, she traveled to a nearby city to have an abortion—in an era and context of powerful social and moral control, especially for all matters concerning women.

The rest of what emerged as the woman gradually spoke of her life, in her analytic sessions, turned out to be just as amazing.

"*Hilflosigkeit*"

"*Hilflosigkeit*," or "helplessness," is a German term that has been used in psychoanalysis since Freud, to speak of the distress of the very small child, whose only means of obtaining the attention and assistance he needs from the elders in his family is by screaming, crying, and gesticulating.[6]

This young woman had experienced this sort of distress. Her analysis would reflect this call for help. Nevertheless, at first, it came from very far away. It gradually became closer, and finally became more vivid and emotional.

She told her analyst, initially in an offhand way, about an odd "game" she had often played as a child, after outings with her parents. On the way home, she would run past them, reaching the house first. She would climb up on the doorstep and lie down in front of the door, chanting, "I am an outcast child, I'm cold and hungry. I need to be comforted."

In the analysis, she gradually returned to this scene, which is difficult to dismiss as ordinary and innocuous. It is so powerful that she came to see it and relive it as a fairly violent and intense condensation, and as a paradigmatic expression, of a large part of her life. Actually, the vision is so paradigmatic that one almost wonders how often, in reality, she actually played this "game." Perhaps it was not as frequently as it seemed to her as a grown woman. For her, the make-believe could have been a somewhat dramatized manner of getting back to, finally acknowledging, and having someone hear what she was experiencing as a child—and what she was still experiencing, in her relationships and disputes with her husband, in particular.[7]

Other situations of rejection, abandonment, and despair came from even more remote sources to be associated with this scene. She knew that her mother had had two miscarriages: one before her conception, and another shortly after her birth. When the mother had described the miscarriage to her daughter, she had done so in rather abrupt, callous terms, speaking of how she "felt the blood running down her legs"—another scene, from the preceding generation, that this young woman talked about early in her analysis as if she were reporting some distant news that had no emotional impact on her—as if she had not been harshly and profoundly scarred by the event.

In generation after generation, from the grandmothers, to the mother, to her own, in woman after woman, violence and disaster were repeated in this way. And yet, for a long time, she remained oblivious to it, measuring neither the impact of it, nor herself in comparison to it.[8]

But her recollection of herself, of what might have imprinted upon her since before birth, soon delved even deeper. It sent her back to her earliest infancy, and also to the very heart of what had caused her to begin an analysis.

In some of her early sessions, she told of another scene to which she returned only two years later, so reluctant to approach it. On the day her mother had her second miscarriage, she supposedly fell from the diaper-changing table when her mother was attending to her—I use the conditional here, because as real as this scene might be, it is obviously just as paradigmatic as the "game" of being abandoned on the doorstep and the call for help she would later address to her parents and, in sum, to anyone willing to listen.

It is understandable why, later in her analysis, these three scenes—the "game" on the doorstep, the scene of her mother's miscarriage, and the fall from the changing table—would become the condensation of what she had to say to herself about her life, and also about death, or at least about the most serious threats of death that had befallen her. She dreamed of an old barn that is slowly but inexorably collapsing while she feels fortunate to have been able to rescue her cat, in the nick of time—along with a few pieces of furniture, including a mirror that had belonged to her grandparents.

This last scene is a dream scene. It says what dwells within, or haunts her, in her inner life, a life that had long been active, inside her. Gradually, from the brutally factual universe that had been hers, to which she had long been subjected, she had been able to make an inner representation and question,[9] that she could then consider and explore, about which she could wonder—although, as this dream tells her, to do so was to take the risk of truly becoming frightened of it, and perhaps truly collapsing.

The worst, in the depths

Inner life may be even less reassuring than the harshest facts, as this young woman learned by experience. At first, she did not exactly realize it. She experienced it from a distance, from too great a distance.

In her very first session with her analyst, she had spoken almost gingerly of a dream she remembered. Actually, it is rather terrifying. In the dream, she saw a vigorous, lively cat—which her mother intended to kill. Her mother wanted to kill the cat with an injection in the head. The cat struggled. The daughter tried to protest. Finally, with the third injection, the cat died.

This dream remained as if waiting, in suspense through months and years of analysis until, very gradually, the young woman was able to relate it to the story of the death of her very old cat, with what she knew of the stories of her grandmothers, with the violence that had become a chill between her parents, with the fall from the changing table, with her "game" of being abandoned on the doorstep, when she was still small, with the death of her teenage love, with the reversible violence of her marital disputes.

Our inner universe may long remain as if remote from ourselves, with its more or less recurrent characters, landscapes, scenes, or smells, and erratic half-memories.[10] Keeping it at bay is a vain effort, for the inner world specific to us nevertheless surreptitiously inhabits us, and drives our relationships to ourselves and to others. If we accept it, this could be a source of great delight in our lives. But it is also true that we may sometimes have reasons for maintaining this distance, ignoring this world or trying to. For venturing too boldly into some regions of ourselves may make us the captives of the terrible depths of ourselves. We sometimes think it wiser to "let sleeping dogs lie" and stay at a safe distance.

It would take this woman six years of careful, attentive analysis to collect the shards of her story and assemble them, finally recognizing herself in the several steps, circumstances, and events of her life that had led up to the present of her analysis—a separate time in her life, a different way of living and of allowing herself to live.

People are often surprised at how long an analysis takes and that the process requires such a stringent approach, continuity, and rules. One cannot really know what will be encountered and discovered, and whether it will be received and confronted.[11]

It was only after five years of analysis that this young woman came to be attentive to dreams that in other times, would have vanished from her memory, or that she would have ignored or rejected, not wishing to delve into them.

In a vividly physical dream that occurred in her sixth year of analysis, she found herself at the home of a doctor friend, with whom she discovered affinities that were expressed, said she, in a sort of "tender, amorous complicity." Suddenly, in this dream, she saw herself sitting on the toilet, evacuating such masses of excrement that she had to use huge quantities of paper, and feared an uncontrollable overflow.

Worse yet, in another later dream, in which she was accompanied by her brothers and perhaps also her father, she saw, or recognized, a woman she knew when she was twenty, a destructive type of person. In her dream, this woman became a sort of small, sexless doll, crawling with parasites and other disgusting, poisonous vermin, which were proliferating. The only way to be safe was to confine it all in a bag, a task it seemed her brothers helped with. In this dream, she wondered whether her brothers were unharmed.[12]

How can such a repulsive world be experienced and survived if the depths of the soul and being pullulate with such nauseating worms, bugs, and larvae? With such dangerous creatures, barely differentiated, uncontrollable, overwhelming, and invasive?

When I noted Jung's familiarity with the images and writings of the alchemists, I mentioned the *materia prima*—the "raw materials" that are indeed so primitive, elementary, and undifferentiated that they could be described as inhuman, where death is such a radical threat that we find ourselves in depths beneath any differentiation in drives—and therefore beneath the distinction Freud makes between life instinct and death instinct.

In this regard, psychoanalysis that explores beneath the Freudian teachings while remaining faithful to Freud mentions sadomasochism. This approach asks the question of the various ways of organizing the life of the psyche long before the Oedipal structure. It makes it clear how a sadistic urge can be combined with a masochistic one, and how each of these positions is labile, swinging uncontrollably to the opposite or complementary position.[13] This approach can give us some insights into the young woman's case, especially when we recall the type of instability she experienced with her husband. But it is still construed in terms that are too bipolar. As a result, it is too rigid to fit the radical lack of differentiation we have to deal with here.

Bold post-Freudian psychoanalysis will then come to speak of a "primal scene" ("*Urszene*" in the Freudian text),[14] orienting our attention toward the representation a child might try to make of parental intercourse. In the intensity of a confrontation with this scene, and the emotions it arouses in the child, the latter can only mingle associations of sex with rape, combining love with hurting or violating the other. The "primal scene" also relegates the child to the position of the outsider, the outcast, where the infant, shut out and abandoned by mother and father, experiences Hilflosigkeit, a distressful condition of helplessness.

Nevertheless, we are again clinging to a fairly elaborate structure. It is a little closer to the brutally chaotic indifferentation we are trying to grasp, but it still stops on the brink.

For we are forced to observe and know that the depths of the soul are even darker and more distressing to face, beneath the representations I have just mentioned. In any case, they can be, for each of us, blacker than blue, having seen Picasso's paintings before and after 1932, and comparing them to what we are looking at now.[15]

Unless some life, some potential and urge for life emerges and wends its way through the infernal chaos of raw materials, all the more violent for being almost formless.

Will we follow Jung, when he teaches that consciousness is born of the rawest and most remotely unconscious depths of ourselves? When he comes to write that the growth of the personality is rooted in the unconscious?[16]

I have said that Jung is "emergentist," and that this perspective in which he places us, disrupted and transformed the primary expectations of psychoanalysis, which wanted to think only in terms of repression.

But what is it that can emerge from a depth that is so unmade, so brutally elementary, savage, and threatening?

What recourse?
What resource?

Perhaps the story of Bluebeard can tell us something. Perhaps it can indicate an approach that is more than just a fairy tale.

At the climax of the story of *Bluebeard*, in the heart of the forbidden closet, the young woman is really alone in front of what she discovers, in front of what is discovered. "She thought she would die of fright," Perrault wrote.

The bodies of the murdered wives, their throats cut, hang in rows along the walls. And there is blood everywhere—uncontrollable blood that indelibly stains the key.[17]

The outsized violence and deadly omnipotence of this ogre Bluebeard are such that we wonder how the young woman in the story will avoid the death sentence looming over her, when her terrifying husband returns. She has just discovered the evidence of it—hence her distress, desperation, and apparently unrelieved solitude—the "*Hilflosigkeit*" we noted before.

In this fairy tale—if it really is a fairy tale—she looks for a subterfuge to save her life. She tries to make her ogre husband feel sorry for her, and then requests yet another grace period, to pray and to live and survive for a little while longer. Her husband has already raised his knife.[18]

But her salvation will not come from that quarter. Her doom is inevitable and imminent. Finally, the event will come from elsewhere,[19] from her appeal to her young sister Anne, who, at the beginning of the story, did not fall into the trap of the Bluebeard's generous promises of largesse. "Anne, Sister Anne, don't you see anyone coming?" the young woman implores. The maidens await rescue by their brothers, two horsemen. One is a dragoon, the other a musketeer, according to Perrault, and they alone can save the young women from death. Moreover, they too come from afar, from the young woman's childhood, the childhood she lost when she married this Ogre in his castle.

The moment of the brothers' arrival is the one Gustave Doré chose to illustrate in his third engraving (seen on the next page). We see the brothers galloping up in a great cloud of dust. The castle looms in the background. Doré shows them from behind, dashing for all they are worth, from a viewpoint that is almost cinematographic. It sweeps us up in a frenzied dolly shot, uniting us with the forward movement of the horsemen and their mounts. We rush to the rescue of the damsel, while sister Anne, a tiny silhouette at the top of the massive tower, calls to them, cheering them on, encouraging them to make haste, to come to the assistance of she who is in dire distress.

Anne and her brothers join forces, in a burst of frantic energy, an effort to save their sister in distress. Life returns forcefully from the

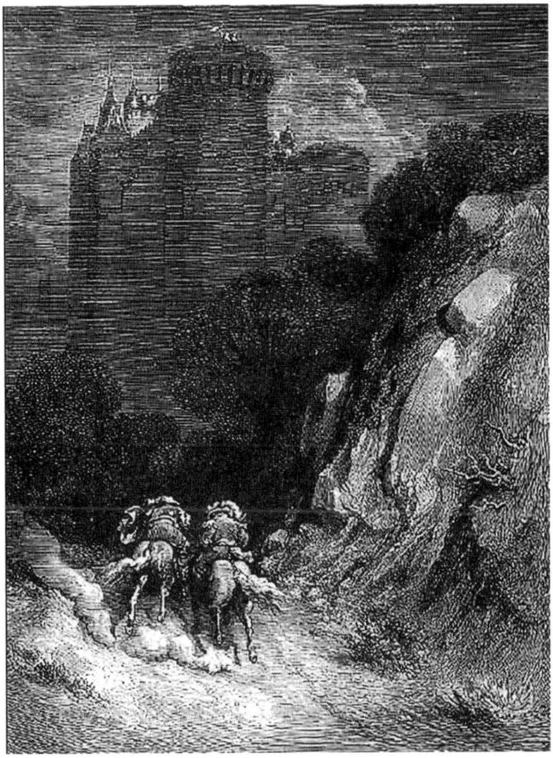

Doré, Bluebeard III

early times, from a time in the past that is still vivid and lively, a time that is a resource when disaster seems inevitable.[20]

That takes care of Perrault's text and Doré's engraving. But the reality—"the Bluebeard reality"—when one truly takes a close look can be worse than what Perrault describes and what Doré shows. How does all of this relate to the young woman in psychoanalysis today?

Her life—in any case, her early life and, especially, her inner life—are just as dark, or perhaps even darker, than that of the maiden in a story from another era.

This modern woman desperately needs help—her only hope for salvation. Who or what can come to her rescue? The account of her analysis may provide answers. First, look at some landmark encounters in her life.

After the death of her first lover, her high-school boyfriend, she worked with an elderly psychiatrist who seems to have known how to soothe her—whereas her parents had bought her a television set, "to distract her" from her grief.

Before the death of the boy she called her "fiancé," she was impressed by his mother, whom she described as an elegant, ambitious, somewhat eccentric woman, to all appearances comfortable with her husband. Our young woman admired her.

In addition to these encounters, we should also note the quality of her intellect, and especially her varied curiosity. They emerged when she started school, and even more clearly in her university years, after her boyfriend's death. These curiosities were highly intellectualized, but they were beneficial, leading her to study philosophy and the arts, and to read psychoanalytic literature, and finally to want to experience an analysis herself.

This experience in analysis was initially engaged from the standpoint of a desire for knowledge. However, gradually it was revealed to be a call for help. The experience did make her attentive and open to implementing the resources needed to soften up the configurations specific to her psychic economy and make them more flexible. They could then evolve, to some degree, and be transformed, changing the ingrained patterns.

This woman's rescuers had come from the people around her, from her social circle, and from certain life encounters she had had, some unexpected or unlikely. But her most decisive resources would come from within.

Session by session, year by year in her analysis, these inner resources would be supported and encouraged by the analyst, delighted to see in them the signs of life—lying fallow, it is true, and up to then treated too harshly but nevertheless attesting to a capacity, a taste for feelings—one that was budding, at least—a taste for the feeling in particular of happiness, awaiting the moment and opportunity to allow itself to be felt.

After a little over three years of analysis, years in which the young woman had succeeded in gaining some appreciation for some of her own qualities and demands, and her own tastes, especially in relation to her husband, her analyst ventured to suggest that she mention female characters from literature or cinema who might have inspired or attracted her as an adolescent or young woman.

At first, the suggestion seemed just as fruitless and futile as when Bluebeard abruptly popped out, in relation to the woman's quarrels with her husband. The only figures who came to mind for the young woman were eminent men, usually philosophers.

Yet at the time that she came to cite the passage in her life of the mother of her ill-fated high-school boyfriend, she had admired the older woman for her strong vision and independence. After that, as if in a kind of reverie that relaxed, she cited a series of other female figures. Women belonging to our collective imagination and history came to populate and animate the young woman's discourse.

The first one mentioned was the beauty Eleanor of Aquitaine, queen of the Franks and England in the twelfth century. Eleanor participated in the Second Crusade, but she also encouraged the troubadours singing of courtly love and of the queen's unfaithfulness to her royal husband.

Next came the Apache heroine Nsho-Chi, she of the long, jet-black braids. From the depths of her nineteenth-century existence in Karl May's novels, Winnetou's sister had inspired this woman's adolescent dreams.

A more recent female figure was also mentioned: Hollywood actress Lauren Bacall. Our young woman enjoyed imagining her, facing Humphrey Bogart, desired by him, opposing her ironic femininity to the superiority he wished to impose on her.

The analysis then began to address some other encounters that had emerged in her life, especially a recent one with the wife of a filmmaker who was a filmmaker herself. This woman's creative, independent mind had impressed her, like the fact that she and her husband managed to work together on films, although they sometimes argued.

The analytic sessions became lighter and sometimes almost cheerful. The analyst discreetly encouraged the new developments in the young woman's imagination, developments that flirted unobtrusively with a symbolic life that was gradually taking on some consistency.[21]

The analytic relationship had also evolved.[22] The young woman had embarked on analysis largely out of what she thought of as intellectual curiosity with some reluctance and resistance, most evident in the way she distanced herself from her emotions, and particularly her most striking memories of childhood and adolescence, as well as her way of avoiding any emotional complicity with, or closeness to, her analyst.

She had nevertheless succeeded in expressing herself a little more freely to the analyst. She took the risk not without, at the slightest alarm, reasserting her control, in a multitude of ways, in the registers she practiced best, including seduction tinted with rivalry, when she spoke to her analyst in the psychoanalytic language she herself had learned to master.

Likewise, sometimes the young woman manifested her ambivalence more directly, making an issue of money or the cost of the sessions, but also, in an explicitly homoerotic dream, reported in the analysis, in which the figures were the analyst and the young woman's mother, brought together and rejected, in the same movement. The scene began in an inn that appeared to be hospitable, and ended in a building that was half-charred and roofless, reminiscent of the collapsing barn evoked in another dream.

The point is that the feeling, driven by emotion, was beginning live in the present analysis under way. The analytic relationship can prove to be an opportunity, lively and vital, to experience and recognize a human relationship and encounter that is not so brutal, unbearable, conflict-ridden, close, or intrusive that it becomes devastating—as a result, in particular, of the protective, protected, stringent setting for this relationship and encounter, and also as a result of the keenness of the analyst's judgment—which is sometimes a gamble.

If feeling thus has its place, gradually aggressiveness can also finally find the paths for expression.

Destruction, proper aggressiveness, and gratitude

Aggressiveness is a word that sometimes frightens and repels people, for it can mirror destructiveness. It arouses fears of destruction. Perhaps our approach to the story of *Bluebeard*, placing Perrault's text and Doré's illustrations side by side with this psychoanalytic story, now compels us to touch upon the matter of aggressiveness to gain more insight into how it compares to the forces of death and destruction, which likely also dangerously dwell within us.

In the tale of *Bluebeard*, after the discovery that the lord of the manor is actually a serial wife-killer, the next event is the long-awaited arrival of the two brothers who rush upon Bluebeard, charging and chasing him. When they catch him, they impale him with a sword, putting him to death.

Here, Perrault's text states only the facts. Upon reaching the end, the reader heaves a sigh of relief and satisfaction.

The engraving by Doré (below) that illustrates and interprets this part of the story with its own means is much more animated. It draws us into the same momentum as the preceding picture, which swept us up almost cinematographically in the two brothers' race to the rescue of their sister. In this way, from one engraving to the next, we participate in their action. We kill Bluebeard with them. There is a difference between our feelings of relief and satisfaction with a job well done, the mood we were in after reading Perrault. Instead, swept up in the

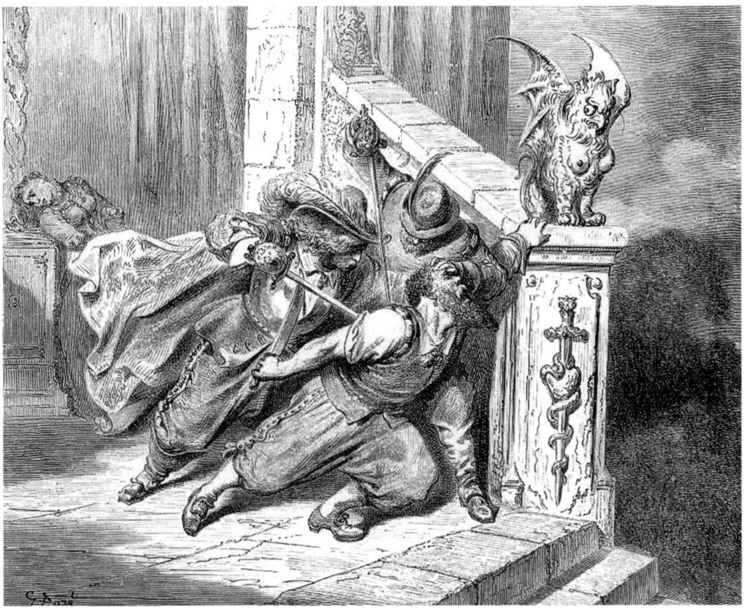

Doré, Bluebeard IV

action, we experience the feeling of the two brothers' deadly strength.

In the background of this scene, the engraving shows us the young woman, so overwhelmed with fear that she is fainting. This seems to reflect the passage in Perrault saying "the poor woman was nearly as dead as her husband." But it now also imposes the question of knowing if the murderous attack, by sword in this case, is really sustainable and if slaying Bluebeard is the only solution.

Perhaps you hesitate.[23] Shouldn't this monster be allowed to mend his ways? Perhaps he could somehow be tamed. Given enough attention and love, he might yet be rescued.

The impulse to heal, which drives any therapist, pulls in this direction. There are many other stories in which the Beast finally becomes human, and they, too, argue for this outcome.[24] But no: neither Perrault nor Doré indicates this path. Quite the contrary, Doré's engravings, by sweeping us up in the two brothers' momentum, tend to encourage us to support the heroine of the tale, so that she too finally assumes this act, which, by its very violence, puts an end to a story that is fated to repeat itself again and again.[25]

But what of the story of psychoanalysis are we dealing with here? How was it settled in this case?

In this present story, the analyst tells us that the young woman gradually opened her eyes.[26] At last, she looked at what had scarred her so deeply that it had almost destroyed her. In any case, it had put her in serious danger, and irresistibly compelled her to find herself in almost infernal situations, engaged in hopeless actions or reactions. She was lost and helpless, for so long, desperately calling for help, but her cries could not be heard.

This young woman had also been led to look directly at the misfortunes and disasters her own mother had experienced—and at those that had plagued far too many of the women in the history of her family.

The gradual advancement of her analysis had enabled her to consider the terrible violence, raw and unnamed, inhabiting the depths of her soul, obsessing her, threatening her, and ready at any moment to invade and overpower her, flooding into her behavior.

What enabled her to make a place for and confront such a harshly unlivable reality?

It is the rhythm, setting, and rules of the psychoanalysis, along with the attention and proper support of her analyst. It is also the shaping work—in German, in Jung's work, it is called *Gestaltung*—that seeks and manages to represent the raw material, as best it can, to articulate, differentiate, and thereby approach and express, via a shape, a figuration, representation, and a dramatization that makes it finally observable. Thus, as if by nature, this primal stuff rebels against any domestication, described as inhuman.

We saw what came next: the evolution and transformations of the dreams the young woman gradually managed to be attentive to. This is the most amazing, vivid, and central experience one can have in the course of an analysis: yes, the unconscious does work for the best possible expression of that which escapes us, that which frightens us, that which we would often prefer to ignore—as long as one is somewhat open to what is being presented and being represented, and as long as one does so with the commitment this attention requires, especially the emotional engagement.[27]

By this very opening, by organizing the reception and commitment, by the sustained attention that is mobilized at the time, we are inclined to collaborate with this work of expression, which starts as unconscious; to take a hand in it, if only by jotting down the dreams we remember, like the young woman in the psychoanalytic story. In other cases, one might draw or paint what we are dealing with, or perhaps dance it: in other words, to express it by any means that might contribute to giving it a form, making it more recognizable and knowable, and also, sometimes, making it something that we can share.[28]

This is one way of confronting it, sizing it up, and sizing oneself up in relation to it. Strictly speaking, it's also a way of getting a handle on it, of evaluating, judging, and adjusting what is tending to be expressed, and also taking a position, by implementing one's natural sagacity and ability to act. As a result, one moves from the subjugation of being overwhelmed to the position of the subject who responds, and becomes responsible: It is indeed truly in this way that the actively ethical dimension of relationships to the unconscious, assumed as a result, is found and practiced.

As a result, one must be able to refuse, reject, and even combat that which cannot be assumed or amended. These refusals, denials, and combats are required, imposed, and necessary. The young woman in analysis was both able and wise enough truly to judge the terrors the women before her had undergone without being able to judge it themselves.[29] She was able to confront, frankly and directly, what she had had to experience as a child, what she had been forced to suffer in childhood, when she had not yet acquired the ability to really see or know it, or protect herself from it.

Last, in her analysis, she was able to mobilize the strength and energy that were not yet hers in childhood and adolescence, and which, prior to her analysis, had found only a hopeless, exaggerated form of expression in the marital disputes that exhausted her.

In Perrault's story, and in Doré's illustrations, this strength and energy come from the two brothers, called to the rescue by her sister Anne. The point is that all is not lost. The rescue and assistance a person awaits come from the mobilization of this strength and energy, which have not been depleted or deformed by one's missteps and mistaken choices. In this story of *Bluebeard*, visual proof of the horror, the refusal to obey, the distancing, the call for help, the aggressiveness assumed in its very violence, and the ruthless attack are all vital requirements.

As for the young woman in our story today, according to her analyst, she is still struggling with brutal, savage dreams, nearly nightmares, where the outcome is uncertain. But she is seriously thinking about separating from her husband, and she has actively resumed work on her thesis in philosophy. She has had a pleasantly close encounter with one of her dance teachers—an enterprising salsa instructor, from the other side of the world—whereas, with her analysis, she has come to wonder more precisely and angrily how she could have been left to struggle for so long alone, without anyone hearing her most desperate calls for help.[30]

This is a merciless endeavor, but it is not thankless as a result. In Perrault's text, the young woman expresses her gratitude for her ultimate rescue in the last lines of the story: "As it happened, Bluebeard had no heirs, and his wife therefore remained the mistress of all of his holdings. She used part of it to give her sister Anne a rich dowry for her wedding to a young gentleman who had long loved her; another part to purchase the ranks of Captain for her brothers; and the rest to her own marriage to a good and honest man, who erased her memories of the bad times she had spent with Bluebeard."

As for our young woman of today, who will soon complete her analysis, she knows what she owes to her analyst.

The heart of the matter

In conclusion, the heart of the matter of *Bluebeard* is the depth of the soul, always present. The question that arises, in the old and new versions of the adventure, is how to reach all the way into those depths, how to emerge from them safely, and also, how to work with them.

Narcissus, interpreted by Ovid and later Caravaggio, pored over this question. But, as far as Ovid's version of the story is concerned, he leaves us dreaming of a flower. As for Caravaggio's depiction, it invites us to the fleeting vision of a sort of unity to be sought within the very tension of our relationships to ourselves.

Perrault shared the depths of the soul as the story of an ogre. He wrote it without being too wary of making a tale for children, with a moral, out of it—unless he merely used this literary form and its societal role as a disguise, to convey the message that structures and animates his text, a message that is both disturbing and also delightful.

Doré showed us what we must look at in this story, even though he too tried to fool or trick us with a red herring, a clue that leads us to believe, falsely, that one key might open the door to knowing all there is to be known.

Despite some people's hopes, psychoanalysis certainly does not offer any key either. However, it does explore the question of knowing how to go into the deepest and darkest depths of ourselves,[31] how to get back out, and how to deal with what we find. In turn, it asserts that what is at stake is our relationship to what is conventionally called the unconscious. Likewise, its role is to accompany and assist anyone willing to engage in the work it permits—the way it helped the young woman whose commitment to analysis was the subject of this chapter.

From Ovid to Caravaggio, and from Perrault and Doré up to our contemporary psychoanalysis, we can see the question of the relationship to the unconscious reconsidered and recast, perhaps moving forward more every time.

The point is to go ever deeper, as far as we can. We try to go even deeper to see, even more precisely, depending on the resources available at the time, and knowing the digging may be dangerous.[32]

8

Jackson Pollock on the Brink of the Well

THE CHALLENGE OF FIGURATION

Jackson Pollock may be one of the world's most famous modern painters, especially in Jungian circles.

Many art enthusiasts enjoy his paintings, which gained prominence in New York galleries in the late 1940s and are now the pride of the world's great modern art museums. But other art-lovers are horrified by his surprising painting technique, the lack of control he exerts when dripping, pouring, or spattering the color on the canvas. Whether we love his work or hate it, he prompts us to wonder what he made of art, and what it has become.

His international notoriety was also boosted by everyone's curiosity about his ups and downs, the trials and errors, the crises and ultimate tragedy of his private life: his instability, eccentricities, and occasional violence; his alcoholism; and the varied psychiatric and psychotherapeutic treatments he tried, including a two-year analysis with the Jungian analyst Dr. Joseph Henderson, from early 1939 to November 1941. His sudden, accidental death in 1956, at the age of 44, when he lost control of his car and slammed into a tree, contributed to the popular image of Pollock, outsized in every way, lost adventurer or creative genius, laboring under a tremendous curse.

However, the reader who wishes to go beyond these superficial images of the artist, the Pollock icon, and to grasp the advancements and issues raised by his work in relation to modern art quickly faces a series of imperious questions concerning Pollock's debates and struggles, debates that belong to an entire movement in modern and contemporary art.

The first surrounds the theme of traditional figuration in Western art, particularly in the New York school of painting in the 1930s and 1940s led by Thomas Hart Benton, who became Pollock's instructor at the Art Students League in 1930, when Pollock was only 18 years old.

A second debate involved the dazzling dominance of Picasso, who exhibited his *Guernica* in Manhattan in 1939, along with hundreds of other paintings. The formal power of Picasso's work and the emotional, social, and political commitment that drove the Spanish modernist quickly made him the center of attention in the art world. Pollock was also involved with the surrealists' practices of automatic creation beginning in the early 1940s.

Lastly, throughout his career, and especially in the final years of his life, in his last creative engagements, Pollock was dealing with very strange presences he had long wished to ignore, overcome, ward off, or perhaps cover up. We can now see how these presences returned to haunt him in the few years leading up to his death.

Pollock's painting was therefore an experiment with the most crucial issues in modern and contemporary creation.[1] He was committed; he struggled, from the beginning of his career to the end, heart and soul. Today, his personal quest and painterly boldness leave some of us feeling outraged; others are stunned. But surely, no one is indifferent.

Let's look more closely at the man and his work, beginning with the famous series of photos showing him seated beside the canvas stretched out on the floor of his studio, brooding. Seeing him thus, we cannot help but be reminded of the fallen angel's expression in the print Dürer entitled *Melancolia I*, the subject of the fourth chapter of this book.

This photograph is from a series of 500 pictures shot by Hans Namuth,[2] in the summer and autumn of 1950. The photographs from this series also often show the painter in action—Pollock is com-

Pollock in his Long Island studio in 1950. Photo by Hans Namuth

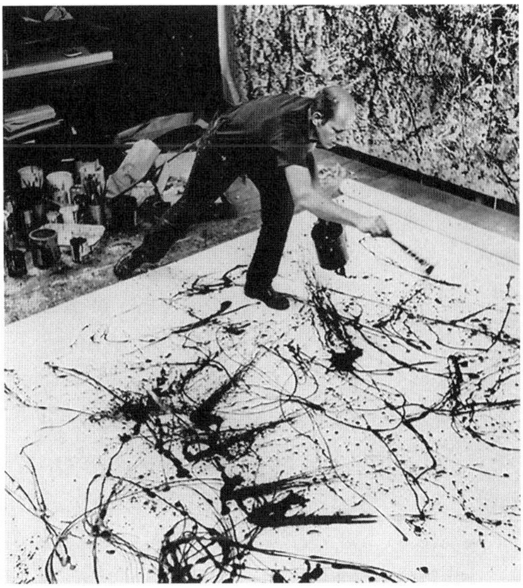

monly described as an "action painter"—in a creative dance around the canvas, circling it with leaps and steps, dominating it, and finally occupying it, investing it, nourishing it with liquid colors that, poured on, form lines and shapes that jump, zigzag, intersect, and squiggle, bringing the space to life and making it a work of art.

The photographer followed the painter, accompanying his every creative move. We see the effect on the canvas. When the movement stops, when the figure is still, the tide ebbs, the action painter subsides, huddled into himself after the choreographic élan of pitching paint, after the liquid gesture that left a trace on the canvas on the floor is spent.[3]

Namuth took these shots from above the painter. He was shooting from high enough to show Pollock beside his canvases, as if he had sunk back into the gravity of his body. "The large barn was filled with paintings. A dripping wet canvas covered the entire floor," Namuth recalled. "Blinding shafts of sunlight hit the wet canvas, making its surface hard to see. There was complete silence. I looked aimlessly through the ground glass of my Rolleiflex and began to take a few pictures. Pollock looked at the painting. Then, unexpectedly, he picked up can and paintbrush and started to move around the canvas. It was as if he suddenly realized the painting was not finished. His movements, slow at first, gradually became faster and more dancelike as he flung black, white, and rust-colored paint onto the canvas. He completely forgot that Lee and I were there;[4] he did not seem to hear the click of the camera shooter. I wore two Rolleiflexes with 80mm lenses around my neck. Both cameras were loaded, and when one was finished, I quickly switched to the other. Then I reloaded both."[5]

Another Narcissus?
Without Echo

Namuth went on to say that Pollock liked the contact sheets he brought him. The painter liked the pictures or, to be more accurate, the painter liked himself in the pictures. At the time, Pollock was a Narcissus so curved in on himself that he had no need of the other, no need to speak to anyone or request anything. He was so completely alone that we do not hear or see him express the question, the call of Narcissus to Echo, in Ovid: "*Ecquis adest*?" / "Is anyone there?"[6]

Pollock's immersion in his ongoing work was so singular and total, so entirely solitary, that he appears as a Narcissus who is even more radical than the earlier Narcissus figures we have considered—a Narcissus who does not call out to Echo.

Yet she is there. Pollock's wife, Lee Krasner, had shown the photographer into the studio. Behind her, there are Betty Parsons, Peggy Guggenheim, and Helen Marot,[7] and, in the background, Stella MacClure, his mother. Also pictured are his brothers and his friends, and in this particular case, Hans Namuth, the photographer: all of them gazing upon him with such consideration that he nearly always found himself confronted by the wonderful promise he then was in their eyes, and for himself.[8] Indeed, the man was especially impressive, and also engaging: so often was he holed up or plunged in an inner withdrawal that it still impresses a person who discovers it. It is particularly evident in Namuth's photographs.[9]

At the time, Pollock was showing his work, to great acclaim.[10] But he was still gloomy, as we see in the photographs by Namuth, despite the brightness of his Long Island studio. He alternated between leaps into creative movement and collapse, in the subsidence that throws him back and seats him heavily on the edge of his work, or clinging to his cigarettes, and also to the alcohol that had already driven him from detox to detox, and from therapist to therapist.

To get a better understanding of all that is involved in the artist's passionate action—something that was totally new, then—go back in time and see where Pollock was coming from, and the source of the energy we see in 1950.

Before 1950
Figuration awhirl

In returning to Pollock's first steps as an artist, as a young man in the early 1930s, long before he was the toast of the New York gallery scene, he was struggling with his master Thomas Hart Benton's esthetic and social vision. Pollock had sought Benton out and was close to him. At the time, Benton was known for his moral nationalism and militant regionalism, his celebration of the virtues of rural America, the healthy grandeur of the American West, and also for his attachment to the painting of the great masters of the European Renaissance: Tintoretto, Rubens, and El Greco.[11]

Hence, Pollock's first works, from 1934 to 1938, such as *Going West*, with the team of horses pulling the cart loaded with a huge log, or *The Covered Wagon*, were rather Bentonian. They express the ideological and social spirit and the rhythmic turbulence that characterize Benton's painting. Even the titles resemble Benton's.[12]

But we see Pollock beginning to come into his own with *Woman*, which dates from 1930–33. The unusually powerful, open woman's body is frightening. The explosive red, yellow, and black shapes in *The Flame*, from 1934–38, tend to invade and almost overflow from the canvas.[13] It is hard to know whether the reptilian writhing in *Circle*, from 1938–41, is seen and experienced from above, through the microscope, or from below, through the telescope, and it is contained only by the edges of the circle. It does what it can to present itself as a classical Italian Renaissance tondo.[14]

And in *Naked Man*, from the same years, 1938–41, although the body and homelike setting of the subject are quite ordinary and conventionally recognizable, the man's head is a total whirl that conjoins or confuses the mechanical movement of a turbine and the threat or assault of the beak of a hawk. This "naked man" is losing his head, which is spinning uncontrollably—or, at least, what is happening to him may make our own heads, or the painter's, spin.

The movement in the painting goes wild—no longer for the benefit of social progress, as Benton would have wanted, but for the sheer sake of spinning and whirling. It's easy to wonder whether the paint is not going to invade or swallow everything.[15] In the paintings of these years—*Birth, Bird, Bull, Naked Man,* and *Naked Man with Knife*— the objects or creatures supposed to be represented by the titles collide, mingle, and blend, sometimes generating each other. It is nearly impossible to make them out; one's eye gets lost in trying to recognize them in the violence of the paint.

Figurative painting does what it can. But it gets lost. Figures are drawn, but are nearly instantly devoured by the force of the colors and movement.

How can one apply the term "abstract" to this art? Abstraction is generally defined as painting in which it is difficult to recognize the subject. But in the case of Pollock's painting, "abstract" seems too loose a term.

This painting, which is grappling with figuration, often attacking and changing it beyond recognition, is quite the opposite of "abstract." The painting itself becomes a living, primary, inchoate, and almost undifferentiated mass. As such, it proves to be an even more forceful engine for the most elementary bodily sensations. It is presented and acts beneath the representations and narrative arrangements that might reassure us.

It does not draw its strength and accuracy from the representation and dramatization of a recognizable scene. This undeniable punch comes from somewhere else: from deep and often savage realities, simultaneously chthonic and volcanic. It shows these forces erupting on the canvas. That was new, even if it took a cue from scenes painted much earlier, in the history of art.

Consider *Composition with Figures and Banners,* from 1934–38: the source of the dynamic structure of the composition is in the interplay between the flames, such a strong presence in the works we have just mentioned, and the power of the vertical black bars, standing erect as if to orchestrate the whole.[16] I consider it likely that, in visual terms, Pollock was thinking of Uccello's *Battles of San Romano*,[17] but in his own way. For Pollock, the shafts of the lances painted in the Quattrocento became an uneven row of black bars pointing at the sky, and the banners are the flames that crackle in the works of this twentieth-century US painter.

This transmutation of an entire pictorial tradition into a modern expression, an expressionism we will therefore avoid describing as "abstract"[18] is what gives energy and range to the work of a painter on an endless quest for the best way for him to paint.

And now Picasso intervenes

Pollock's Bentonian period lasted until the late 1930s. As a follower of Thomas Hart Benton, Pollock sought himself in Bentonian themes and, through Benton, in the history of Italian painting. Like his first master, Pollock felt like, or tried to feel like, the heir to the Renaissance tradition in our time. This dual heritage, one nested inside the other, nourished Pollock. But at the same time, he tried to free himself from it as much as possible, by subordinating the objects and subjects he was supposed to represent—the pioneers of the western frontier, with horses drawing covered wagons, and soon the heads of bulls or birds, a birth in progress, whirling eyeballs, disfigured sorts of human beings, and then standing flagpoles—to flaming movements that lead the onlooker's gaze from one place to the next in this dynamic of so many shapes and poles that all landmarks are lost, and everything may soon be lost. The figure and figuration resist and adapt, transforming themselves. But soon even this concept is drowned or, actually, set aflame, in the very movement of the painting.

In 1939, Picasso came to New York. His painting *Guernica* had caused a sensation when it was first shown at the Spanish Pavilion of the 1937 World's Fair in Paris. Picasso had just been lost for several years, in his life and work.[19] But now he had found his path, as a painter engaging with some of the most radical social and political events of his time, like the bombing of the town of Guernica by Franco's forces in the Spanish Civil War—and by his artistic treatment of the most human and most poignant pain, distorting form to make the drama in the picture more expressive than ever. In those years, he was at one of the highest points in his career and his fame. His works were touring Europe and the United States, eliciting heated debate.

In 1939, *Guernica* was exhibited for the first time in New York, at the Valentine Gallery, along with sixty preparatory sketches or studies. The painting and studies then embarked on a tour of US cities, going to Chicago, Los Angeles, and San Francisco. In November of that year, a 40-year retrospective of Picasso's work, featuring 344 pieces, opened at the Museum of Modern Art in New York City. It was the event of the year. And it was a shock. Everyone in the US art scene attended and was amazed. Pollock was one of them.[20]

Pollock was overcome with awe at the sight of *Guernica.* But he struggled, feeling some ambivalence toward Picasso, especially in relation to the latter's treatment of figures. The Spanish painter was brutal with these representations, attacking them, destroying them, deconstructing and reconstructing them the way he deconstructed and reconstructed the composition, the better to bring to life the depths of a screaming despair that was still visible, still legible, and by that very token still profoundly human—up to and including the whinny of a horse in agony.[21]

Pollock hesitated, seeking his path. He was divided, as a man and as an artist. His admiration for Picasso was infinite. But he guarded himself against it, rather violently. More than once, he growled that he had heard more than enough about Picasso. The damned Spanish artist seemed to have defined painting once and for all. Pollock wanted to free himself from Picasso, just as he had tried to free himself from Thomas Hart Benton.[22]

At that point, feeling overwhelmed, he sought out Dr. Joseph Henderson, who worked with him until Pollock left for California, in April 1941. Pollock was tormented by his own instability, his inhibitions, his alcoholism, and his violence. It was difficult for him to speak. He showed Henderson the drawings he was making at the time, often variants on Picasso's style with *Guernica.* The analyst decided to consider them with him.[23]

In the aftermath of this analysis, the works Pollock painted between 1941 and 1943 are among the most balanced and structured paintings he ever made. *Male and Female* (1942), *Guardians of the Secret* (1943), *The She-Wolf,* and *Pasiphae* (also from 1943) involve forms of figurative representation that are fairly typical—even archetypal, or at least explicitly mythological. At the time, Pollock had just met a circle of surrealists, with whom he engaged in "automatic writing" exercises. These paintings make it look as though, for a time, he was able to combine the Jungian experience of the power of images, clarified by his work with two analysts, Joseph Henderson and then Violet Staub de Laszlo, with the more freely associative inspiration of surrealism. As a result, during this period, his work steered between a figurative representation that permitted a sort of dialogue on a scale that was nearly human, and a pictorial writing that crosses the canvas and links one work to the next at great speed, in a much more stenographic way.[24]

The large "drip paintings," from 1947 to 1950

The large canvases Pollock made in these years are the best-known of all of his works. At the time, they were considered to be his masterpieces. Generally, the same opinion prevails today, and the art market reflects it. They are also the paintings that are most likely to alienate art-lovers unfamiliar with contemporary painting. Their attitude can be understood, for the drip-painting movement was truly exceptional in the history of art. It could even be called extremist.

The first of these paintings demonstrates the artist's conflicted relationship with one of the most remarkable movements in art history, Impressionism.

In 1947, with *Cathedral,* Pollock seized an opportunity to create his own vision based on Monet's numerous views of the cathedral at Rouen. However, due to Pollock's approach to painting, the monument that is named in the title is totally unrecognizable. It is even impossible to make out any cathedral whatsoever. Could it be that Pollock has pushed the borders of Impressionism to the ultimate limit, and that what he depicts on the canvas is the perception, impression, and feeling the artist might experience in front of a cathedral, a landscape, or a haystack? Or perhaps because the artist has gradually freed himself from a relationship to the outer subject, it may finally and truly be a painting that is only about painting. For, as Maurice Denis said, "before it is a battle horse, a nude, or some other story, (...) essentially it is a flat surface covered with colors arranged in a certain order."[25]

Both suggestions are fairly accurate. We would benefit, however, by taking our observation and thinking further. We might indeed perceive the object of this painting as being our inner life, rather than perceptions or impressions of the outer world. Its object is truly internal.[26] This is a very new experience in the history of art, even if it had been announced long before by the arts that had to serve religious spiritualities.

I've mentioned *Cathedral*, from 1947, but its specifically pictorial effect, and that of *Gothic* (1943) and *Tondo* (1948), along with their very titles, show that Pollock's work drew upon what our churches and temples, and especially their stained-glass windows, were able to offer in terms of sensation and emotion, in the times when religions still brought crowds together to call upon each individual to meditate and go beyond him or herself.[27]

For isn't the stained-glass window in a middle place, physically and spiritually, between a power and light that are simultaneously outside and inside? Hence the liveliness of the light, playing with the changes that one might experience from one hour to the next, in a day, while creating a suspended time that abstracts us from ordinary moments and gestures. Pollock's painting, especially from 1947 to 1950, lives in a temporality outside the quotidian and creates a space-time that is also apart. One could say that it is presented as a ritual.[28] But the experience is more than disconcerting. You cannot know the scale at which it occurs. Do you see a thousand eyes, a thousand cosmic, cosmological spiral galaxies, or the boiling of oceans and mountains and pits of the primeval chaos? A macrocosmos or a microcosmos?

In the late 1940s, Pollock was taking every risk and daring us to follow him, especially with *Black and White* or *Summertime Number 9 A 1948*. It is notable that, starting in 1948, he began to number and date his canvases in the titles he gave them. It is as if he himself were conscious of needing to register the passage of time in the rushing flow of creation that had swept him up.

But in this flow, he found an invigorating dynamic balance—which can nevertheless be frightening, and rightly so. For these rapids can be dangerous, if only for the artist himself. No longer possessing a sense of the scale at which his paintings place us is unsettling, for the artist and the viewer. How can one continue living and breathing in a world devoid of familiar objects and figures—a world of total chaos?

From the taste for nature to the boundaries and risks of "all-over"

In the late 1940s, Pollock's large drip paintings, which today we tend to call "classic Pollocks," were encountering success, a triumph that gradually established and asserted itself. The artist was finally deriving a more comfortable income from the sales of his work. So Pollock and his wife Lee Krasner decided to relocate their studio from the city to East Hampton, on Long Island. Surrounded by trees, wind, the sea, and nature, Pollock was enchanted and inspired.[29]

He usually enjoyed these natural surroundings alone, however. And he painted in a refurbished barn, a studio where he admitted only his wife. When a friend asked him why he did not paint outdoors, in nature, he is said to have replied, "I am nature."[30] It's an impressive statement, just like the works he was making at the time: *Lavender Mist*, from 1950, and *Autumn Rhythm*, the same year.

The works of the early 1940s, entitled *Bird, Birth, Bull,* and *Naked Man*, and those that followed, *Male and Female, Guardians of the Secret, The She-Wolf,* and *Pasiphae*, all presented in a more mythologizing or archetypal spirit in both subject and composition, were structured and organized masterfully. The forces and presences conjured up on the canvas were in ideal balance. However, the ones he created on Long Island starting in 1950, which speak of lavender and autumn, prevail merely on the basis of the dynamic equilibrium of their lines in action. No recognizable form or presence emerges, but there is a dynamic, a deeply and radically natural dynamic. And Pollock makes us active, delighted participants in it.

But is it sustainable? Livable? "I am nature," Pollock proclaimed. But is that possible? The inner movement expressed by these works is unlimited and, seemingly, still uninhabited. Can one be human and yet be nature?[31]

The answer to this question might come from the art itself: from what the paintings show and become.

The year 1950 is also when Pollock created *One*. It is tempting to call the painting "Pan," it seems so all-encompassing. The whole world seems to be there, moving, alive, and absolute. The painter is engaging in an accomplishment intended to be so incredibly and tangibly total that one wonders whether the distance between subject and object, the distinction, is not abolished, and if the painter is not abolishing himself as a subject in it.

The art world of the time was more than amazed. Critics were stunned. Until then, no canvas that could also be the very world had ever been seen.

Let's look closer at *One*. Something sets it radically apart.

Unlike what we believed we saw and experienced with the earlier drip paintings, here, the paint does not go beyond the limits of the canvas. It stops and goes back, before overflowing. Like *Autumn Rhythm* the same year, the action stops before the edge. Certain works from 1950, unlike those of the 1940s, and unlike some later canvases, are not boundless. They stay within the limits of the canvas, contained.

These works are drip paintings. But they are not "all-over" paintings. The network or tangle of drips poured onto the canvas leaves a blank margin all around, like a narrow ledge.

Moreover, in these two works, the painting is organized. It does not go every which way. Should we mask our vision and look at only one half of the canvas, the balance is broken. Turned upside-down, the paintings lose their foundation. We discover that the colors are distributed in such a way as to obey the law of gravity. The "heaviest" part is at the bottom.[32] The work obeys an order, and has a physical direction that gives it consistency.

Still more remarkable: although you may let your eye travel along the innumerable bending or broken trails in the tangle, it does not sink into them. Instead of creating an abyss, instead of offering the promise or dizziness of drowning, the painting resists it with its frontality. It faces your gaze, whereas Ovid's *Narcissus*, as you may recall, did not have a ledge or border to hold him back from falling. Not knowing how to differentiate between the upper and lower regions, he could not find a way to resist the attraction of the depths. He was fascinated by them. And as for Caravaggio's Narcissus, who braces himself against the fall with all his strength, clinging to safety, it is hard to see how he could escape his doom.[33]

With regard to Pollock's 1950 paintings, the question nevertheless remains: how can you stay on the brink without falling in? The painter contains the painting; we see and perceive the center of gravity of these works, and their frontality confronts the threat of sinking. But will these features be strong enough to enable us to resist being swept away when a whirling motion emerges and takes over?

There is some likelihood Pollock saw the crucial nature of this question and asked it of himself. He probably experienced it in all its urgency, at that point in his career, quite tangibly and physically, with his own body.

Not only does he limit some of his paintings from going "all-over," he also occasionally writes his name on the border of certain canvases—that of *Lavender Mist* in particular. He had occasionally signed his work in the past, but it was not at all customary for him. He also made handprints on the canvases—just like the Paleolithic painters I mentioned earlier. They may have done so precisely because they wanted to mark or inscribe their human presence on a world they had dared to represent, the world they were bringing to life on the rocky walls, a world that of course dwarfed them with its natural powers.[34] Perhaps they deliberately made these handprints to avoid getting lost in the wilderness. The power of the natural world was so awe-inspiring that humans needed some protection from it. They needed something to cling to, to avoid drowning.[35]

Pollock was also clinging. It was 1950: could he have escaped all of the risks and traps of the headlong action painting he had so successfully indulged in since 1947? Unfortunately, no. Although he was wise enough to exert some control over his creative action, and even stand back from it to reconsider it, he wanted to go still further.

Actually, with *One, Autumn Rhythm*, and *Lavender Mist*, Pollock had constructed a triptych, which surrounds the viewer as it opens up to him. Soon he is included—enclosed, even—in the whole that is formed by the three parts, a whole that might even absorb him, and us with him.

Pollock's first drip paintings were now long behind him. He had hurled himself into them, body and soul, since 1947. They were totally devoid of any figures. No presence was admitted, or admitted itself. Even his own was getting lost there.

William Rubin, one of the most prominent American critics of the time, called Pollock's drip paintings prior to 1950 "his victory over Picasso"[36]—the Picasso who remained figurative, even though for decades he had been treating the figure with a violence that had never been seen in the history of art. *Guernica* had taken this direction even further. French critic Marcelin Pleynet interprets this "victory" in a similar way, as a beautiful way for Pollock to go beyond the painter from Europe who had awed him so much: to surpass him, the way a

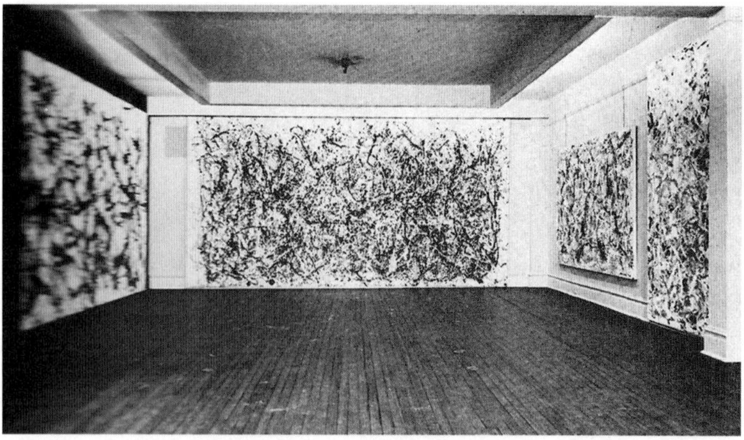

One, Autumn Rhythm, and Lavender Mist, as they were hung at Betty Parsons Gallery in Manhattan, in 1950. Photo by Hans Namuth

son feels obliged to surpass and vanquish his father. Pollock's need was all the clearer after he had surpassed and overcome his master Thomas Hart Benton and American figurative art.[37]

This psychologically oriented interpretation, largely developed in the psychobiographical style,[38] is relevant. But what is at stake at this point in Pollock's work, at the very beginning of the 1950s, is also of a much broader scope. It is a crucial issue, and may even be vital.

Facing this arrangement of *One, Autumn Rhythm*, and *Lavender Mist* as a triptych, I find it nearly impossible to avoid thinking of the Rothko Chapel in Houston. This chapel is deliberately ecumenical, making absolutely no reference to the various figures and narratives of religions. It dispenses with belief altogether. Whoever enters it—alone, if possible—and takes the time to sit down for a while, is bound to be gripped by the dark suspense surrounding him. Meanwhile, bit by bit, the large black panels on the wall reveal their somber spectrum of different dark hues, barely perceptible at first. In these surroundings, as one gains this awareness, one is gradually gripped by an awe-inspiring, wordless experience of a dive into bottomless depths, or an emergence from an unknown source. It beguiles and fascinates you,

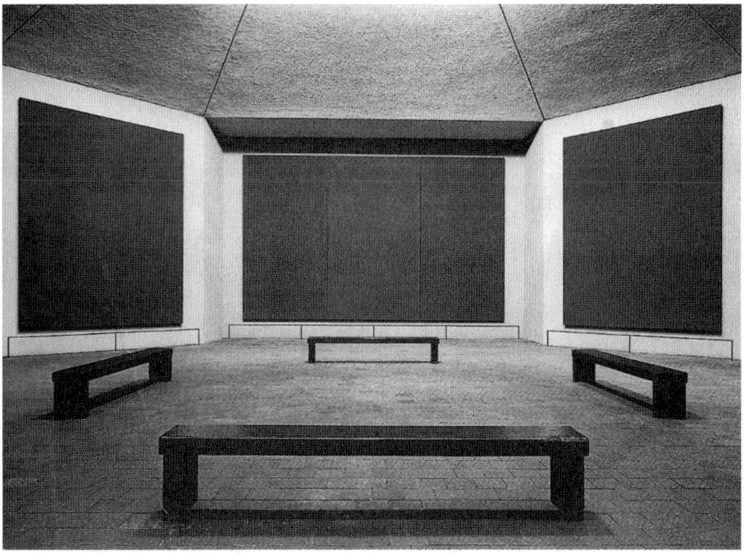

Rothko Chapel in Houston. Photo by Alix Dermigny

putting you almost outside time. Actually, you are within the time of an attention so suspenseful that you can hardly qualify your fascination: it is either exhilarating or too dangerously captivating.[39] And one is forced to be aware that shortly after completing this octagonal, almost circular "chapel," Rothko committed suicide.[40]

Naturally, my point is not to overdramatize Pollock's engagement and the risk he took. But we are concerned for the painter—and with him, and for the direction being taken by painting.[41]

It is quite possible that both Pollock and Namuth, who accompanied him so eagerly in the headlong "action painting" that had led to the canvases that preceded *One, Autumn Rhythm,* and *Lavender Mist,* were also alert to this danger. They may even have been groping for something solid, some wall, ledge, margin, or boundary, to avoid the looming threat of being swallowed up.

An Echo?

Have we paid sufficient attention to the other photographs Namuth and Pollock snapped that same year, 1950, taking turns in front of the lens?

The photographs of Pollock in the tall grass on Long Island, as a philosopher with a skull, in action painting, smoking, withdrawn, curled up into himself, are almost too familiar to us and seem posed.

But now the painter took the camera into his own hands. He wanted to photograph his photographer. Namuth played the game, switching places with Pollock, assuming his position in the same corner of the room while Pollock took the picture.[42] As a result, in these twin images, each man is a double of the other, sharing the composition with the same cross-shaped sculpture—a detail I will return to. Each seems to be pinned to the white wall, possibly even cornered.

In this mutual photo-shooting session, the corner of the room, framed to include both the angles of the ceiling and floor, serves as a limit, closing the perspective. Speaking of Pollock's large drip-paintings, from 1947 onward, I noted an attraction to a bottomless pit, and therefore a threat of being swallowed up. However, in 1950, the year these two photographs were taken, *One, Autumn,* and *Lav-*

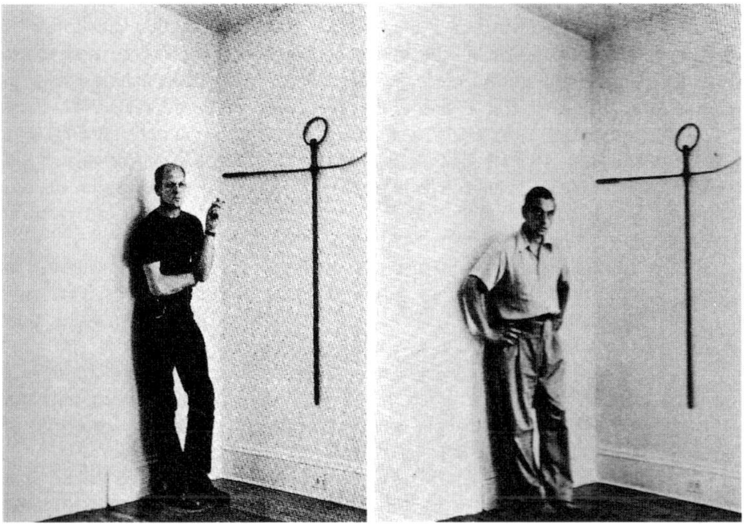

Pollock by Namuth, Namuth by Pollock

ender Mist seem to attempt to respond to this tendency, with their frontality, their relationship to the frame, the consistency of their composition, and the weight of their center of gravity.

In these two photographs of each of the men, they are doubles for each other, simply trading places. The camera remains in the same position. Only the subject changes: Pollock or Namuth. The distance from the camera is the same. The two mirror images are purely visual, mute, suspended, fixed, rigid, and fascinating—and therefore all the more disturbing.

To follow Freud here, he elaborated his approach to what he called narcissism from the story of Narcissus. Freud is neither Ovid nor Caravaggio. He considers all questions as being sexual, from the outset. According to him, narcissism arises from tension between the development of the ego and the relationship to the other, at the different stages of childhood, in the name of what he calls "object-libido." He writes that the subject's first love-object is himself, his own body.[43] This soon leads Freud to blurt out something about homosexuals. He states that homosexuals identify with women and become their own sex objects. Freud postulates that homosexuals are driven by narcissism to seek out adolescents who resemble them—actually "*jugendliche und der eigenen Person ähnliche Männer*"—to lavish upon them the same love they received from their mothers. Freud adds that often, these so-called "inverts" are not at all insensitive to feminine charms, but they transfer the lust aroused by the opposite sex to a male object. In doing so, they would merely be reproducing the tendency at the source of their attraction to their own sex. The compulsion driving them to seek out male lovers would be triggered by a constant flight ("*ruhelose Flucht*") away from women.[44] We know how Freud approached and interpreted the life and work of Leonardo da Vinci in these terms.[45]

It is an impressive analysis and a tempting approach to explaining homosexuality. As an observation, theory, and interpretation, it can be relevant. Except that when we begin to wonder how the individual is shaped, and what shapes the relationship to the other, we are continually reminded of the insistent question Ovid lends to *Narcissus*: "*Ecquis adest?*" / "Is anyone there?" This appeal is intended as an opening. Would it lead only to a dead end?

Jung suggests a different way. Certainly, sexuality is a big deal, starting in childhood. But neither Jung nor we can be satisfied with reducing the relationship to the unconscious to the repression of sexuality and to the compromises, accommodations, and transformations required at the successive ages in life. I have applied the term "emergentist" to qualify Jung's approach to and practice of the relationship to the unconscious. Let's specify this approach using two words: complementarity and compensation.[46]

In Pollock's face-to-face with Namuth, the question is whether the situation offers some chance of meeting someone who is enough of an other: someone who is similar and close, and yet different enough to engage Pollock in emerging from the depths of his world sufficiently to take a chance with an encounter.

The answer is likely to come from an examination of what follows in Pollock's art.

By September 1950, Hans Namuth had documented Pollock as an "action painter" with a long series of photographs. Most of these pictures were shot from above. But Namuth, increasingly captivated by the painter's movements, observed that although the pictures described his creative motion well enough, they were disappointingly immobile. It was at that point that he decided to experiment with filmmaking rather than still photography. He later wrote that he felt dissatisfied to show merely the painter painting. He wanted to show more: Pollock inside the painting, coming toward the viewer through the paint. Soon, they figured out how.[47]

Namuth decided to film him from below, an idea that literally knocked Namuth over. The novice filmmaker would have to lie down in order to shoot the painter, who was painting on glass for the first time.

Pollock was so taken with the idea that he built a wooden platform to support a piece of plate glass. The film immortalizes the moments when Pollock pours paint onto the glass, occasionally moving around other elements, pieces of colored glass, chips of plaster, and pieces of string and screen. Namuth recalls that after much trial and error, he finally managed to focus the lens on Pollock behind the glass directly above him, as he lay on his back with the camera on his chest.

The painting on glass in the film is entitled *Number 29, 1950.* Like the film, it is the result of trial and error. At different times, Namuth's film shows Pollock the painter hesitating, stopping, and then abruptly wiping all the paint off the glass and starting over. Pollock's voice comments, "I lost contact with my first painting on glass, so I started another one."

Moreover, for several weeks during the winter of 1950, Pollock left this *Number 29* outdoors behind the studio, in the weather and the rotting leaves. He never followed through on his original plan for the painting, which was to be built into the porch of his house.

Still more remarkable, when the MOMA exhibited *Number 29, 1950,* there was some hesitation as to which way to hang it. In the end, it was actually hung upside-down. Even Pollock presented it that way in a Namuth photograph, immediately after he painted it.[48]

In this adventure, the painter lost his momentum and resources, and the work lost its consistency and direction. What does that mean in relation to the issues in Pollock's art up to then? Where was he headed?

The onset of winter

A new era in Pollock's life and work began. It is the period in which he painted what are called his "black pourings," and experimented with ink on very thin rice and silk-mulberry papers.

The very large "black pourings" are dominated by strokes of thinned black enamel. The background is the raw beige duck canvas, which is largely unprimed. These pourings were a radical departure from his earlier "all-over" paintings. Moreover, the "black pourings" are much fewer in number than the large drip paintings of 1947 to 1950. Also, Pollock applied the enamel to the unprimed canvas by squirting it out of a turkey baster, in addition to using the hardened brushes and sticks he handled for the drip paintings.

What happened? The black streaks and spots sank into the porous canvas, creating a movement of more or less distinct silhouettes. From the depths of the picture, they emerge, and then are stopped by the more rigid layer of primer, applied after the paint.

Thus, these silhouettes sink in, and vanish, or are covered up. But at the same time, they rise up again toward the artist painting them, or toward the person viewing them. Actually, a form of figuration is emerging, although the figures are still often difficult to make out. It is quite the opposite of the representational art Pollock struggled with in his Bentonian period, or in his debates with Picasso's *Guernica*, or in the intentionally mythologizing or archetypal works he produced in the aftermath of his therapy with Dr. Henderson. Figures are re-emerging, but their vocabulary is experimental, fleeting, fleeing perception. This figuration is not inherited or learned. It is as if figuration will from now on be inevitable, although it will also be diverse and uncertain.

The ink blots on rice and mulberry paper are small—measuring about 18 inches by 12 (45 cm × 35 cm), with only a few slightly larger pieces. The format is more "domestic," extremely different from his previous canvases. The paintings on paper were made indoors, because in the winter, the barn was too cold and drafty.

Pollock usually proceeded by pouring ink, black or occasionally colored, onto the top sheet in a pile of porous paper. He would then work with what had bled through onto the second or third sheet of paper, on the obverse or reverse. Again, in this period, nameless figures emerged. The vestiges of one representation suggested the outlines of the next, directly or as a blurrier reflection of the first. The artist smudged them even more, or, on the contrary, defined them.[49]

In this research into the depth of the paper medium, into what returns to the surface or is reflected by it, Pollock explored what had until now escaped him and what was returning to him. He explored it in the first shaping, then in its obverse and its face-to-face. He seemed to be trying to identify what was emerging and presenting itself for an encounter—almost for a dialogue.

The paintings are an intensely exploratory, groping reconnaissance effort, an attempt to identify what haunts, obsesses, and compels him from beneath and behind but also from in front. Something calls out to him, although it still hovers largely beyond his reach. These figures escape from him, and then return. They return to him as much as they escape him. They loom over him, yet are evanescent.

One or several Echos, of one gender or the other, are emerging for this Narcissus, who had held himself aloof from such encounters in the desperately solitary and manifestly non-representational drip paintings he had been making between 1947 and 1950.

But after Namuth had been such a presence in the very field of Pollock's creative action, after there had been an exchange of gazes, accepted and perhaps sought by the painter, in the papers Pollock worked on during the cold nights of the winter of 1950, these encounters beckon, insist, and impose themselves.[50] The question is now to let them come, to receive them, to work on them, to face them, or to let them flee.

With his early drip paintings, later contained in borders, from 1947 to 1950, and with his "black pourings" and the indoors work on thin papers during the Long Island winter, Pollock had been seeking the proper distance at which to allow an encounter, so that at last, in addition to the gaze and touch, he could hear the voice of someone else, other than himself, and not a mere echo.

But the story of his life and work willed it otherwise.

Yet another proposal for Pollock: this time, for the sky

In the same years, a second friend charmed Pollock. Tony Smith, an architect, convinced him to undertake another project, a mad one, for the painter: to decorate his church.[51] Pollock was asked to create the church's skylights—a series of plates that was to surround a transparent dome, open to the sky.

The artist had yet to install his glass painting *Number 29, 1950*, made at Namuth's behest, on his porch in East Hampton. Now the same idea, or a surprisingly similar one, was recurring, but on a much grander and more ambitious scale. And this time, the artist was being invited, solicited, and encouraged to launch his creative energy skyward, to make art as huge as the sunny, starry, or cloudy skies of Long Island. It was an outsized challenge, and again, a friend was daring him to do it.

Nothing ever came of Tony Smith's church. Pollock's sketches for the skylights, if they ever existed, have never been found.

Why didn't anyone at the time see that as a succubus beneath the sky, Pollock was doomed to lose himself and his balance, which had carried him through the dance of creation around a painting on the floor? That Pollock had been walking a tightrope, merely working within the confines of his studio?

Why do the keenest Pollock scholars insist that his previous large drip paintings might have been sketches, studies, or an inspiration for the church project, when this project, unlike the earlier works done on the floor, would force him to take flight into the sky?[52] The post-Namuth "black pourings" and experiments with rice paper[53] arose from a wholly different attitude and attention, as we have seen. They were practically the opposite of the hubris of this church project. The process they required had awakened the artist's sense that an emergence was possible: fragile, uncertain, but awaited. At last, figures and presences that were sufficiently consistent and shaped could emerge.

The church-skylight plan was a mistake, even more than the painting on glass, with Namuth beneath him, had been. It was an aberration. Pollock's creative movement does not turn skyward. On the contrary, it is directed downward, toward our depths, where life seeks its shape, in the chaos of a lumpy night clotted with matter in its most undifferentiated state.

A Pollock church, of all structures, was a total incongruity. The luminous heights to which those in the know urge us to rise, teaching us lessons, were not Pollock's element. Sublimation did not befit his perspective.

This much can be read in the works he made after 1950 in the years just prior to his death. His last works may show us some of the issues that were most crucial to his creative adventure.

The Deep

This impressive canvas, tall and wide (220.4 cm × 150.7 cm, or 86.8 in. × 59.3 in.), dating from 1953, is for me one of Pollock's most profound and most amazingly accurate pieces. The Museum of Modern Art at Centre Georges Pompidou in Paris acquired it. The question of the shaping, composition, and execution of *The Deep* is quite other than that of the most fortuitous gestural and pictorial grace, or of the great risks taken in his earlier action paintings.

One is invited to wonder what is emerging, appearing, and being represented. The equilibrium in the action paintings gives way to the unexpected, coming from God knows what sources, and destined for God knows what purpose.

Is that a figure we see? Who can say whether it is appearing or disappearing? *The Deep* is not a mural like the one Pollock created for Peggy Guggenheim when he embarked on the drip-painting adventure, even though *Convergence*, like *The Deep* from 1953, is another action painting. Nor can *The Deep* be an opening—as if the canvas had been ripped open—to reveal some recognizable, familiar face.

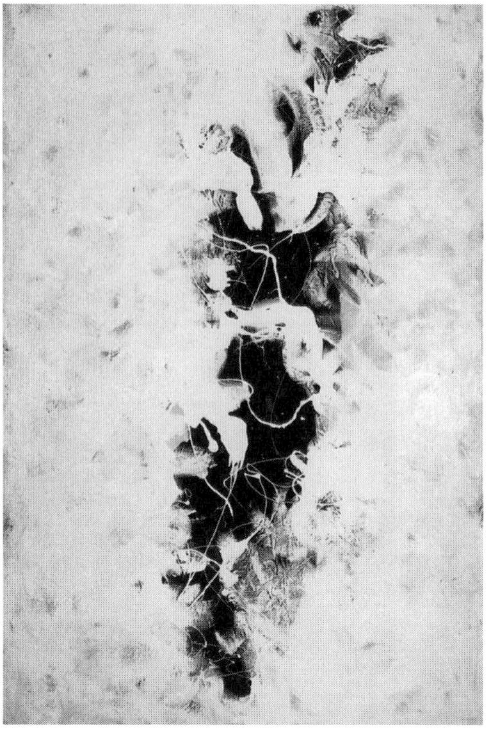

The Deep, Paris, Centre Georges Pompidou, Musée National d'Art Moderne

The Deep is a presence, at last—possibly a feminine one. But it resists representation. It calls out—to whoever is looking at it, and calling out to it. Only the viewer has to adjust his gaze. One must find the proper distance, the distance at which a voice can be heard. An erotic is at play, one that escaped the Narcissus of Ovid and Caravaggio. But the figure sinks in and hides, through the very medium of the paint.

"*Huc coeamus*" / "Here, let us meet," cried Ovid's young man, addressing the nymph. "*Quoque petitus abis?*" / "Where do you run, when I look for you?"[54]

"*Quid videat, nescit.*" / "He knows not what he sees." "*Sed quod videt, uritur illo.*" / "But what he sees consumes him."[55]

Still more: "*Liceat quod tangere non est, aspicere and misero praebere alimenta furori.*" / "Let me at least contemplate that which I cannot touch. Let me feed my miserable folly."[56]

In *The Deep*, the other is escaping to a bottomless, undifferentiated wholeness, and we remain on the brink of the yawning pit, which momentarily revealed a presence we perceive as feminine. One might wonder if this presence is not more maternal than feminine—the type of maternal presence that can carry you away, absorbing you into her immeasurable depths and the bottomless well from which there is no return.[57]

Pollock is always groping his way forward, alone, not really knowing what he has found, or what he is about to find, or how to deal with it.

Blue Poles

This canvas painted in 1952, another of the Jackson Pollock pieces I admire, is another way for the artist to explore further, without getting lost. It appears to be another drip painting. However, the labyrinthine, undifferentiated scribble of paint poured on the canvas is powerfully structured and punctuated by a rhythmic series of more or less vertical raised bars.

The "poles"—dark bars, bands, or sticks—support the equilibrium of the pictorial whole of the canvas, which is quite large (210.8 cm × 497.6 cm). While asserting their presence, they allow the wild tangle of colored drips and spatters of paint in the background to come to life. As a result, the viewer is not in as much danger of being swallowed up by this chaotic mass—a background that gives not a hint as to its scale or its limits.

The series of poles—which are as the title says dark blue, rather

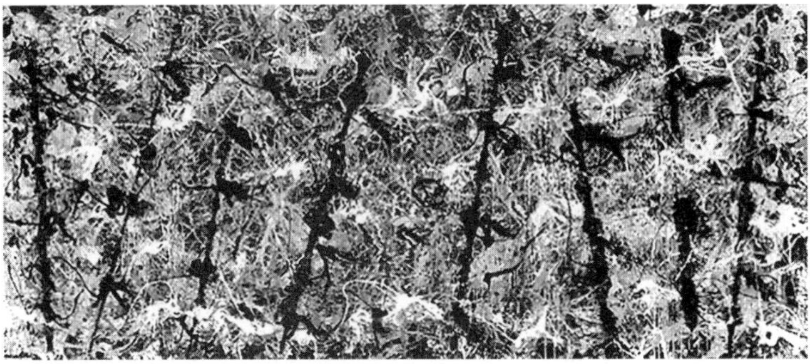

Blue Poles, National Gallery of Australia, Canberra

than black[58]—give us a safe mooring, and they may have served the same purpose for Pollock. Otherwise, the Brownian motion of the vortex swirling behind them could well have swallowed him, and us with him.

It is as though Pollock had recalled a painting he had done over fifteen years earlier. In the 1938 *Composition with Figures and Banners*, there was practically no question of either figures or banners, despite the title. The painting did not tell any story whatsoever, unlike Uccello's *Battles of San Romano*. In fact, the Composition of 1934–38 seemed to be about the raised staffs and lances in the Battles—as if they had been reduced to a purely pictorial expression and function. It invited us to experience and perceive the inner coherence and dynamic of the paint and painting.

It is the same way with the *Blue Poles* of 1952: impossible to find any narration that would situate or resituate us in the world we know. Now the paint itself finds, creates, and offers us a journey into the depths and waters that are just as fascinating and dangerous as in the most absolute drip paintings of 1947–1950. The invitation is even more evident than the earlier ones, and yet it offers us a mooring. The "poles" manage to stand, and they give our eyes the power to gaze into the depths without getting lost in them.[59]

Yet a question halts us. Is it really possible to dispense with narrative so readily, so radically? Perhaps without even realizing it, the painter was relying upon some remembered scene or story. After all, Uccello's *Battles* obviously haunted *Composition with Figures and Banners*. In *Blue Poles*, perhaps some other scene could be operative, a part of our culture that is nearly but not quite forgotten.

Some critics and commentators on Pollock's work are of this opinion. They are often described as Jungians.

Is there any Pollockian iconography?

What of the Crucifixion?

These art critics and commentators, who claim Jung as an inspiration and wrote largely in the United States in the 1970s, often turned their attention to Pollock's figurative paintings predating 1947, the year he began his drip-painting period.[60] Likewise, they were especially interested in the "black pourings" of 1951–52,[61] as well as his return, which I have discussed, to what is generally called "abstract" painting.

Their hypothesis, asserted as a thesis, is that Pollock was always drawn to figurative representation, but that he was also driven to conceal, camouflage, and veil such figures under the non-representational action and colors of his drip paintings. Evidence for this statement is based on what Pollock allegedly told his wife Lee Krasner, when she questioned that he was no longer painting pictures on his canvases. "I would rather veil them," he said, according to Krasner.[62] These critics believe Pollock repressed his relationship to images, even though it was one of the subjects he worked on in therapy with Dr. Henderson.[63] Having been suppressed, the images flooded him later. Various prescription drug treatments and self-medication with alcohol could not stem this tide of figures. Neither did the "decorative" (as they say) nature of his drip paintings, or the return of some representation in his "black pourings" of 1951–52.[64]

As for the figurative themes that would then be identifiable in the Pollock pieces that do not eliminate images entirely, these authors notably mention that of the Crucifixion.[65]

Such a thesis suggesting difficult-to-recognize but nevertheless underlying figuration deserves close consideration, because it demands that we wonder what we are dealing with, in the arts, in particular—but not only—once we venture further into the relationships to the unconscious. It is a fundamental question.

To approach this question from the standpoint of Pollock's personal journey, we must recall the impact the painting *Guernica* had upon him, when he saw it in New York in 1937. Indeed, the memory of this show, as I pointed out, was lively and operative until Pollock's life and work ended.

The drama of *Guernica* is not centered on a cross. Nevertheless, the painting is animated and organized by the expression of agonizing torment, a theme that Christian iconography may convey the best in depictions of the Crucifixion or the Descent from the Cross. Moreover, as we know today, Picasso himself painted a *Crucifixion* in 1930, a painting that was so important to him that he always kept it for himself.

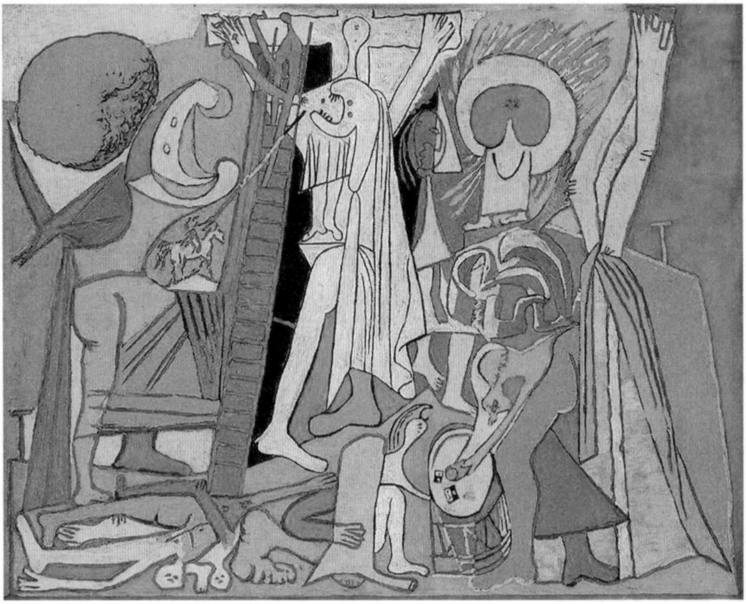

Picasso, Crucifixion, Paris, Musée Picasso

Pollock was in all likelihood unaware of this painting, for with very few exceptions, it was made public only after Picasso's death in April 1973.[66] However, it makes sense to try to see, in the strangely powerful and perceptible tension created by the vertical stripes of the Blue Poles, something of the tension that Christian tradition has succeeded in representing in the scenes of Crosses standing the same way, often at night, at Gethsemane, the yard where Christ was crucified alongside two thieves sacrificed with Him.

We could consider these Jungian approaches as an exercise in association—or, more precisely, amplification. As we have seen, this exercise is relevant insofar as the associations provide evidence for, support, and nourish the themes at play in a work of art, even surreptitiously, and especially in the way they contribute to its emotional reception.

Except that this narrative approach, which actually tries to be archetypological, is part of a more than debatable project: an effort to track down images, even in Pollock's works where they cannot be seen—including the least figurative drip paintings. Naturally, these interpretations also hunt for images in the "black pourings" of 1952—those that are contemporary with Blue Poles.

Veiled figures?

These Jungians can be praised for their questioning approach to Pollock's works. It contrasts sharply with the general consensus celebrating his "classical" drip paintings, long held to be his most successful pieces.

But, I consider them fundamentally wrong. Their approach is based on a premise Jung would certainly never have endorsed, a premise from which we have distanced ourselves throughout this book.

According to this premise, usually implicit in these critics' writings, the depths of the soul consist of images that seek only to be expressed. But this comes from a partial reading of Jung that is ultimately erroneous, due to two notable omissions.

This approach leaves out the difference Jung gradually but clearly established between archetypes and images that are possibly archetypal. The former are in fact structural potentialities, always present, it is true, and full of energy. However, they only go into action under certain conditions.

Mainly, this approach omits that Jung, through personal experience—particularly the one he reports in his *Red Book*—by his clinical practice, by his familiarity with the arts, including the images of the alchemists, and lastly in his theoretical writings, demonstrates that a person who ventures deep within him- or herself soon learns that the depths of the soul he or she encounters are actually far from being a treasure-store of images. The inner depths of the soul are almost always radically chaotic, archaic, and undifferentiated, well beneath any recognizable shape. The encounter may prove terrifying—or, on the contrary, ideally blissful: the fulfillment of the hope of perfect happiness, finally attained or found again.[67] Hence the question of knowing what can be done with the encounter and how to go about it.

These authors are misinterpreting Jung, but it does not exclude them from consideration. Their most serious error is that they put us on the wrong track when we are trying to identify some of the issues that are crucial to Pollock's work, especially as concerns the theme of crucifixion they detect in his "black pourings," in his experiments with very thin rice or silk mulberry paper, or his plans to paint glass for the dome of Tony Smith's church.

The true cross

Doubtless, as we have seen, Pollock was haunted by Picasso's work. He was more than impressed by *Guernica*, as well as by the themes that flow powerfully through the work like an underground stream, bringing this painting to life. One of these themes is the Crucifixion.

It is not entirely by accident that Pollock showed an interest in designing a church, a project Tony Smith had suggested to him, and on which he worked for a time.

And it is not at all absurd to look for Christian themes, particularly the theme of the Crucifixion, especially in the outlines of shapes and figures Pollock allowed to emerge from the ink blots on either side of the thin paper, shapes and figures that he later explored and reworked during the winter of 1951–52.

So it might be true that these American critics of a Jungian bent have found an important source of information for understanding Pollock's wanderings and struggles throughout his career.

But does it make sense to speak of these images as "archetypal" without specifying the source from which they come, and their hopes for life, or perhaps their tendency to elude us? Even an expert on contemporary art as well-respected as E. A. Carmean, who is openly critical of these Jungian approaches, speaks of Pollock's painting in the "tension between the ego and the self," but without explaining any details about this particular interplay.[68]

So, since the question certainly seems to involve a Cross and Crucifixion, why has no attention been drawn to the crucifix that is deliberately shown in Namuth's photographs of Pollock, and Pollock's photographs of Namuth?

Refer again to the photographs on page 153. We have noted how impressive and even disturbing these photographs are, due to the precise and inescapable symmetry in which the two men are placed, a symmetry in which they may have placed themselves, one in relation to the other, and one in the place of the other.

This scene, or pair of scenes, mirror images, arouses extreme tension. When we contemplated Caravaggio's *Narcissus*, we could feel afraid of what the turbid and worse-than-disturbing waters beneath him might contain. The way Pollock and Namuth mirror each others' gazes, like twins, is even more disturbing and difficult to experience.

Why? It could be because it shows the failure and futility of the quest for the other, when that person is nothing more than the reflection of the seeker. The dead end, represented so graphically by the twin framing of these two shots, is tragic.

Many an art historian and critic has noted and even pointed out the mirror effect between Pollock and Namuth.[69] But none mention the dissonance created by the closeness between them, which twins them, and the painter's desperate and solitary dance, as he embarks on the creation of the bottomless, soul-less world of his drip paintings. This tension is so painful that it happens to be signified, represented by the cross flanking the lone figure in each photograph—although we do not know which man, Pollock or Namuth, wanted it to be in there.

The challenges of this art

And so the question returns: "*Ecquis adest?*" / "Is anyone there?" Anyone who is close enough, similar enough, and yet different enough—to meet, in other words. Who? Where? How?

It is an ego waiting, asking, and doubtless calling out. But he remains alone. It is Pollock when he is not an action painter, and Namuth, the painter's mute twin. Each is alone, immobile, tightly locked into himself, at the same time as he is torn apart, as if crucified—derelictus—or, when leaping into the frenetic movement of dripping paint or, as a twin, like Echo, in that of the photographer with 500 shots. Identifying with each other, unfortunately.

On the other hand, there is the abyss of a world that is too whole and too anonymous, to avoid oscillating between a natural, but fundamentally inhuman happiness—as in *Lavender Mist* or *Autumn Rhythm*—and, the infinite turmoil of a boiling chaos—as in *One*—still devoid of all human presence.

The experiment with painting on glass with the photographer underneath him, the face-to-face shots twinning painter and photographer, as well as Tony Smith's church proposal, fizzling out in the sky, all destabilized the painter. These experiences scrambled and broke the limitless momentum of the painter, driven to animate and perhaps people the canvas by pouring himself into it, by throwing himself into the abyss opening before him.

The presence that glimmers in *The Deep* emerges from this pool. Sometimes, a dynamic equilibrium is created in the tangle of the bottomless depths, its structure and grace the product of sheer serendipity. Then, Pollock has *Blue Poles.*

But soon the painter withdraws into himself and closes himself off, alone again, and the painting hesitates between the delight in bounding into the air again, with renewed momentum, and the somber return to a ground that is figureless and flowerless, alas. "The water's pain is infinite," wrote Gaston Bachelard in *L'eau and les rêves.*

Conclusion

VESSELS ARE BROKEN AND A BOOK OPENS

The creative rush of Jackson Pollock's adventure, with its commitment, thrills, and terrors, now asks that we speak more explicitly about our journey through this book.

Are there images underneath emotions?

A cursory interpretation of Jung can be misleading. The casual reader might assume that the human unconscious is universally endowed with a huge bank of ready-to-use images, and that all we have to do is make a room for these images to emerge, willy-nilly. Artists would be the ideal candidates for this task, for they lend themselves most readily to the manifestation of images.

In his old age, Jung recalled the anguish that followed his crisis and departure from Freud. He withdrew to Zurich almost entirely alone in 1913, when the threat of war was looming over Europe, and then the world:

> I was living in a constant state of tension; often I felt as if gigantic blocks of stone were tumbling down upon me. One thunderstorm followed another. My enduring these storms was a question of brute strength. Others have been shattered by them—Nietzsche, and Hölderlin, and many others. But there was a demonic strength in me, and from the beginning there was no doubt in my mind that I must find the meaning of what I was experiencing in these fantasies.[1]

"My enduring these storms." That speaks of the sturdiness required, the resistance, constancy, and continuity. All of these qualities and capabilities are the work of the ego. So the ego is needed for this matter, with the determination that it alone can possess. For the risks are great—the risk of being totally overwhelmed, the risk of utter defeat.[2]

And ego formation is not a simple matter. It's quite an enterprise, beginning with our prehistory. In the first chapter of this book, we looked on as the earliest humans, our ancestors, gradually struggled to become aware of their singularity. We noted their surprise and amazement to discover they were so different from other living creatures. In their daily lives, subsisting as hunters and gatherers, they faced fascinating, awe-inspiring animals. At the same time, they drew and painted these beasts on the walls of their caves or shelters, discovering that apparently these animals also dwelt within the human, in an inner world. In the paintings, the beasts were at least as powerful as they were outside, on the hunting ground.

Also, this discovery or awareness each person may acquire of his or her singularity can end tragically. Young Narcissus, the hero of Ovid's song and later of Caravaggio's painting, was irresistibly attracted to the image he had forged of himself, an image that was also irresistibly attractive to his friends and lovers. He was so fond of himself that he was oblivious to the coming dislocation, the quasi disintegration of this magnificent young man, in whom he fervently wished to believe, until he bent over the pool and peered into the depths, into a warped reflection that is terrifyingly archaic, impersonal, undifferentiated, and, by that very token, quite inhuman. Yet, such as they are, they may also be a part of ourselves with the power to swallow us up forever.

"I had to find the meaning of what I was experiencing," Jung adds. Then he writes, "To the extent that I managed to translate the emotions into images—that is to say, to find the images which were concealed in the emotions—I was inwardly calmed and reassured."

"To find the images which were concealed in the emotions." What does this statement mean? Is it saying that images are surreptitiously lingering there, inhabiting or haunting the emotions of the moment? Would the point then be to uncover them, to hunt them down? Or to invite them to appear, so that one might identify and recognize, and perhaps even finally master, that which threatened to upset and overwhelm us, or to swallow us up?

This is a tempting interpretation. It even has some virtues. It might be useful not only for our thinking, which might get some traction on the source or cause of that which had escaped it, or assailed it, but also and especially to soothe us. That way, we might not only recover some peace of mind, but also find the art and manner of facing a new or terrifying event. Such a summoning-up of the images that would be hidden inside the emotions of a discovery, of an initially unnameable, unrepresentable experience, too challenging to approach, might indeed prove useful—like the shamanistic cure of the Cuna Indians of Panama, so well described and analyzed by Claude Lévi-Strauss in *Structural Anthropology*.[3]

It's a beautiful story: the story of a successful psychotherapy. The problem was a difficult birth, so difficult that the outcome of the process was in considerable doubt. The laboring woman was in excruciating pain. She was desperate. A shaman was called. He arrived at the scene, went to the woman's side, and began to sing, or chant, a long tale, repeating again and again the terrible crisis this woman was in, her pain, her confusion, her call for help, how he had come to her side, and then how he had prepared to intercede: the work he had done to create a whole army of figurines modeled from various materials and objects. His song told of how the figures had embarked on the journey the unborn child would have to navigate, a path strewn with obstacles and dangerous traps, including bitter combats that would have to be waged against contrary spirits to deliver the "*purba*," the vital force, or the soul of the patient until finally the birth happened. Delivery came. And the shaman's song accompanied it still, describing "*Muu*," "the dark inner space, the muddy spring," which, for this Central American people, is the original source of the power of life and procreation. The idea was to get "*Muu*" to return to the proper place, and to be ready to start moving again but in a less violent, less terribly dangerous way.

This chapter of *Structural Anthropology* is entitled "The Effectiveness of Symbols," with good reason. The symbol, or more precisely, symbolic life, really does have an effect—many effects in fact.[4] These effects begin when the symbol is shaped. These effects go to work. In the form of a song or incantation, mobilized as a ritual, among the Cuna people, it released the flow of a process that had been brought to a standstill or blocked, the process of a birth that needed to take place.

In the case of this Central American people, symbolic life, spoken, chanted, and ritualized, is supplied by the shaman, who is the agent or vehicle of local culture. Through him, thanks to him, thanks to the evocation and convocation of an entire mythology in which the members of this culture participate, life can resume its course. The life energy, the soul, is liberated by it.

In other cases, situations, or contexts, the mobilization that frees the energy is not as simple. The tale of the fifteenth-century Swiss hero Nicholas of Fluë comes from another place and time, in quite another culture. It is one that Jung and his circle enjoyed telling.

One fine day, this stalwart peasant from "primitive" Switzerland, the respectable father of a large family, left wife, children, and village to go into the mountains alone and become a hermit. At that time, he had a terrifying encounter with an enormous, faceless, speechless power and presence. The encounter was such a frightful, terrible experience that he was more than distressed and marked by it; his own face, it is said, was deformed as a result.[5] This lasted until he was able to recognize the teachings of the Church and the Trinity in what he had lived through in solitary bewilderment.

And, it is said, recovering his composure, he returned to his countrymen, then on the brink of their worst fratricidal war, ready to tear each other to pieces over the loot they had won in their victory over Charles the Bold. And Nicholas was able to speak to them with such wisdom and authority that together they settled upon rules for sharing peacefully, recreating the agreement and brotherly bonds that saved Switzerland from the feuding that could have shattered it.

In this story, still told today to Swiss children and their parents,[6] we can recognize how an initially unnameable, unrepresentable, unbearable experience[7] comes first. It precedes and serves as raw material for an event that must come to pass, even if the event is liable to upset or destabilize the person experiencing it. Shape, shaping, and language come next, at first to deal with the event, and also to share the experience initially felt in solitary, helpless anguish, and to regain or weave bonds of life.

Sometimes the shape is already there in the surrounding culture. It is accessible, as was the case for the Cuna Indians Lévi-Strauss described, and also for Nicholas of Fluë, in Switzerland.

At other times, the shape must be created. But how does one go about that?

Regression and shaping

In the aftermath of his break from Freud and his departure from the psychoanalytical institutions in Vienna, Jung felt this question. He found himself in the overwhelming tumult and confusion I have just evoked, almost all alone, no longer sure which saint or father to swear by. He was utterly lost. Let's look closer at what he was able to tell us about this situation, and what he was able to do with it.

At the time, he was a well-known, prominent, and promising gentleman, greatly admired, especially by women. His knowledge, skill, and authority as "Professor Doktor" earned him widespread respect, as the photographs we have of him at this time attest.[8] His career and family life appeared to be following a smooth course.[9] But oddly enough, whenever his clinical work, the rhythms of his household, and his other commitments left him some free time, he would go out in the garden of his home by the lake to indulge, alone, in bizarre construction games—activities that actually did come to him from childhood.[10]

One might find this amusing, and the good people of Zurich probably did laugh at Jung behind his back, so smug was their faith in the superiority of their university and their upper-middle-class refinement. In those times, unlike today, spontaneous expression, even accompanied by sculpture, drawing, or painting, was much less acceptable as a hobby or pastime.[11] So imagine what an uncharted adventure Jung was embarking on—and actually, what a humiliation it was, for this brilliant psychiatrist and psychopathologist to be dabbling with his hands from day to day, and in fact, we now know, for months and years on end. He would have been an embarrassment to his circle of friends and, especially, to himself.

In torment, Jung had resolved to abandon himself to the uncertain groping of his hands. Often the hand knows how to decipher an enigma the intellect struggles with in vain.[12] With his hands, he began to sketch, and then to build, and then to transform little villages made of odds and ends, of pieces of wood and stones that washed up on the lake shores, and then a path, a church, and scenes developed, without any real idea of what they might become.

Such an experience is sensorial and gestural. It is the work of a lone body groping its way forward, not knowing what will ensue. And it is ritual, in that it demands that one detach and free oneself, from ordinary routines and temporalities. This process of regression and shaping can only move forward at its own pace. It takes time, time devoted to it alone. And it also requires a willingness to undertake the effort without knowing why and where it will lead, or even if it will lead anywhere.[13]

This exercise is a serious regression. It sends us back to ways of being and doing, to means of expression that one might believe are consigned to the past, to means of expression from which one ordinarily has good reasons to forbid oneself.[14]

Yet this practice of regression can turn out to be a source of another becoming, but only if it meets certain conditions.

The first of these conditions is that one engages in it with utter abandon—by allowing oneself to relinquish the control that usually serves as a means of planning, mapping, and guiding a journey. Instead, the subject returns to simple, exploratory attempts, guided only by the senses at the moment, notably the perceptions that were ours in other times, when our sensations, feelings, intuitions, emotions, and thoughts found their expression without too much hindrance from the rules and inhibitions to which we submit as adults. However, this regression may be repugnant to the ego.

The second condition, following from the first, is that we commit to shaping that which emerges. It may be almost impossible to discern at first. It may sometimes be downright disturbing or, on the contrary, blissful. But in any case, it is unexpected and always new.

These experiences or experiments with the exercise of regression and the work of shaping were activities that Jung engaged in for years, after his first building games in the garden of his home in Küsnacht. He continued assiduously, always largely alone and almost in secrecy, making himself attentive to the appearance, in his fantasies and dreams, of a variety of recurrent characters—a rather primitive warrior, an old man, a young woman, snakes, and other animals, and also certain settings: a sort of volcano, a boat, a fortress—and abstract patterns. These elements often interacted or dialogued with each other. Jung began to draw and paint in a big red book, to note how the drawings made him feel, then to shape captions for the images, lettering them carefully, like illuminated manuscripts. But the whole process was so secretive, and almost shameful, that this *Red Book* has only recently been published for the first time.

Structures and the work of figuration

For Jung, drawing, painting, and lettering the *Red Book* were an opportunity to recover a grip on and re-elaborate experiences that had initially almost overwhelmed him, while renewing the liveliness of these impressions. They had flooded over him rather obscurely, arousing fears of being overcome by them. But, at the same time he felt the thrill of an encounter with a powerful autochthonous force, apparently largely autonomous, that had been waiting with some impatience to be allowed to emerge in the form of a shape, so that this truth could at last voice itself.

I have just mentioned some of the characters, encounters, and scenes that are introduced to us, from one page of this book to the next. It is inhabited by presences and events that sometimes recur and are quite astonishing. The figuration running through the text and illuminated pages[15] proceeds from a stirring in the remote depths, operating surreptitiously in an underworld until an expression is traced, then outlined more firmly, and, at last, imposed. Structures are at work there.

The term "structure" ordinarily connotes an abstract, hypothetical object, a sort of mind view or intellectual option with which one may or may not agree. But that definition is far too shallow. It is related to a conception of human functioning that has been roundly denied. Contemporary developments in linguistics, after Ferdinand de Saussure, at least, and up to Chomsky and his school, as well as approaches to ethnology and anthropology since Lévi-Strauss, have all emphasized the centrality of structure.

We saw a glimpse of Lévi-Strauss's structuralism when I mentioned the text he wrote on the effects and virtues of the chanting and other rites practiced by the Cuna Indian shaman in Panama when it was crucial to restart the course of a woman's labor, and to accompany her and the baby through to delivery.

The point is that these structures are actually living, active realities, acting upon us, in the sense of the *Wirklichkeit* (the reality as Jung understood it).[16] They are so lively, active, and powerful that they are the source of figures, the site of a figuration and also of configurations; that is, of scenes and dramas that impress us, compelling and mobilizing us. They serve to animate and engage us in an amazed reflection about ourselves, about what usually escapes our notice, but which nevertheless never fails to haunt us, and which is quite likely to strike us at inopportune moments in the course of our lives, causing us to act, often without our knowledge, or at least without our wishing to know too much about why.[17]

Thus, in the Roman world at Herculaneum, we witnessed how an initially puzzling meeting between a man and a woman of the time—in this case, a gladiator who seems a bit preoccupied and a lady who makes us wonder why she is being taken for a landscape—could lead more or less surreptitiously into other scenes and encounters, arranged differently, but structured identically: the scene of an Ariadne expecting momentarily to be swept up by Dionysus to a celestial wedding or, on the contrary, that of a young princess about to be raped. Our observation and reflection, from one scene to the next, are initially perplexed and then amazed. Our minds venture forth, find themselves outflanked, but then are freed to hurtle forward again, until they are traveling in disturbing directions, sometimes infused with joy, but at others, quite uncomfortable—directions they must nevertheless explore.

We also saw this at another time in the history of Western culture, when we made ourselves attentive to the transition, in a matter of years, from Dürer's *Black Melancholy* to the *Red Melancholy* by Cranach—the transition from an angel who has fallen heavily from the skies to a tantalizing, and somewhat bewitching woman who beckons to us to join her in God-knows-what ordinary and extraordinary game: from work to work, the heroes and heroines may differ, like the setting and context of each, but the progression from one configuration to the next, in the name of a structural movement of transformation and interpellation, is the all-encompassing whole.

These powerfully dynamic, creative structures, which help organize our representations, and thereby our ways of being, mobilize our observation, reflection, and discussion, from the very earliest times of psychoanalysis. They are also at the core of current developments in the psychoanalysis of the arts.

In the beginnings of psychoanalysis, Freud approached these structures from the bias of fantasies he described as "primal" or "original"—he spoke of "*Urphantasien*." Wishing to inventory them, he counted four in all. According to him, they are related to our intrauterine life, our difficult position as a child between father and mother, the even more difficult representation we might formulate for ourselves of the relations between our parents, and the risks and threats of castration and seduction.[18]

Starting in particular with his first studies of the attraction of incest and the taboo against it, and the metamorphoses and symbols of the libido, Jung rapidly entered the debate. Gradually, he dug beneath the Freudian lesson. Jung radicalized the question. He freed himself from the overly confining listing suggested by Freud and, at the same time, from the narrowness of Freud's exclusive focus on sexuality. Jung saw these structures as a creative potential, of a capacity for expression, which could be activated at each of the most crucial transition stages—some of them matters of life or death—the bridges all of us have had to cross since the beginning of time and the challenges they bring, where each of us has had to situate himself or herself from one age to another. In this respect, he spoke of "archetypes."

Following him, we see that although these structure-types are much more numerous than the ones Freud theorized, they are still not infinite. Nor are there an infinite number of the most nodal, most decisive situations or phases we all have to deal with. We also see that, contrary to what one might think, even in certain Jungian circles, these structure-types are not eternal, immutable, and timeless. Actually, they are activated at rhythms and in time frames that are all their own and that can be observed at different scales—that of the evolutions and transformations that mark the successive phases of every human life, the time frame described today as transgenerational, and also the one that could be classified as "long term," operating at the pace of cultural history. As a result, these structures themselves turn out to be evolving in a transformation process. In the last part of his work, starting in 1944, Jung invites us to observe this on the scale of the history of our cultures, particularly that of the history of Christianity.

But deep down, it is terribly risky

So far, our thinking is fairly satisfied, for thinking is fond of research and debates that arise from the convergences and divergences between different schools of thought or ways of thinking. Intuition, pleased to perceive the structural order and the outlines of the whole picture, the forces driving the whole story, is even more attracted than our thinking was. As for feeling, for the moment it keeps its opinion to itself.

But what a surprise! Undercover, masked by respectable and even apparently idyllic scenes, a strange brew is simmering, fermenting, steaming—on the brink of boiling over out into the open at any moment.

Look at the image of *The Garden* in Frankfurt, where Eve or the Virgin Mary is ensconced, wise and well-behaved, a book in her hand and the holy women surrounding her, busy gathering flowers and fruit, playing on the psaltery or drawing water from a fountain. The tableau is a bid to qualify as paradisiacal, or would have us believe in Paradise. Only when we study the illustration more closely do we begin to worry.

Do we not see odd and disturbing figures lurking on the edges of the scene? Do they not make us wonder what role they are about to play, in what appears to be a garden celebration of virginity? Certainly, they can still be mistaken for honorable saints, and they take great care to remain on the outskirts of the promising garden of delights. But is it not clear that at least one of them is also a warrior, and that they are gazing at the ladies or maidens with great interest and increasing intensity? Are they not about to cause a serious disturbance in the pleasant order of the garden, perhaps overthrowing or perverting it? Evil has crept into the landscape. It is still confined to the edges, but for he who knows how to sense it, it is indeed present, incognito, surreptitious, sneaky, and perhaps about to pounce on its prey.

A few years or decades later in Florence, in the terrible *Story of Nastagio degli Onesti*, we found ourselves in another garden, believing we were attending a properly orchestrated wedding ceremony, when suddenly drama—or rather, tragedy—struck. A young woman was savagely pursued by dogs and even a furious horseman, and then mauled in an endless and truly infernal chase. This young woman is stripped bare in the picture, and not in a way we expect of an elegant and ideal *Quattrocento* Venus. Instead, she is the helpless victim of the most vicious attack possible, an attack we are forced to witness in all of its ruthless brutality. The painting imposes the evidence on us: undisguised aggressiveness and brutality, violence that is virtually or veritably animal, far below the culture of a virginity or sexuality contained by society and religiously consummated in marriage. It is revealed here, glorying in its carnal and actually murderous rawness.

As far as we know, Freud was not familiar with this work. Would he have been astonished by it? His own tastes ran to classicism, and he might have been disgusted or repelled by this depiction of an assault. Except, it is true, as we noted earlier, that although Freud enjoyed celebrating Michelangelo and his *Moses*, he did not fail to pay attention to the extreme tension expressed in that particular sculpture, between the brutally clastic and potentially destructive violence experienced by the prophet, and the control he had to exert to serve God and his people—or, at least, so he believed.

Moreover, it is not by accident, but rather by a necessity born of the advances in his research, despite the temptation to celebrate the great accomplishments and promises of sublimation, that as his writings continued, and until the end of his life, Freud came to speak of a powerfully regressive and destructive force that incessantly aims at the disintegration of the other, of oneself, and of everything, a force he called "death instinct." He would show the radical opposition between this instinct and the life instinct, which strives, on the contrary, to create, to develop, and to nourish.

Similarly, it is no accident if, on the basis of what he had initially said about the unconscious in its relationship with the preconscious and the conscious, that Freud would later speak of the "id"—a reality so strange, so strangely worrisome, that he resorted to the remarkably impersonal German term "*es*" to convey its primal chaos or lack of organization. Freud would show that the formation of the ego and superego proceed, as well as they can, from the id.

The point is that Freud saw Eros—life and its bonds—as being opposed to the stubborn remanence and chaotic aggression of the forces of disorder and death, determined to return to states that are inorganic and actually inhuman, or at least prehuman.

As for Jung, one can certainly admire and celebrate the careful calligraphy and illumination ornamenting his *Red Book*, the delightful shapes, colors, curves, and flowers. But any familiarity with the book makes it clear that at its nerve center, when the subject is the shadowy underworld and a journey down into the realm of the dead, a nameless, fragmented, shattered creature is represented—barely represented, to tell the truth—reduced to shreds and fragments, so abject that the eye must strain to distinguish the outline or emergence of some recognizable presence.[19]

There is no doubt that we are truly and physically exploring uncanny, upsetting regions of ourselves beneath any figure and figuration, in depths so abysmal they are repellent to thought and intuition, and suffocating for sentiment. Sensation alone rules. It is a sensation, or several sensations, that are so primal, elementary, and impossible to distinguish, that a person is overwhelmed and lost in great distress. These are the sensations James Joyce aroused in Jung, with his novel *Ulysses*, a chaos that enraged Jung. But finally, he was able to recognize the turmoil as the adventure that he and many of his patients had had to experience. In later years, he would discover another gripping, thrilling expression of that sensation, in much of the iconography and literature of the alchemists.[20]

The experience is a terrible ordeal, so dangerous that one has serious reasons to hesitate on the brink. In fact, one may even give it a wide berth, shunning it completely.

Ovid's story of Narcissus can be read as an attempt to avoid approaching the edge: first we admire the physical beauty and attractiveness of the young man in love with himself, and then we allow ourselves to be charmed, convinced, or consoled by the miracle of the flower, sung by the poet. But as soon as Caravaggio takes up the story, the dark pit is impossible to ignore—the depths of the pool, shattering and fragmenting the self-image so beloved of the young man, and so beloved to all of those who surrounded him. The painter shows Narcissus in a state of utter captivation, and in mortal danger. The young man is about to lose himself. The painting demands that we witness and experience this person's painful disintegration, the shapeless chaos in which he is about to be drowned—a morass that may swallow us up with him—in depths where young Echo will never be able to join him.

The story or adventure of Narcissus on the brink, about to be swallowed up, and the struggles of Pollock on the edge of the same abyss, are central to this book.

But whereas Caravaggio's *Narcissus*, like Ovid's, left young Echo behind him, without deigning to see her, Pollock grappled with the expected emergence of a feminine figure or presence, facing him but hovering just out of sight, as if held off or refused. She finally takes shape and answers him: hence his debate with figuration with the heritage of our history of representation, with his master, Benton, and with Picasso and his *Guernica*. It was a debate that was also a challenge for him: how to go forward even further with the delights and successes of his action painting and also make a place, finally, for an encounter with another person.

This challenge, a battle he waged again and again by changing his painting circumstances and techniques, left him alone, derelictus, wholly abandoned to crucifixion. It caused him to lose his life, body, and soul, in one last desperate race, ending in the form of suicide by colliding with a tree.

Hence the question that insistently runs throughout this book, forcing itself upon us when it is time to conclude: the matter of how to contain or hold in both senses of the word: How can one hold what is emerging, often in such a chaotic and abyssal form, and shape it, or represent it truthfully, and also how should one hold oneself?

The painter and sculptor Anselm Kiefer, one of the most boldly creative artists working today, has adopted this double question for himself, explored it, and reworked it, putting it into play in his own way—and his work should help us take a step or two further.

Anselm Kiefer's Palette

Anselm Kiefer was born in Germany in 1945 immediately after the war. Disaster weighed on everything, everywhere—on landscapes, minds, and hearts.

Kiefer's first paintings were often immense canvases—over 6 by 6 feet for *Maikäfer Flieg* / Maybug, Fly, 1974, for example. They represented and interpreted in painting all the ballast of the German land, plowed up, ravaged, and devastated by war, scorched and still smoking here and there, as if the landscape were wounded flesh, poorly stitched back together in utter pain, without any hope on the horizon, and devoid of human figures.

The overwhelming mood of hopelessness and sorrow is quite similar to the feeling we get from the print Dürer entitled *Melancolia*, discussed previously: the fallen angel plopped down, surrounded by a mishmash of objects, tools, and instruments from the artist's time. Yet in this painting by Kiefer, there is really no one at all.

It is airless. We also miss the sight of the sky pushed all the way to the top of the landscape. The scene is invaded by the thick strokes of paint applied with the knife, expressing the weight of the earth harrowed by war. The mud rises almost as far as the eye can see to the horizon, the top of the canvas.

But up there in the distance, what do we see? What do we read? There are some handwritten words, difficult to make out, written by the painter. He has noted a nursery rhyme, familiar to German kids. It is a sad tale, but it rises above the wounded land as best it can:

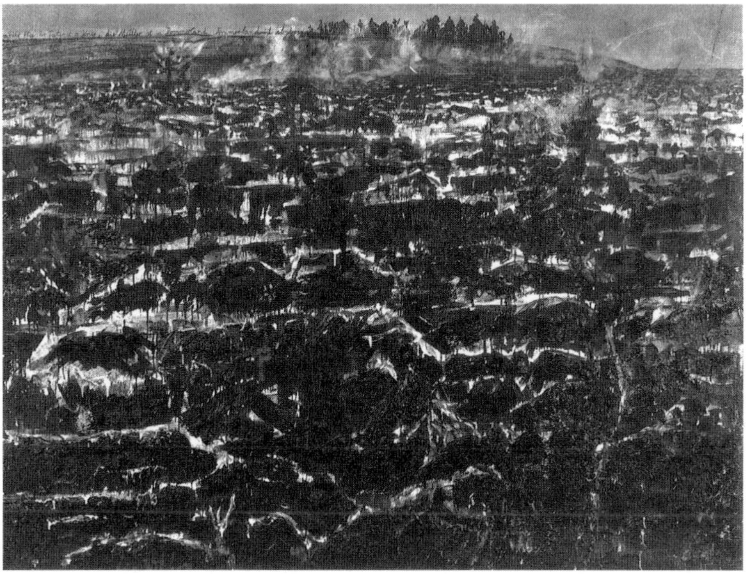

Maikäfer Flieg / Maybug, Fly, 220 × 300 cm, 1974, Nationalgalerie, Staatliche Museen zu Berlin

"*Maikäfer flieg. Der Vater ist im Krieg. Die Mutter ist im Pommerland. Pommerland ist abgebrannt*" / "Maybug, fly. Your father's at war. Your mother's in Pomerania. And Pomerania is all burned."[21]

This nursery song, a lament about wartime placed there by Kiefer, comes from far away, from his childhood perhaps, or from that of his parents. It says, as best it can, the anonymous desolation of war, the lost or doomed presences, the solitude, absence, and death.

Throughout this early period, Kiefer continued to paint these mournful canvases, on the same theme and in the same way. Meanwhile, another series of works from the same years took us to other places. The painter entitled them *Innenraum* / Inner Room. They show empty attic rooms—in reality, rooms where the painter had set up his studio. In the pictures, these disused, inanimate spaces are as if haunted by ancient presences: the heroes of old Germanic mythology. In fact, we can read their names written on the canvas, and some of us know their strange and disturbing family histories: Amfortas, the impotent old king, with the wound that will not heal, or Arminius, the chieftain who vanquished the Roman armies, or Parsifal—and in this painting, instead of the Holy Grail one would expect, one sees a chipped enamel basin, sitting on a stool.

By the early 1980s, Kiefer was a well-known, successful contemporary artist, whose works were exhibited at the Venice Biennale. Certain critics were outraged. A controversy raged: Wasn't Kiefer too ambiguous to be honest in his references to a mythical German past, a legend Nazism had co-opted and exploited for its own purposes?

The point indeed was the relationship of this painter, and this painting, to history, and demonstrably to the history of his country. But was the distancing, or *Verfremdung*, as Brecht called it, of these works from Nazism not immediately noted? This distancing, or "defamiliarization," as it is sometimes translated, is actually quite similar to the relationship Joyce maintained, in *Ulysses*, with his own home, the very Catholic, fatherland Ireland.

Yet another series of images from these same years showed and explored the relationship to history in still another way. They are woodcuts, nearly totally gray and ghostly, dense with tangled leaves and branches between tall black tree trunks, the nearly impenetrable forest undergrowth. Some of them are entitled *Wege der Weltweisheit* / The Paths of World Wisdom. The viewer's eye alights upon disembodied heads, the great minds of Germanic tradition, and Kiefer labeled them with their names: Hegel, Feuerbach, Marx, Schopenhauer, Heidegger, and Nietzsche. In tightly-knit cohorts of wandering souls, a procession from beyond the tomb, they float like startled zombies, without any of these great men seeming to answer readily to the roll call. These collective values now sound hollow. There is definitely nothing to be expected from them. Nor is there any reason to hope that the German land will ever recover from devastation.

This is when a shape appears in Kiefer's oeuvre. It is initially somewhat puzzling. Although we are accustomed to seeing these things in the painter's studio, they are hardly ever depicted on the canvas; but surprisingly, a Palette appeared. It was followed by several more, for the painter enjoys going forward by series of works, over the course of which he reveals and explores a single formal and thematic element.

This Palette is not really presented as a perfect or ideal shape. It is

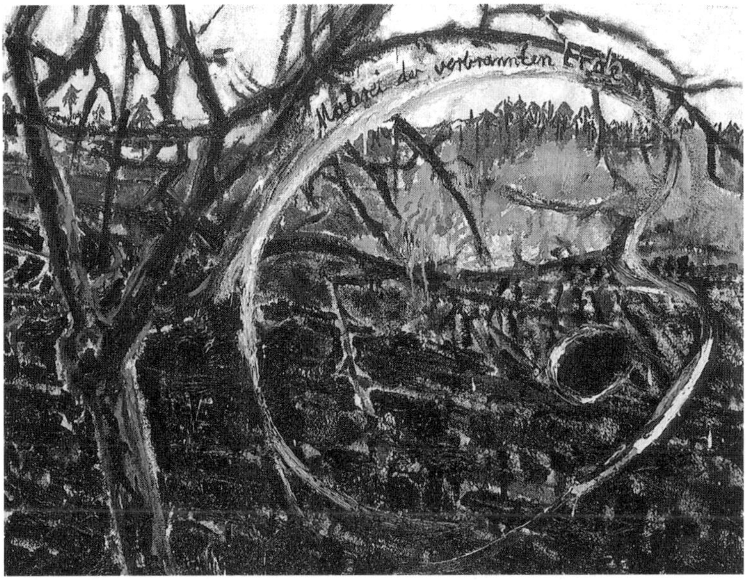

Malerei der verbrannten Erde / Painting of the Burned Earth, 1974, 95 × 125, 5 cm, private coll.

roundish, without truly being round. In fact, the painter draws the outline of a palette, instead of the real object.[22] The Palette, Kiefer's many Palettes, appear to be a somewhat abstract shape, like a virtually geometric container. One might try to describe them as conceptual, at the same time that each Palette is quite tangibly there, exactly the right size for a human hand, especially for this painter's hand.

The shape is precariously but perfectly balanced, despite its asymmetry, one side containing the hole for the painter's thumb. It appears in the middle of landscapes of the ravaged German land. Like an eye, looking. As a result, the disaster is contained, measured, related to a human scale—to our own scale. Alongside the painter, we confront this wounded and devastated terrain.

Now, the palette is certainly an odd object. Doubtless, it surprised Kiefer himself. One wonders how to understand it. We have encountered a similar shape in our travels. It, too, was combined with the strong emotional charge of another scene: I am referring to the near-perfect circle bisected by a horizontal line, the thin line to which Caravaggio's *Narcissus* was clinging, as he crouched on the brink of the depths that threatened to swallow him. In the works of both painters, Kiefer and Caravaggio, although they are separated by huge differences in context and style, an enigmatic round shape appears, organizing the scene. It takes on a strikingly prominent position in the composition of the works, and it is also strikingly prominent by the question it elicits in us as to the role it plays in conveying the meaning of the painting to us.

Kiefer's Palette is sometimes shown hovering in the air, as if to free itself from the brutality of war and the wounds war has inflicted. Kiefer paints it with wings. It's a little silly, yet touching. The artist is doing what he can to give the Palette a boost, but at the same time, he takes care to bring it back into proper proportion. We see the Palette struggling.

A winged Palette—but now its wings are black as it crashes to the earth—still the same German desolation. The name of the painting is *Icarus.* Sometimes, learning to fly, an ideal falls from on high.

Actually, the Palette is in danger. Thus, in the 1977 *Palette am Seil*

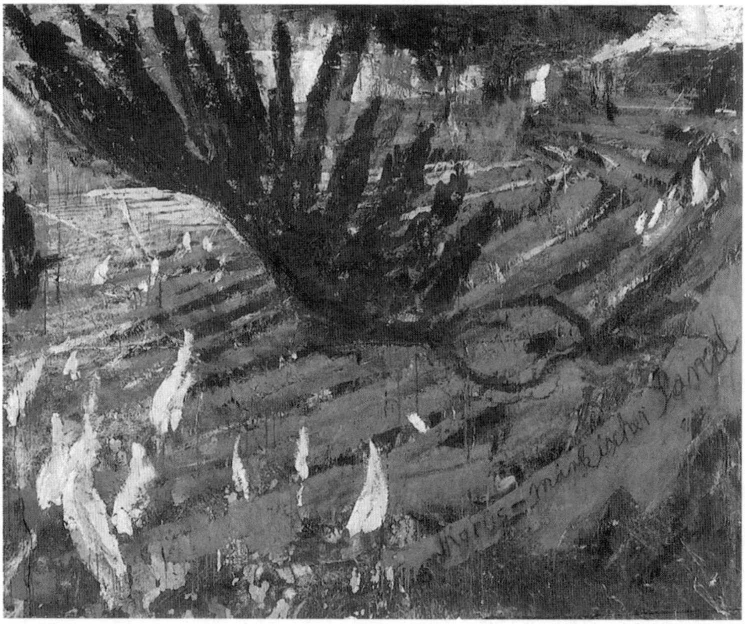

Icarus. Märkischer Sand. Icarus / Sand of the Brandenburg March. Icarus, 290 × 360 cm, private coll.

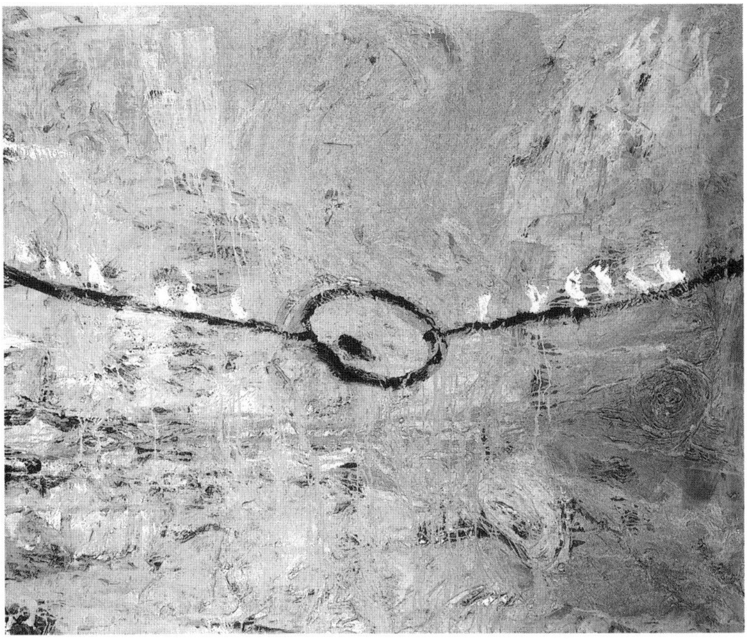

Palette am Seil / Palette on a Rope, 1977, 130 × 160 cm, Städlische Galerie, Munich

/ Palette on a Rope,[23] we see it teetering on a tightrope, precariously balanced high in the air. Wim Wenders, the German filmmaker who is Kiefer's contemporary, might have painted it that way if he were a painter. Kiefer added little flames that have singed the rope in places, placing the Palette at even greater risk of falling.

This is a more powerful and striking work than the earlier *Icarus*, because there is no explicit depiction of the fall, or reference to the myth in the title. We simply feel that the Palette on the rope is in mortal peril, and all we can do is wait for the fall, certain it will happen.

In other works constructed on the same theme, we see the Palette clinging to a tree. With *Icarus*, Kiefer had just learned to paint black wings. Now he invents the use of lead as a medium, integrating the heavy metal into his canvases. The first is *Baum mit Palette* / Tree with Palette from 1978 (seen on next page). To me, it is one of Kiefer's most beautiful works, because it is one of his most moving.

This Palette hanging from a tree, stuck to the trunk, is made of lead, and ribbons that are also real lead on the canvas, dangle from

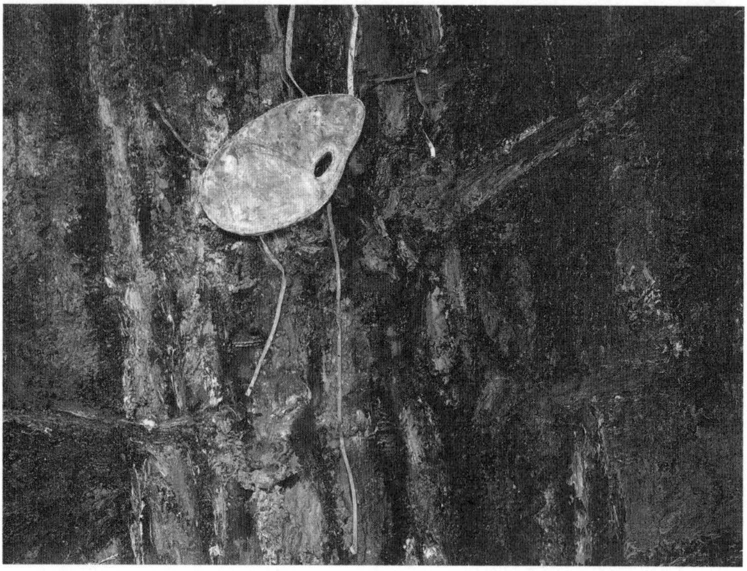

Baum mit Palette / Tree with Palette, 1977, 290 × 195 cm, Bayeler Foundation, Basel

its body, subject to gravity. Despite its almost ideal shape, the Palette is suffering. It looks like a wounded bird. This beauty, deprived of flight, can only remember soaring. It still has the flying motion, and can aspire to fly. But it has returned from flying, too. It has learned resignation. Kiefer's work does not seek the sublime. It does not bet on sublimation. It seeks sentiment and creates it through sensation.

Weight of lead and lightness of flight

Becoming a sculptor as well, the artist integrates the rawest natural elements into his pieces—sand, clay, straw, plants, ashes, hair, lead—that Kiefer is learning to articulate, like a language. The work becomes increasingly sensorial and again obeys the laws of gravity. It finds its true gravity.

This work proceeds by a regression that takes us back to our most elementary sensations and experiences, all the way to the deepest foundations of ourselves and nature to free us of our overly ideal movements and to support us in a gathering or clustering of ourselves that might make us breathe and go forward in some other way, if possible.

So what is this Palette that, in its variety of expressions, attracts a whole world that is familiar to us, through our history of forms, spiritualities, and thought—the wings of angels, the myth of Icarus—and combines it with an ordinary, everyday object, a painter's palette, in a movement and in media or materials that are natural ones, whose center of gravity draws our attention downward? Perhaps Jung can help us perceive it more clearly.

We know that in 1916–17, in Château-d'Oex, Jung had been called up to the army and was serving as an officer. It was during the First World War. At the time, he had had to take a leave of absence from his ordinary duties and responsibilities as a clinician and researcher, and also from his work with writing and painting. He was still groping in his efforts with his *Red Book.* What he did sometimes delighted him, and often he was seriously disturbed by it. But he was always surprised. He never knew what he was going to find, and even less what he was going to become. Actually, he was in a state of severe disorientation.

It was at that point in his uncertainty, tormented inside by endless questions, that he found himself drawing—or rather, allowing shapes to emerge from beneath his pencil or pen, shapes that were more or less rounded, circles that were more or less complete, sorts of flowers with petals radiating from a central point, more or less symmetrical, sometimes in color, and sometimes not. He was not yet speaking of "*mandalas*"—or of the "self."[24]

Drawing by drawing, day by day, he observed the outlines, shapes, distortions, and transformations that were emerging, and also how the shapes varied, as a function of his mood at the moment he was drawing or painting.

When he began to speak of the "self" in this context, he spoke of the kinship of these spontaneous mandalas with many shapes or representations expressing an ideal balance or search for perfection. Such a quest is the theme of many a myth, religion, or spiritual pursuit, Tibetan Buddhism being among the most notable. Many material realities and accomplishments reflect the same striving for equilibrium.

Jung dreamed of various species of trees, including a magnolia.[25] He drew objects that looked like flowers, and also contemplated square, round, or star-shaped buildings: churches, temples, or Vauban's fortifications, for example.

These formations might make one think of a complete whole, or the dream of accomplishing one. They might be held up as ideal. For such is the way they may appear to us, and we are quite tempted to believe it is true. Jung, however, observed them. He took an interest, but resisted being captivated by them. Hence, his attentive analyses were open to but constantly critical of the plenitudes celebrated or promised by religions. At the same time, he observed the striking particularity of Christianity. It is a religious tradition centering on the figure of the Cross, of the Crucifixion, on a tension inherent to the way it presents itself, and is seen, strictly defined, as a torture, a quartering. Likewise, the cross also symbolizes a violently opposed double polarity, given to us to see and live, between the vertical movement upward and the weight that soon, ineluctably, drags it downward.

The experience, observation, and analysis of these formations tending to be rounded out, accomplished, and idealized in the imaginary, but which are also able and wise enough to be presented in an inner tension that is sometimes unbearable, like that of the cross, led Jung to speak of the "self" as a structurally active, dynamic, creative reality that can also evolve.[26]

Hence, he developed terms for the relationship to the unconscious that bespeak the tensions, or even power struggles, involved: complementarity, compensation, and also contradiction—an approach that is easy enough to describe but harder to practice.[27]

The term "totality" is not really fitting.[28] It would be more accurate to speak of a set: a compound or complex set that would strive to be accomplished, like a work in progress or in process. Actually, the process counts as much as the structure,[29] with a decentration effect as well.

It might be a surprise, for very often, quite the contrary of obeying what might be expected of it, and also quite the contrary of placing us on the orbit of the ideal, which might fulfill the expectations of the ego, the centration that comes over the person is arranged around a center at some point removed from us. It is usually lower. Hence a dynamic disequilibrium that is disconcerting, to say the least. It makes us wonder where we will end up.[30]

Jung experienced and observed it. And he lets us know. Or, at least he tried to allow us to perceive it. The arts make us experience it.

This is why we were able to feel the weight of the body of the doleful angel, who had fallen from on high despite his wings: the angel Dürer put at the center of his *Melancolia*. And with Caravaggio's *Narcissus*, we held on tight to avoid the danger of being captivated by the depths opening beneath him. At that point, the metaphysical or graciously worldly high ceases to be as easy as it was in the past.

Pollock committed to it and threw himself into these depths that to us are seemingly bottomless. He dove into the process by means of the dance of creation that brought him, and us along with him, the rewards and joys of experiencing *Autumn Rhythm*, *Lavender Mist*, or *One, Number 52, 1950*. But these joys, this bliss, this nearly total participation or immersion in the movements of the world remained the success of a fleeting and perilous moment. Pollock tried so hard to find the safest position, above and around the canvases lying on the floor of his studio, or in the layers of thin rice paper, or when he accepted the challenge from the photographer Namuth underneath him, or that of his friend Tony Smith who, on the contrary, wanted him to project his colors towards the sky, or also when, with *The Deep*, he was able to allow the strange emergence of a presence that looks to us like a feminine one, the faint outline of a woman's body. Sometimes he got it right, but at other times, he got it terribly wrong. We support his movement and his search; we go forward alongside him. But one can only be awed at the risks he took, the obstacles he had to overcome, the traps he struggled to escape from, at the adjustments he attempted, and at the somber successes of his art.

As for Kiefer, whose creative power is no less impressive than Pollock's and may even exceed it, he has undoubtedly read Jung's work. More than one of his interviews and of his works attests to his respect for Jung. I do not know if he would speak of the "self" in relation to his Palette opened onto the infinite ruin of the German land. In any case, we can see that he knows the meaning of the terms wound, pain, loss, and disaster.

I would have liked for Pollock and Kiefer to meet, for they have gone through similar moments or phases in the story of their art-making, and faced similar challenges as they navigated their individual processes of creation. There is a response to the nearly absolute expansion, nearly "all-over," of Pollock's large drip paintings, and to his attempt to give his work a more stable mooring, with the structure and rhythm of the composition of *Blue Poles*, in Kiefer's *Johannisnacht*, from the late 1970s.[31] It gives us the fragility of straw and the threat of fire. However, it departs from Pollock's *Blue Poles* due to the fact that the St. John's Eve midsummer bonfire to which it refers really is a time of transition and renewal, in the course of the seasons, and also in Kiefer's work. To my way of seeing, starting with *Johannisnacht*, Kiefer has learned to hold and convey to us most keenly the pain, the passing of time, evil, and grief his Palettes attempted to circumvent. Now Kiefer permits us to get closer to these risks. Starting with this representation of the bonfire, his work went through another renewal, in its themes, in his manner and matter. Human presences finally take part.

From the Palette to the books

Kiefer's Palette goes through many an ordeal as his work progresses. It is sorely tried.

In the 1974 *Resumptio*, we see the winged Palette fluttering over a dark tomb that dominates the foreground. Is the Palette about to soar away from the scene into the sky? Or is it struggling to avoid being swallowed up by the tomb and annihilated?

Oddly enough, commenting on the piece, critics who know Kiefer's work well usually speak of it soaring away.[32] But how can they be unaware that the one-word title of the piece, the seemingly Latin name, "*Resumptio*," is not really Latin? It is a word Kiefer created. That fact should make us even more attentive. Is this not his way to turn the real Latin word "*Assumptio*" inside out, like the finger of a glove, or to counterfeit it?

Here, the Palette is experiencing the impossible flight of which it might have dreamed. It is deliberately deviating from the "*Assumptio*."

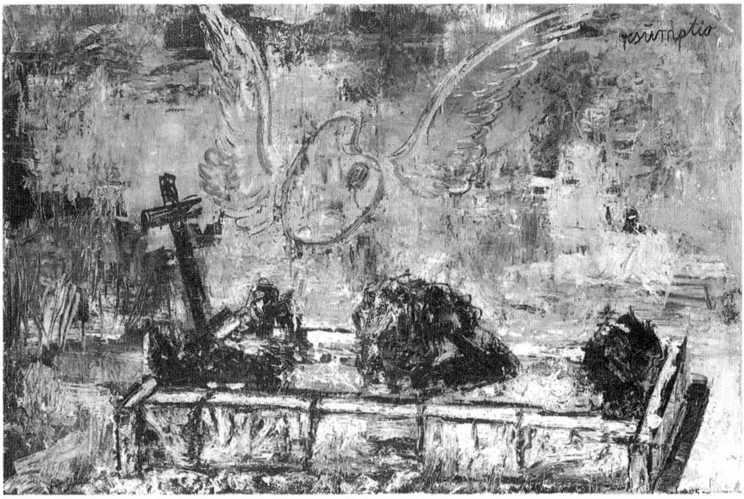

Resumptio, 1974, 115 ×180 cm, private coll.

It is in the midst of falling, being pulled back to the ground, to the land and to the tomb. Understandably, it does not resign itself easily. It struggles. Actually, Kiefer's Palette is about to find itself prostrate, on the ground and on the brink of shattering.

In the following work from 1980, we see the Palette grounded, surrounded by almost broken threats. It is about to be crushed by tanks in battle array, aimed straight at it.[33] A fire has broken out, and the flames will soon destroy the wooden Palette, or at least the wooden floor where the artist has placed it. It is the same wooden floor we saw in the first works of the 1970s, the floor of the studio.

The Palette is besieged. And the tension in which we see it is also an inner tension. Moreover, the title Kiefer gives to the scene, "*Bilderstreit*," which can be translated as Battle of the Images, seems clearly to refer to the conflicts and combats provoked in Byzantium by the radical determination to banish all imagery and representation, from religious worship and edifices.

Here, the image is under attack, taking a beating from outside and inside. Figuration itself is challenged. The art and manner of containing that which occupies us, of giving us some grip on the very thing that is liable to overwhelm us or escape from us, is liable to lose out.

The Palette isn't what it used to be. The painter, or rather his paint-

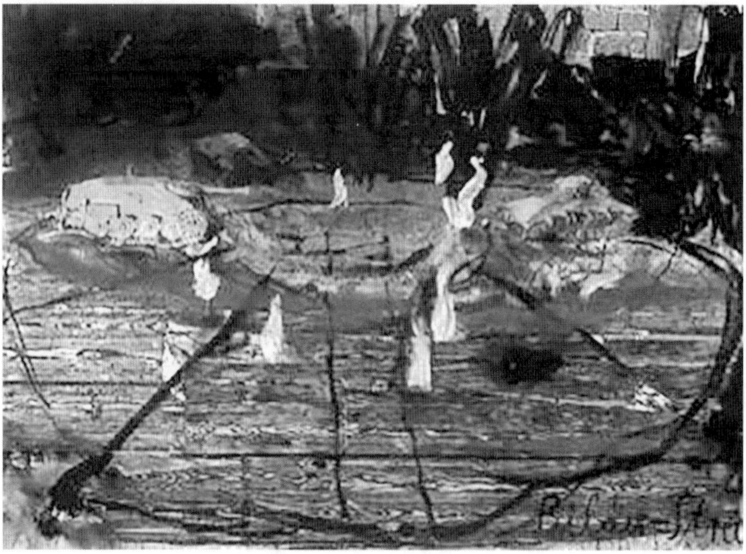

Bilder-streit / Battle of images, 1980, 295 × 406 cm, Museum Boijmans Van Beuningen, Rotterdam

ing, is aware of that, and it informs us. In *Gefallene Bilder* / The Fall of Images, from 1986, the image vanishes, receding completely, lost in the chasm the work depicts. Figuration is lost.

Except, in the dynamic of Kiefer's progress, another event occurs. Suddenly, the Palette yields to another object—just as tangible and identifiable as the Palette, and just as eloquent, but in another way. It is the Book. It takes its place, and appears again and again as a subject for Kiefer. It differs significantly from the Palette in one primary respect: instead of being transparent or translucent, it is heavy and opaque. It is made of lead: its pages, sheets of lead, give it thickness and weight. Naturally, it is necessary to prop it up somehow, to give it support, because it is so heavy. The painter, who is also a sculptor, gives it a pedestal or stand, keeping it off the ground, stabilizing it, and showing that even though it, too, has wings, like the Palette, it cannot take flight into the heights; it cannot soar into the skies.[34]

It becomes increasingly clear that the Book is replacing the Palette as the subject of Kiefer's paintings. Now it is the Book that the painter hangs, suspending it on wires above a ground that is also increasingly real—the wounded, harrowed German soil. Sometimes the sea is beneath the Book.

The fold in the Book's page is itself a furrow, and the Book contains the wound of the earth or the sometimes-violent trough of the wave. It also leads us to the wound and furrows where the sea forms troughs. It contains and perhaps holds the secret to what one is seeking there. How can one know what the Books really do contain, what might be found there? Kiefer's Books are simultaneously open and secret.

One could be tempted to handle them. That is what a book ordinarily permits or invites a person to do. But until now, Kiefer has exhibited them very little. Certainly, he allowed some of them to be photographed, and with his permission, the photographs were published. But it was only in 2015 that he showed them, at the French National Library in Paris, the BNF.[35] Even then, only a few were open. Many more were on display, but from afar—placed on high shelves,

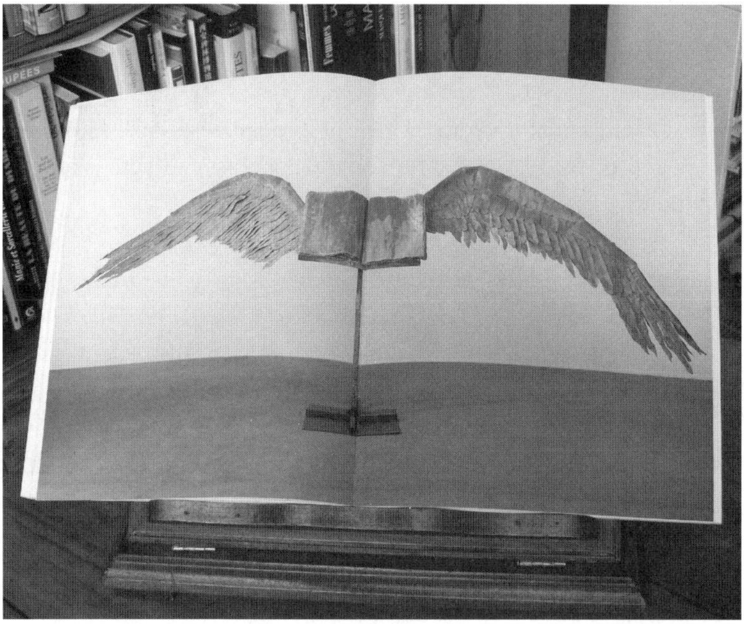

Buch mit Flügeln / Book with wings, 1992–94, Modern Museum of Fort Worth

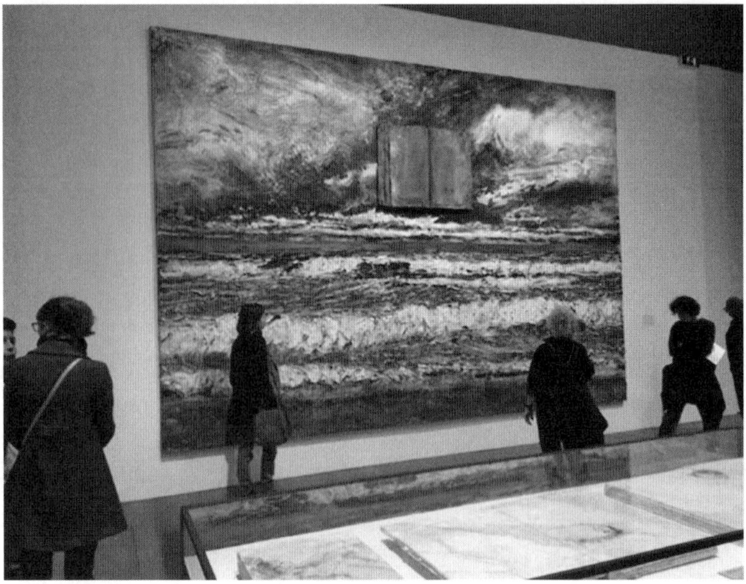

Das Buch / Le Livre, 2015, Bibliothèque Nationale de France, Paris. Photo by Alix Dermigny

and often in boxes made of metal or cardboard. That is how the artist created them. Most of them are so big and heavy—especially the ones made of lead—that they are evidently impossible to take into one's hands and open. How can one know what they contain? Will they keep their secret?[36]

The vessels are broken

Books lend themselves to sharing. They are a means of communication—from the author to the readers, from one generation to another, from one era to another.

Could it be that Kiefer, who is an avid reader, who lives surrounded by books, and who, by his own account,[37] knows how to nourish himself with readings, new or old, is deliberately keeping us apart from the contents of the books he created? Or might it be that he himself is still awaiting what might be found within them?

The answer to this question comes from another form—another history—that haunts his work: that of broken vessels.

They can be found at various times in his work even up to our day. For the exhibition at the BNF, Kiefer created one version of them. It is not a painting, nor, strictly speaking, a sculpture—at least, the way a sculpture is usually understood. Instead, it is what today's artists call "an installation." A sort of bookcase supports heavy leaden books, from which glasses are falling and have fallen. We see the broken ones on the floor.

This piece might inspire a dissertation about the "*sephirot*," the Kabbalah, and Isaac Luria's vision of the creation of the world. It has engaged many scholars. And Kiefer himself has studied these analyses.

However, it may be simpler, at least for most of us, and perhaps more accurate, to accept these works at face value by drawing the most obvious meaning they present to our eyes: these vessels are shattered ineluctably.

Kiefer's vessels, which, in his work, are often associated with books and collections of books, can be seen as containers that were doubtless quite useful for a long time. They served their purpose well. However, they are now inadequate and useless.

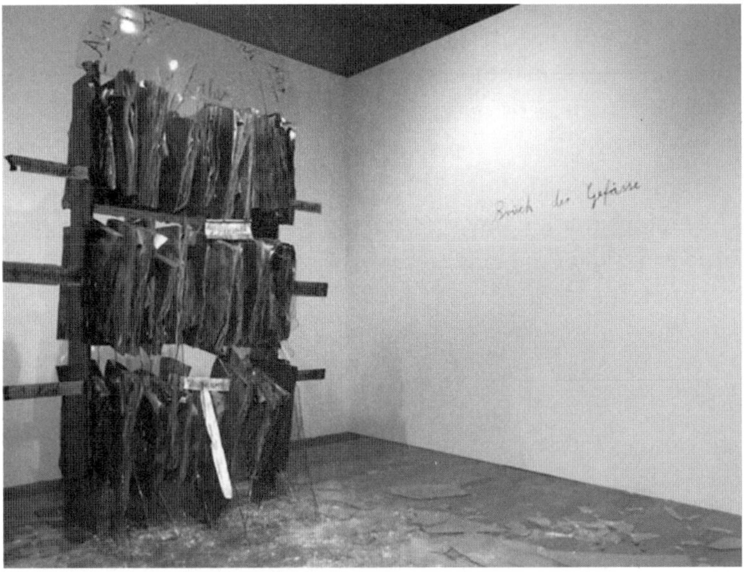

Shevirat-Ha-Kelim, 2011, Bibliothèque Nationale de France, Paris. Photo by Alix Dermigny

These shattered vessels are a blunt expression, dramatic in its very rawness, of the representations and also the concepts, conceptions, and theories that have kept us busy for so long, from one generation to the next, from one era to the next, in our culture. As such, they also stand for the books that, for so long, contained and transmitted these representations, concepts, and theories to us.

Kiefer's work has always been eloquent and insistent in speaking of ruins, of the past: obsolescence, loss, and grief. The viewer can only be gripped—choked—by the emotion.

One might therefore also wonder why this body of work, so often described as melancholic, nevertheless does not convey utter despair. To my way of thinking, there are two main reasons for this.

Presences that come from afar

The first reason why these pieces, from one painting, sculpture, or installation to the next, prompt joy rather than despair is that the progression amazes us. The manner and matter of the work, the materials from which it is shaped, are continually being renewed. We discover and admire this capacity for renewal with astonishment, and it is even more powerful than the themes of grief and loss we mentioned above. There is a single basic movement, a deep, powerful current, driving Kiefer forward. These works are the vessels, the new vessels, of the creation of our own times. It therefore ensues that sentiment is born of sensation. Intuition allows itself to go with the flow and to be nourished by it. As for thinking, it can wait.

Another powerful reason to rejoice in being around this work is that something is emerging from these new forms and substances, these new vessels that consciously remember the ones we used for so long that served our purposes. In the thickness of the paint, clay, sand, straw, lead, grasses and flowers, and glass, and in the many photographs we see the outlines of something that is about to appear: creatures, presences, souls, about to approach us, when we call out their names.[38]

Margarete and Shulamith are the figures the artist, or his work, evokes and summons, calling them by name, these feminine first names, so near to us and from so very far away.

Margarete of the golden hair has haunted German letters since Goethe's *Faust*, at least, where she was betrayed, abused, convicted of murder, and thrown into the dungeon to rot.

Shulamith and her raven locks come from the Song of Songs or Canticle of Canticles, the Song of Solomon in the Jewish Torah. She was King Solomon's first and greatest love, a young woman of ideal beauty and grace—and, in Germany, she was subjected to the worst of fates, the death camps.

Kiefer's work does not show these women's faces, but one can feel their powerful presence. This presence brings his work to life. It is a force that has been strengthening for a long time, drawn from books—the oldest and most classical stories of German literature and mythology. These female figures have been slumbering for years in Kiefer's work; I see one in Siegfried's *Difficult Way to Brünhilde*, from 1977, stirring up a great torment of suspense.[39] Likewise, the beautiful *Brünhilde schläft* / Brünhilde sleeps, from 1980, shows her stretched out in the chill of falling snow with her eyes closed, as if immersed in shallow waters, like Ophelia.[40]

A feminine presence gradually becomes more explicit in Kiefer's work because the transformational movement in his creation, both material and thematic, in the diversity of his means of expression, promoted such an emergence.[41] But there is another factor. Kiefer had a decisive encounter, with a poem by Paul Celan, a poet who is quite close to us.

Kiefer discovered Celan's *Todesfuge*, or Death Fugue. It sings of the beauty of two women: "*Dein goldenes Haar, Margarete. Dein aschenes Haar, Sulamith.*" / "Your golden hair, Margarete. Your ashen hair, Shulamith."[42] Celan wrote this awe-inspiring poem in 1945—the year of Kiefer's birth—in a concentration camp. The fire he invokes is more than an artist's device. It was a crematorium. The ideal was turned into ashes. Celan committed suicide in 1970, at the age of 49.

Kiefer, reading Celan in the depths of disaster—a disaster that is now no longer anonymous and devoid of figures, like the one in his first canvases that made one say, in the night, "this is war,"—brings Margarete's presence to us. The wounded German soil is still in the background, and Margarete dwells in the real sheaves of straw he adds to the canvas, glowing golden against the blackness of the earth. These clusters of yellow straw are fragile in every way likely to fall off when the painting is moved. They are threatened from inside by tongues of flame about to destroy them.

Still accompanied by Celan, or meditating upon him, the painter causes us to see and feel the shadow of the golden straw. After writing Margarete's name out on the canvas in his own hand, he shows us the shadows that bring out the blacks and cinders he has learned to incorporate into his creation, as a terrible, ominous presence.[43]

From that point, his work in recent years, exploring an entirely different register of sensuality and sensibility, makes us attentive and sensitive in an entirely new way to a womanly presence and body, by sketching it in watercolor on the skin and in the soft thickness of pages that are attentively erotic.[44]

For this powerful painter and sculptor, who also knows how to entrust his art to the watercolor, is truly attached to eliciting sentiment through sensation. This faculty is one of the virtues of regression. It can give rise to the shaping of a new expression, and to a contemporary figuration, which recalls the sources and pathways of its elaboration. No less is expected of an artist.

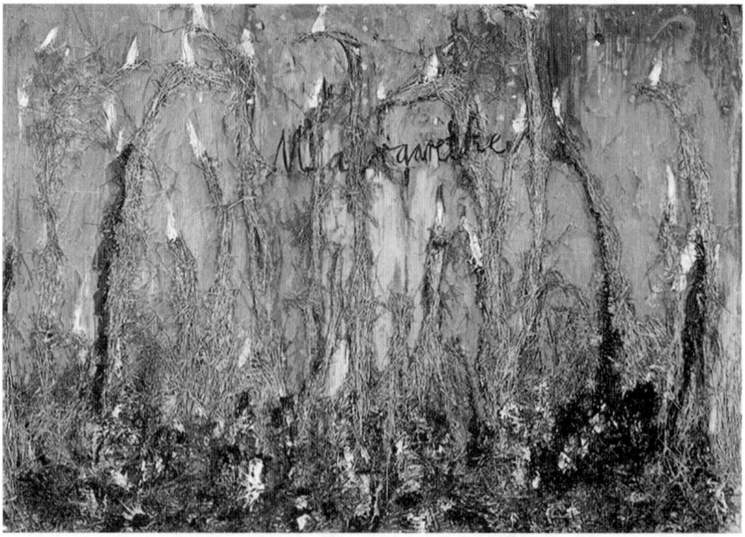

Margarete, 1981, 280 × 380 cm, San Francisco Museum of Modern Art

One wonders how Pollock would have seen the emergence, the eruption, in Kiefer's work, of these strongly felt feminine presences—Pollock, who struggled so hard to reach the point where he could allow the vague figure of *The Deep* to show herself. How could he, too, perhaps, have made room for these women, with the means belonging to his own art and his own progress in life?

To say the truth?

Psychoanalysis, as a clinical practice and form of thinking, regardless of the tradition in which it develops, is engaged in meeting a similar challenge, when the ego is willing to let go of its needs for coherence, continuity, and control, and when, yielding to a regressive movement, the deepest and most abysmal insides of ourselves have been reached, those which are sometimes the most dangerously energetic and active. Psychoanalysis seeks a shaping, an expression, for the most accurate container for what was experienced in the depths. Something that would enable us to share it.

Yves Bonnefoy, a poet and specialist in the history of ideas and of the arts, and a professor at the Collège de France, has written a beautiful text that mentions vessels and pottery in this connection. Speaking of clay vessels and pots is a direct consideration of *Gestaltung*, or shaping. Pottery is a craft that is relevant to the question we are examining.

Bonnefoy expresses the idea: "Making vases helped elaborate, if not invent, language."[45] Naturally, I was delighted to read this: the point is to shape a language.

However, let us note that next Bonnefoy issues a warning: "Not all pots tell the truth."

Again, he is quite right. The clay vessel is only a container one is happy to use. For a time, it may be suitable. But it may also become obsolete or shatter. Kiefer showed this to us and enabled us to experience it. The history of the arts, in all of their diversity, can be read from one chapter to the next in this book—as the history of the gradual or simultaneous crafting of ways of doing, as themes call out and respond, contradicting each other, crumble, shatter, and are renewed. The history of psychoanalysis is the same way.

Look at how the various traditions and orientations of psychoanalysis are continually challenging and testing the various expressions of the theories that seem to be taken as its bedrock. Psychoanalysis, by nature, questions what came before, redefines or reconsiders its basic terms and concepts, transforming them and sometimes shattering them, to renew them, not without difficulty.

This habit of self-examination and necessary adjustment elicits the amazement of its observers and, even more, its own practitioners. The latter may even become defensive about it. Freud experienced this reaction as soon as he began writing, and at various stages in his work, from one phase to another in his psychology. As for Jung, although he did not have to shatter all of the Freudian vessels he once thought would contain his thinking and his experience of the unconscious, he did have to reshape them radically.[46]

Hence, the processes of creation and those of psychoanalysis are cousins. But can we therefore decree that psychoanalysis is an art? One is tempted to believe that it is. At one point, Jung nearly fell for the idea.

Jung liked women. He also had a few reasons to be wary of this inclination. We know that one of the young women in his circle tried to convince him that he was truly an artist, and should pursue a career in this direction—a bit like Echo trying to love Narcissus, or like the photographer Hans Namuth, eager to support Pollock and join him in his adventure.[47]

Jung was close to believing in her, and believing in him an artist. But he was not, and he was not fated to fulfill that destiny. His purpose in life was different—he had something else to do and to create.

Jung was a clinician and a psychologist, and he had done all that it was within his power to do to make his clinical practice and thinking—his professional identity itself—fit into the mold of Freudian psychoanalysis and its institutions. But his experiences of the world and of his inner life, starting in childhood, his scholarly work and intellectual heritage, particularly the philosophical education he had received, had failed to find their best possible expression in Freudianism. Jung had to express himself differently. He had to push forward differently. He had to create his own way of thinking and practicing psychoanalysis. Jung's psychoanalysis had to be differentiated or set apart from the turn Freud wanted to give it. It had to make itself creative—and it did.

The concepts Jung created and implemented in psychoanalysis are indeed singular objects. They are strangely alive and amazing. They are animated, figurative, and—most surprisingly and curiously of all, coming from a concept—they can be presented anthropomorphically. They even have sexual characteristics. Thus, when I speak of the "*anima*" figure, of one of my "*anima*" figures, I am talking about a certain reality that dwells within me, a certain feminine inner presence. I can make room for this presence, learning to recognize and associate with it, or her; she may inspire, seduce, or betray me. It is also good for me to learn how to outwit her, for she often is merrily projected here or there, without my knowledge, onto one of the women I meet. In fact, this is how Jung experienced the anima, and it is one of the lessons he drew from his conversations with the lady who wanted to convince him that he was actually a great artist, and that art was evidently his calling.

Surprisingly enough, these concepts, which actually articulate an experience, have no equivalent in other traditions of the psychoanalytic movement.[48] They are suggested only as a living approach and only for a time. They are simply the best expression, at a given time, in a certain context, and for a particular individual, of what could not be expressed in a better way, or experienced otherwise. They are distinctive in that they are presented in the very way the largely autonomous and unconscious autochthonous work of representation is manifested—that is, the work of figuration and dramatization, especially. Each of us can observe and experience these expressions, notably in the theater of our dreams.

Hence what I have called the "emergentist" nature of Jungian practice and thinking. This is the clearest kinship between Jungian psychoanalysis and the work of creation to which the arts attest. The Jungian approach shares another distinctive feature with the arts, with the works we have been studying so far: it knows it is not telling the truth. Telling the truth is not its purpose. It is forever only a gradual, partial attempt, a series of near-misses and adjustments, always striving toward but never reaching the truth, the best possible recognition, at the moment, of what dwells within us and animates us, at times obsessing us or overwhelming us, but largely escaping us. Such an approach is the source of its aversion to orthodoxy, doctrine, and for any sort of belief—a characteristic it shares with the arts.

However, this psychoanalysis sets itself apart from the fine arts by the artisanal nature of its practice. By the fact that as creative as it may be in its ways of thinking and its processes, it is aware that all it will ever be is a container, a "vessel," a protected and protective setting with its own rules, particularly for the training of its practitioners, to be most useful to the becoming of those who solicit it.

This psychoanalysis is aware that it has its own means of going forward, its own ways of orienting and holding the attention of each in the four directions that must be explored when the issue is our relationships with the unconscious, relationships that prove to be all the more crucial the farther we venture into the most primal, archaic, unfamiliar depths, the ones we shrink from exploring because they are the most inhuman parts of ourselves, as we saw in the tale of *Bluebeard* written by Perrault and illustrated by Doré. The four directions we mean are the ones we saw reactivated in our own time in the course of an analysis: the re-living of a childhood that left a mark, a mark that despite its indelibility is in most cases largely forgotten or repressed; the expression and the transformations of the imaginary and symbolic life; the vicissitudes, encounters, and discoveries that arise as the individual makes his or her way through analysis; and last, the experience, in the transference of a therapeutic and human relationship that often had never taken place until then.

As you will have understood, there is yet another dimension of our psychoanalysis.

The history between us

It is often said that the analytic process involves two individuals: that it is a duet. This is somewhat inaccurate. Actually, there are three players. Naturally, the analysand and analyst are involved. But, between them, there is a third element at play. This third is the emerging being, the underlying, axial, active process, seeking its path and its fulfillment. Its current suffuses us, carrying us. We activate this flow, and yet we also try to be its subjects.

In perspective, this movement of becoming, characterized by emergence, shaping, and transformation, is called individuation. It flows on different scales—on the scale of an analysis and more largely on the scale of each individual lifetime. It also flows on a transgenerational scale, and in the long term of a culture. It even occurs throughout the longer duration of our humanity, starting in prehistory.[49]

This movement or process is not at all linear. It cannot be likened to a constant, continuous work in progress. Instead, we could think of it as a work in process, able to evolve at the rate of slow changes, but often enough leaping ahead suddenly by bounds and by crises. At those times, acquired realizations and representations are discarded like old vessels that are no longer useful. We have to struggle to free ourselves from them. It is sometimes difficult for us to let go of the vessels we have used for a long time, because the experience may be rough and fraught with uncertainty. It is quite the contrary of mustering our energy to reach some ideal goal or accomplishment. This journey is a descent that takes us, at our own risk and without very much warning, into the sometimes-raw, brutal depths, all the way to the most radical, inorganic, undifferentiated chaos, beneath all representation and even the most elementary articulations and structures making it possible to distinguish between the life and death instincts, between life and death.

However, the return or regression to the darkest and deepest insides of ourselves, which we have seen are suffocating and actually uninhabitable—I called them "inhuman"—can also be the source or one of the sources for becoming. Then the question or challenge would be to attempt, and to create, new expressions that are weighted differently, notably by practicing sensation and today, often by putting the body into play, and thereby sufficiently marked by the experience of such a plunge into the nether regions of ourselves. Artists and also analysts engage in this work, each by their own means.[50]

But the question returns, demanding an answer: how is one to hold oneself during such an adventure? There is some chance that Kiefer's work may again show us the path—at least his own.

In 1986, Kiefer made a large piece (380 by 560 cm, or 150 by 220 in.) he entitled *Jerusalem.* It followed upon his travels to Israel, and his discovery and study of Jewish traditions and culture—as well as his explorations and friendliness with Mesopotamian cultures.

Two skis are firmly set there in front of us, open and heading forward, as if awaiting the feet that will be placed upon them. The background is still in turmoil, but it now resembles birch bark, rather than the ravaged German land of his earlier works.

It is cold, but we are moving ahead. The rails, the rails of death leading Siegfried in search of Brünhilde are behind us. A sort of axis is being tried and becoming firmer. It does go forward. It will also require two legs that work well together, something that remains to be seen, but we know that balance is found in movement.

Here, one might think of the "self" Jung speaks of. Caravaggio made us feel the tension of such an array in search of itself, but he had made a cut through the question, as if he had wanted to stop it in passing to show it to us better. Kiefer shows it to us in movement. With the explicit, manifest consciousness of the diversity of cultures moving forward and the movement of history, a lively consciousness is remembering yesterday today.

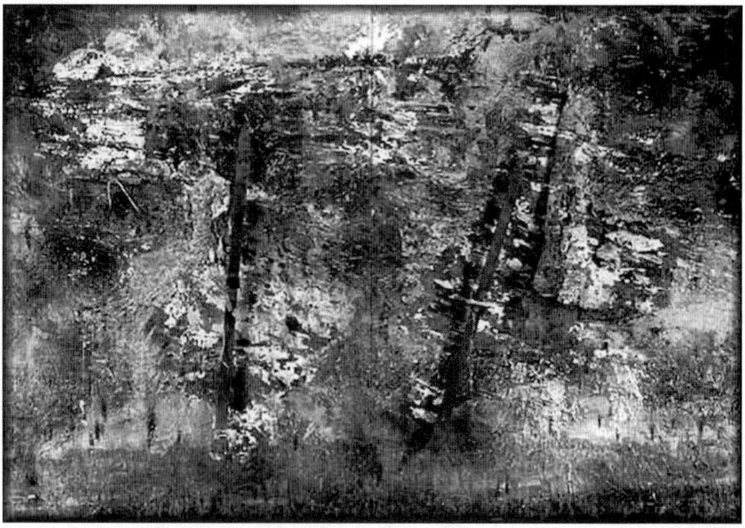

Jerusalem, 1986, 380 × 560 cm, private coll.

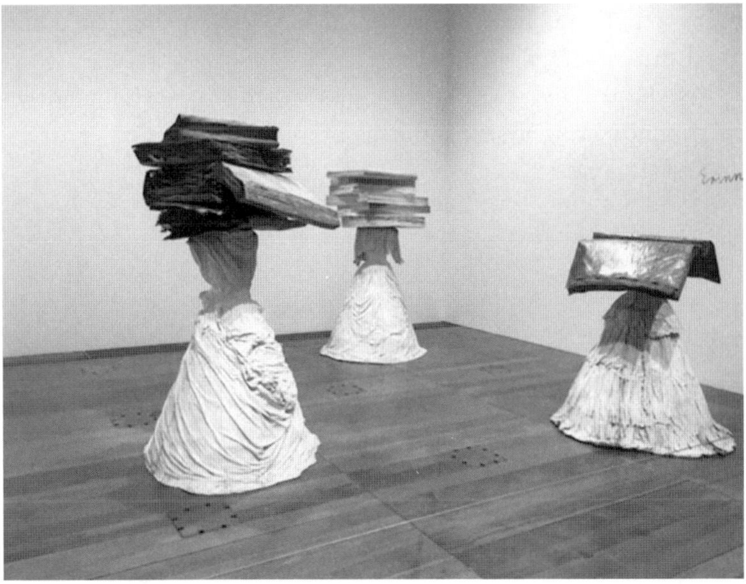

Praxilla, Sappho, Erinna, 2015, Bibliothèque Nationale de France, Paris. Photo by Alix Dermigny

Kiefer implements and stages this life, of a memory open on what it contains as well as onto a future that still lies ahead, in another set of pieces, which are also on a life-sized scale. These works associate women, their bodies, and the presences of women from the past with books that look at us. These books, the women's faces, are sometimes closed and sometimes open—as if, in Kiefer's work, starting with the Margarete of the German tradition and the Shulamith of the Jews, the woman, or women, were the containers, repositories, and libraries of memory, more than anyone else among us, as if they recorded the history to which we belong, the history we carry and that carries us, the history we must move ahead.

In these women standing there and the open books, Jung, who was also a man of the book, might have recognized the Salome of his *Red Book*, and especially his debate with the *Book of Job*—a book he addressed as an elderly man. Jung responded to Job himself, telling him how he himself analyzed and assumed the history of the Jewish people and the history of Christianity. Knowing himself to be the heir to those traditions, he also knew he had to work on seeing and fulfilling their becoming.[51]

Yes, the arts and psychoanalysis go forward with the same movement, if not the same step, for better or worse.

And art precedes us.

Notes

Foreword

1. Harry J. Shafer, *Ancient Texans: Rock Art and Lifeways along the Lower Pecos*. Austin: Gulf Publishing Co., 1992.

Chapter 1

1. Vialou 1996, 2006.

2. Since then, with him, I have participated in a research group on prehistory, which brings together paleoanthropologists, anthropologists, and psychoanalysts—most of them Freudian or Lacanian—on a regular basis. We have the privilege of visiting prehistoric sites in France, Italy, or Spain together, and to discuss the latest advances in research, as well as our own thinking and writing on the subject.

3. Lewis-Williams 2003, 2005.

4. Gaillard 2008, 2009.

5. Langaney 1989, for instance.

6. See my double chapter entitled "The Arts," (2007), in *The Handbook of Jungian Psychology*, R. Papadopoulos ed., London/New York: Routledge.

7. Freud GW/CW 12.

8. This brings us to a discussion that is difficult but epistemologically and methodologically useful, on the distinctions to be made between multidisciplinarity, interdisciplinarity, and transdisciplinarity.

9. Among French publications, cf. M. Lorblanchet, J.-L. Le Quellec, P. G. Bahn, H.-P. Francfort, and B. and G. Delluc, ed., 2006.

10. Five years after the first French printing of *Les chamanes de la préhistoire* in 1996, J. Clottes and D. Lewis-Williams published the expanded work, *Les chamanes de la préhistoire. Texte intégral, polémique et réponses*, to which I refer. If

more scholars responded to criticism in this way, it certainly would give impetus to our research!

11. Vialou 2006.

12. The reader will have noticed that this is the first time the word "soul" has appeared in the text. Keep that in mind. It is my hope that we will gradually understand what perception and conception we formulate of its role in the arts and, generally speaking, in the progress and regress of our collective history.

13. Lewis-Williams 2005.

14. Lewis-Williams 2003, 2008.

15. On these observations and so many others, cf. the works of D. Vialou, especially in *La Préhistoire* and *Chasseurs et artistes. Au cœur de la préhistoire.* Mentioned in the bibliography as follows, these works constantly allowed me to check my own work and served as a guide.

16. See his *Septem sermones ad mortuos* and "Adaptation, individuation et collectivity," both written in 1916.

17. Cf. Humbert 2004.

18. Cf. the article I wrote for this term in Mijolla 2002.

19. I recall the advice given to us by Roger Bastide, our mentor at the EPHE/EHESS research unit, when some of us were preparing for ethnographic field work. He emphasized the importance of leaving our books, hypotheses, and research methods behind when we arrived at our destination. Instead, he suggested we should simply sit down and look around. We were to concentrate on observing body language, tones of voice, gestures, signs, exchanges, and interactions within the community of human beings we were setting out to understand. In fact, the gestures, signs, and exchanges that mystified us completely, that were seemingly meaningless and superfluous, were the ones to which we should pay the closest attention. For, according to Bastide, they were the ones where aspects of these people's lives that went beyond the immediately material were manifested. They could reveal how these people practiced symbolic or spiritual life; their vision of the world, society, and themselves.

20. See Parkington 2003, in particular p. 106 sq.

21. In "The Transcendent Function," another decisive essay from 1916.

22. De Mijolla-Mellor 2009.

23. Note in passing that, to speak of reality, Freud ordinarily uses the term *Realität* (which is a classic connotation of a limitation, as in *Realitätsprüfung*, for example), whereas Jung is much more likely to apply the word *Wirklichkeit.*

The latter is much more active, coming as it does from the German verb *wirken*, which means "to have an effect, to be efficient, to act or operate." Jung even goes so far as to write "alles was wirkt is wirklich." More than once in what follows we will return to this Jungian conception of reality.

Chapter 2

1. Gaillard 1985, 1987.

2. Goethe 1818.

3. Shefold 1972, Barbet 1985.

4. Later in this book, we will discuss how to engage in association and amplification, the source of these practices, and their differences. But, for the moment, we can allow ourselves to be carried by the questions this work asks and the perspectives opened by them.

5. "Ariane, ma sœur, de quel amour blessée, vous mourûtes au bord où vous fûtes laissée," ("Sister Ariadne, by what love your heart cleft, you perished on the shore alone where you were left,") Racine wrote, in Act I, Scene 3 of *Phaedra*. We could associate the doleful music of these verses with that of Monteverdi or Handel who, with their own talent and emotion, composed themes to accompany the poignant and engaging figure of young Ariadne, abandoned.

6. Freud GW V.

7. This could lead to a discussion of terminology: to what degree, and for what reasons, should we differentiate between "analytic psychology" and "psychoanalysis"? Briefly, let me say that the question is clearer if we consider that each of these terms designates a different reality. The term "analytic psychology" applies to the concepts and the investigation elaborated by Jung and the analysts who refer to him for the development of their way of thinking and their clinical practice. The term "psychoanalysis" is applied more broadly to an array of theoretical and clinical developments initially suggested by Freud. Today, they are widespread, although very early they were reworked, rethought, renewed, and transformed, within the context of specific traditions and perspectives. I am referring mainly to those of the Jungian, Kleinian, Winnicottian, and Lacanian movements. Hence, it pleases me, as a Jungian psychoanalyst, to paraphrase Jung to those who are wise enough to listen: "*psychoanalysis nostrum non est psychoanalysis vulgaris*."

8. Readers familiar with Pompeiian painting will be reminded, like me, of

another touching scene, on a wall of the Villa of the Mysteries. It shows a very young woman, the "*panisca*," suckling a goat. In another essay, I have developed an analysis of the scene, one of the happiest, most musical, and closest to nature of the frescoes in this Villa (Gaillard 1981, Gaillard, Sauron 1985).

9. More than once in this book, we will reconsider this return to the child and childhood. To my way of thinking, it is one of the dimensions of any psychoanalytical practice, regardless of the tradition and perspective in which it has developed.

10. Here, recall what we observed in the preceding chapter, regarding the discovery of oneself and the other, an amazing, joyful experience that is nevertheless fraught with difficulty, as attested and manifested by the first expressions of art, from the first times of humanity.

11. Hillman 1972, Lopez-Pedraza 2001.

12. Note that I am resorting to terms from the Jungian vocabulary for the first time. I would prefer to keep the vocabulary at a distance as long as necessary—to allow the art to speak for itself. On this subject, it is instructive to read the discussion between James Hillman and Sonu Shamdasani, published under the excellent title *The Lament of the Dead* (Hillman, Shamdasani 2013).

Chapter 3

1. The artistic style referred to as "international gothic" developed between 1390 and 1420 in Western and Central Europe. Bohemia, the Upper Rhine, northern Italy, and France were hubs of creation for these thirty years of grace and profound change. The late Middle Ages seemed still to be dreaming of what they once were, whereas scientific and technical achievements were about to disrupt this cluster of countries and their culture. Cf. on this subject some of the books mentioned in the bibliography as follows.

2. Here is another occasion for us to enjoy associating scenes freely: images that respond to or echo each other, shedding light on each other perhaps by their differences. This sort of thinking gives us the time and fortune to become better acquainted with the scene that stopped us short, or the event that popped up. Looking back on such situations, we can and must engage with them emotionally and accurately. For the moment, the practice Freud called "free association" seems nearly identical to the exercise Jung promoted, "amplification." Perhaps we will later be able to make out the differences between them.

3. Mondzain 2004.

4. Hence, the practice of so-called free association, like that of amplification, is not limitless. It does in fact lead us to amazement, and from there to questions, and often discoveries, where we must then pause, to size them up as accurately as we can, and compare ourselves with them.

5. We will see that this pose, and from it, the theme of melancholia, will be on our minds in the rest of this book.

6. While I was on the faculty of the Ecole Nationale Supérieure de Beaux-Arts in Paris, the National Fine-Arts Academy, I developed a detailed analysis of these four paintings by Botticelli, and their importance in and effect upon his life's work (Gaillard 1979).

7. This is an example of how the combination of free association and amplification can lead to the experiment in consciousness called "active imagination" in the Jungian tradition—an exercise in "active imagination" observed here on the scale of the evolutions and transformations of our culture (Cf. Jung GW 8 II et VIIIG).

8. Actually, it seems likely that these four panels were assembled to form a chest, a "*cassone*," that the young couple could use to store linen or clothing, perhaps, in their future home.

Chapter 4

1. About Sabina Spielrein, cf. Carotenuto 1980, Kerr 1993, Covington, Wharton 2003, Gaillard 2006, 2009, 2012.

2. Cf. Ragon 1992.

3. Cf. Wehr 1989, p. 110.

4. Cf. Yiassemides 2014, Gaillard 2015.

5. Freud liked this photo of himself. It is quite interesting to note that it was taken by his sons, so we see him as his sons saw him—and that it was the one he sent to Jung in 1907.

6. Later in the book, I shall return to the idea of "psychobiography," which was long one of the canonical guidelines for research in the psychoanalysis of art.

7. Jung's letter to Freud dated June 17, 1910. Because both the English and French translations of this letter have aroused some controversy, I will quote it here in the original German: "*Leonardo ist wunderbar. [...] Ich habe 'Leonardo'*

gleich durchgelesen und werde ihn bald noch einmal vornehmen. Der Übergang zum Mythologischen wächst aus dieser Schrift mit innerer Notwendigkeit empor, eigentlich Ihre erste Schrift, deren innerer Richtlinien ich mich a priori gänzlich gleichgerichtet fühle." Cf. Gaillard 1994.

8. Cf. Hillman, Shamdasani 2013. This is one of the questions that will stay with us throughout the book.

9. Klibansky, Panofsky, Saxl, 1964.

10. Cf. Hersant 1991. With all these instruments attesting to man's technical skills and scientific knowledge, the scenery has changed radically from that of the *Garden of Paradise* of Frankfort, and even more radically from that of the *Rose Garden* of Verona.

11. Gaillard 1998.

12. Bonardel 2012.

13. Here, the reader who feels free enough with his associations may recall the lion and eagle we saw in the painting from the Herculaneum that stopped us in an earlier chapter.

14. The spiral staircase, an object that is special and especially rare in architecture, is a powerful component in the dynamics of the scene.

15. Hersant 1991, p. 74.

16. I like this etymology of the word "desire," an etymology perhaps disputable or uncontrolled, this etymology says that the word is derived from the Latin desiderium, and that desire would therefore be a good way to emerge from states of paralysis or stupor that may always be a threat to us. Desire, from the Latin word "*de-siderium*," from the verb "*de-siderari*," could be understood as a way of breaking out of a state of paralytic stupor (*sideratus*).

17. The alchemists, our chemist-philosophers of the Middle Ages, were already aware of these dangers and had experienced them. They coined the term *nigredo* for this state. Jung refers to this threat that is shattered, as *Zerstückelung*. It is another idea or experience that will come up often in the book.

18. Let us note in passing that, just as Cranach obviously knew the work of Dürer, I would hope that all of today's Jungian analysts are aware of Freud's work—and thereby more generally the current developments and genealogy of psychoanalysis.

Chapter 5

1. This leads us to the difficult task of agreeing on a definition of the term "baroque." I will discuss the matter briefly later.

2. Longhi 2004 [1927], Ebert-Schifferer 2009, Spike 2010.

3. According to recent epigraphic research, notably that of the Hellenist Denis Knoepfler, traces of it would survive on the isle of Euboea as early as the end of the Bronze Age there (Cf. Knoepfler, to be published).

4. Whereas at the Basilica of Herculaneum, as we recall, faced with the enigma of the pose of Arcadia and her encounter with Hercules, the Romans of the time, like us today—at least, those who wondered about what was being shown to them—could, by condensation, identify contemporary scenes in the lady and her entourage. Although obviously different, analogies could be found in the story of Auge, grappling with the same Hercules, and that of Ariadne abandoned by Theseus. This knowledge gives viewers some insight into the meaning of the fresco.

5. As early as the fifth century BCE, Parmenides allegedly remarked that no man can step into the same river twice.

6. Unless one wishes to join the Surrealists in describing this world as surreal.

7. Ovid, *The Metamorphoses,* Book III, verses 432–6. English translation from *Ovid's Metamorphoses: An Introduction to the Basic Aspects.* Galinsky, University of California Press, Berkeley and Los Angeles, 1975, quoting translations by Rolfe Humphries, copyright 1955, by Indiana University Press.

8. We will see a good example of this process in the next chapters of this book, when we discuss a tale where the meaning goes far beyond the nominal moral of the fable that concludes it. The storyteller may have used the more modest moral for a variety of reasons: to avoid arousing fear in the listener, or perhaps to lighten for him the ramifications hinted at by his story.

9. "*Ista repercussae, quan cernis, imaginis umbra est,*" Ovid writes, v. 434.

10. Perhaps at this point it is useful to recall that when Jung speaks of the "shadow," he wishes to draw our attention to the less honorable or even really ugly and evil parts of us of which we are unconscious. In most cases, we wish to know nothing of them. As a result, we project these attributes onto other people, near and far. The "shadow" also can be recognized in the plot of many myths, tales, and other collective lore of various cultures, as well as in our dreams, fantasies, nightmares, or delusions, in the form of a figure that is dark, danger-

ous, or directly evil. In fact, clinical experience shows that recognition of the "shadow" also can lead to the engagement of personal potential that has been neglected for too long.

11. Note that Leonardo da Vinci had already dared to bring these two figures close enough for confusion, and for the confusion of genres. I am speaking of the painting he made in 1516, entitled *Saint John the Baptist,* and the *Bacchus* he painted in 1510–15. We might wonder to what degree he deliberately emphasized the ambiguity out of pure provocation.

12. This canvas, originally supposed to hang in the Basilica of Saint Peter, is currently displayed in the Borghese Gallery, a setting that suits it better.

13. How the cardinal who commissioned the painting would have reacted is unknown, for he died in 1585, before the work was completed.

14. The customer saw no harm in this image—true, he was a banker.

15. His contemporary, Annibale Carracci, knew how to remain more illustrative of the Greek and Roman myths, and to demonstrate more classical balance in his compositions—hence his success on the heights of the Palazzo Farnese, currently the French Embassy in Rome. Thanks to a recent restoration of his fresco, his success is more famous than ever.

16. I venture here, after prominent specialists in these times, including Paul Veyne and Françoise Frontisi, who speak of their own work as "controlled anachronism," in the sense that one may speak of a "controlled skid"—that is, sufficiently measured.

17. Today, experts on this painter are reconsidering the image, gladly cultivated in the past, of a tragic, accursed artist. But the facts about his life, the conditions leading to his exile, and his death are nevertheless eloquent.

18. Marin 1977.

19. In the field of theoretical approaches to art, particularly psychoanalytical, beginning with that of Freud, this gives rise to investigations in terms of sublimation. We will have to return to this subject.

20. Hence the exhibitions in Montpellier and Toulouse in the summer of 2012 on Caravaggism and Caravagesques, and that of spring 2015 at the Musée des Beaux-Arts of the City of Paris, entitled *Les Bas-fonds du Baroque. La Rome du vice et de la misère.*

21. The baroque style, whether it concerned architecture, sculpture, music, or painting, was still young at the time Caravaggio painted *Narcissus.* But the painter rapidly assimilated the baroque taste for the expression of feelings and

the dynamic of shapes. Likewise, there is a baroque way of playing with illusion, and then, especially, unmasking it, by distilling from representations inherited from earlier cultures the beliefs that might be attached to them. I have always been surprised that the Roman Catholic Church was willing to use these arts to lure back into the fold the faithful tempted the stay by the Protestant Reformation. The baroque arts are often a blithely risqué challenge to the attachment required by belief, piety, and convention. Cf. on this subject the fundamental work by Heinrich Wölfflin, *Barock und Renaissance*, published in 1888. Also, a century later, *Vous avez dit Baroque?* by Philippe Beaussant, the musicologist, essayist, and novelist, founder of the Centre de Musique Baroque de Versailles, published by Actes Sud.

22. The work was supposed to adorn the Carmelite Church in Trastevere, but it was rejected by the church's monks.

23. We will recall the position of this body later, when we study another work by Caravaggio, even though it is quite different from this one.

24. Although Roberto Longhi firmly maintains the attribution to Caravaggio, other specialists on the matter are at something of a loss. They suggest it was painted by Orazio Gentileschi, father of Artemisia Gentileschi, one of the rare female painters of the period. Her most famous paintings are her depictions of Judith, especially *Judith Beheading Holofernes.* It has also been attributed to Niccolò Tornioli, whose career postdates that of Caravaggio significantly.

25. We will subsequently see the use to which other analyst colleagues—not Jungians, but neo-Freudians—would like to put this knee.

26. For the sake of argument, perhaps, some of my students, young artists educated at the National Academy of Fine Arts in Paris, tried turning the painting upside down, with the lower half on top and the upper half on the bottom. But they concluded that the painting's center of gravity, the compositional element that anchors it in space, facing us, is clearly the lower part. It is the darkest, heaviest part, attracting all the rest of the composition. It is unthinkable to play with falsifying the effect to avoid the obvious discomfort it causes.

27. Here, it is useful to recall the overwhelmingly heavy burden depicted in the engraving *Melencholy*, where we saw Dürer's "angel." Nearly eighty years earlier, he, too, showed that he was gripped by what he discovered, with his eyes wide open, in the confusion of tools and instruments of his knowledge, while a sort of bat screamed in the night sky.

28. In many cases, double-image play is an effort to avoid discovering and

confronting the parts of oneself one would rather not know about, and especially not recognize as one's own. I demonstrated this phenomenon at work in Dostoyevsky's novella entitled *The Double,* in my essay called "*L'étrange histoire d'un petit pétersbourgeois*" (Gaillard 1980).

29. This should be recognized as a strong trend that is actually one of the biggest pitfalls in psychoanalytic approaches to art. "Applied" psychoanalysis is eager to reduce every object to a supposed all-terrain wisdom held to be the absolute truth. I have criticized this tendency on several occasions.

30. Lacan 1977.

31. I often hear my Jungian colleagues complain of this feeling of solitude or even rejection. But I must say that I do not share it—if only because for years, I have had opportunities to work with Freudian and neo-Freudian colleagues. The panel discussions I have had the privilege of organizing at each of the international congresses of the International Association for Analytical Psychology and International Psychoanalytic Association since 2004 have enabled us to work together on where we agree and disagree, with regard to clinical approach, theory, the history of psychoanalysis, and also in relation to anthropology or prehistory, for examples.

32. Rather paradoxically, he developed these ideas at the same time as he was conducting his debates with Jung, and almost in conjunction with them, starting in the early 1910s.

33. Freud GW XII.

34. In this regard, Freud speaks of *Entbindung.* In German, and in Freud's German, the word refers so strongly and eloquently to a physical phenomenon that it is also applied to a part of the birth process: the "delivery" of the baby.

35. I must say that this is quite interesting to me as a Jungian, after what Jung said of the usefulness of "mythologizing" ("*mythologein*")—but his own myth, as we will see, is radically different from that of Freud's.

36. I will return to the adjective "anachronistic," a word that can be understood here as a precautionary instruction on a rule of method. It raises the insistent question of our current point of view on the course of our collective history, and hence that of our role, means, responsibilities, and tasks today, at the point we have reached in our collective history.

37. In his notebooks, certain pages of which were published in Sonu Shamdasani's *Jung: A Biography in Books*, one can clearly see the rapt and rigorous attention Jung devoted to this vocabulary, and to the reflections that he developed

from these sources from one step to the next, in the writing and painting of his *Red Book* (Shamdasani 2012).

38. On several occasions, I have explained the role played by Jung's *Red Book* in shaping his clinical practice and thinking (Gaillard 2012). The subject will come up again before the end of this book.

39. Extraordinary, but not absolutely unique, as we will soon see.

40. Jung GW/CW 10.

41. Thus, he discusses particularly a painting of a twelfth-century codex, the *Rupertsberg Code*, by Hildegard of Bingen.

42. In German, Jung makes a strict distinction between Vollkommenheit, which I have translated as perfection, and Vollständigkeit, which I have translated as wholeness. I will later return to the question of the Jungian approach to totality.

43. This demonstrates that the Jungian problematics of the self really cannot be solved in these forms of amazed, painless, gentle Jungianism, springing up here and there like the dream of the flower in Ovid's poem. In fact, it is more than likely that Jung himself would have found them unbearable. We know how he worked on Christianity, and that he kept a representation in stained glass of Christ on the Cross near him, in his office (Wehr 1989, p. 110). In fact, the cross, particularly the Christian one, places us in quite a different position from the bodhisattvas. Although the latter evidently have their own strength, qualities, and virtues, it can be feared that the use to which people put them, from afar, serves to cultivate the dream of an ideal perfection (of Vollkommenheit, Jung would say). As for the mandalas he analyzes, at least those we have encountered in our Western cultures, including the ones he drew at Château-d'Oex, he speaks of them not in terms of beatitude, but in reference to his own condition in his here and now, which was not entirely peaceful.

44. Here, his body is represented in an altogether unexpected foreshortening. However, there is a precedent in Mantegna's painting of *The Dead Christ*, currently in the *Pinacoteca* di Brera, in Milan. It was painted much earlier—in 1480—and, like this painting, is fairly unique in presentation and composition.

45. Thus, Rembrandt's *Philosopher in Meditation*, a 1632 painting hanging in the Louvre, can still be seen as a fairly conventional representation of a monk or scholar immersed in reading—until the viewer perceives, or really sees, that the subject of the work, and in fact the object of the painting, in relation to and in contrast with the *Saint Jerome in his Cell*, is evidently the spiral staircase. It is

the element that makes the composition and the movement of the composition, a downward movement, in fact. It runs quite physically and darkly, to the lower depths (Gaillard 2015 [1985]).

46. The work caused a scandal. First it was rejected by the authorities on beauty of the time, and could only be presented at the Salon des Refusés. Monet took the painter's side in the battle, actively defending him and his canvas. This 1863 *Olympia* is the modern cousin of Titian's *Venus of Urbino* (1538), Velásquez's *Rokeby Venus* (1647/1651), and Goya's *Maja Desnuda* (1790/1800). Certainly, Manet recalled it. But a painted nude had never looked at us with as much intensity combined with detachment, in such a way that, instead of arousing desire or identification, she stops us and makes us think—like the "*Arcadia*" of Herculaneum, but in the case of the latter, the encounter was disguised as the illustration of a myth.

47. Jung, in his essay on Picasso.

48. On this subject, cf. Kandinsky's 1910 manifesto *Concerning the Spiritual in Art,* and Maurice Denis's famous statement, also a sort of manifesto, in 1890: "Remember that a painting, before it is a battle horse, a nude woman, or an anecdote of any type—is essentially a flat surface covered with colors assembled in a certain order."

49. This is especially evident in *Narcissus,* but it is also demonstrated by the fate of Paul's body. In and by the painting, the figure is treated with a foreshortening that is comparable only to the one in *Death of the Virgin,* at the Louvre; a foreshortening preceded only by Mantegna's *Dead Christ,* at the Brera.

50. French historian Fernand Braudel (1902–85) renewed historical writing and our relationship to history, transformation, and crisis. The scale of Braudel's contribution will become clearer as this book continues.

Chapter 6

1. The derogatory term "art pompier" designates nineteen-century paintings and sculptures illustrating themes from classical history. Often, the figures wear shiny helmets, like those of French firemen or "pompiers" (firemen)—hence the adjective applied to this art, which also cultivated Oriental exoticism or the "Pompeiian style."

2. It is interesting to note that Botticelli, who is usually remembered for his

paintings of female beauty, also immersed himself in Dante's *Inferno*. True, he took it on in his later years.

3. Hence the French expression "*la clef des songes*" (the key to dreams), an expression I've never particularly liked. Hence also the ambition or pretension of so many psychoanalysts, from the origins of the field up to our own time, to be omniscient about everything, to have the last word on every subject—often inappropriately, alas.

4. An English translation of Perrault's text appears as follows, before the Bibliography.

5. Jung demonstrated the importance of confronting what emerges in a dream, fantasy, work of art, or simply in life as frontally as possible—he uses the German term Auseinandersetzung—but he also specifies that it is helpful to look or listen to what is not in the center. On the edges, our attention often frays, or is reluctant to venture. This point might open or reopen the classic debate in psychoanalysis on the respective purposes of the couch and the "face-to-face," as we will do later.

6. Like you, I am thinking here of the admonition Ovid addresses to his Narcissus. We strove to see what it might hide from us about the relationship of this Narcissus with the abyss into which he gazes. Another version of the tale of *Bluebeard*, which we will consider in the next chapter, could carry us one or two steps further toward this reality, or these realities.

7. http://www.gutenberg.org/files/29021/29021-h/29021-h.htm#Blue_Beard.

8. In fact, we must wonder if this story is really a fairy tale, and also to whom it is addressed. On this subject, cf. Soriano 1977.

9. True, in the same book, written in French, Perrault designates other characters using the definite article. "*Le Petit Poucet*" *(Tom Thumb)* and "*Le Petit Chaperon Rouge*" (*Little Red Riding Hood*) are examples. In those cases, the character is then obviously a certain type, or a generic character, like Bluebeard, in fact, which refers the reader to a certain type of encounter or adventure. Cf. Bellemin-Noël 1983.

10. Here, we might recall that it is not altogether innocent if Dürer's *Melencholy* is an engraving, in black, whereas Cranach's painting plays on the color red.

11. This is one of the questions to which we will return in the next chapter.

12. Bruno Bettelheim, whose works on fairy tales currently serve as the

authoritative reference on the subject, claims Perrault's version is the only one he found (Bettelheim 1976). Yet Verena Kast reports a few others, particularly from northern and eastern Europe (Kast 1998). And I discovered still more, at a recent lecture by Henri Gougaud, a great storyteller and writer himself, and Bernadette Bricout, who also researches these questions. Bluebeard-like ogres live in tales from the West Indies, Brittany, or the Pyrenees (Gougaud 2002, Bricout 2005).

13. Here, Verena Kast quotes the scholars Bolte and Polvka.

14. It is surprising and noteworthy that Gustave Doré did not illustrate this crucial event in the story.

15. Are we brave enough to associate or amplify our thinking here to Hercules, the warrior or gladiator at Herculaneum, who seemed to be divided between approaching Arcadia and his attention to the child looking at him, who may very well be his son?

16. An attentive reader of Perrault's story will note that the writer has already hinted at a strange connivance between the maiden's mother and "the ogre." This mother has practically made herself the monster's accomplice, by encouraging her daughter to accept his advances.

17. Here, we again find what we spoke of earlier on the practice of "amplification," as Jung called it when he pioneered it. But since then, it has often been neglected in Jungian circles—perhaps out of fear that an uncontrolled comparatism would result. I'd like to note in passing that this risk exists only when one fails to return to the initial question, the enigma that triggered the amplification. Cf. Gaillard 2001, an article published in a Freudian journal after a talk I gave that year in Versailles at the congress of the International Association for the History of Psychoanalysis.

18. Sonu Shamdasani's earliest research into the conditions surrounding the writing and publication of this book made it clear that it must not be read as a work that was wholly and simply by Jung. But the first chapter is allegedly among the most authentic in the book.

19. Jung (1963 [1961]), Chap. I. Note that an ogre also appears in this chapter. Gaillard 2013, p. 12.

20. The detail about the cookies is surprisingly missing from Richard and Clara Winston's English translation of *Memories, Dreams, Reflections* published in 1963.

21. De Mijolla 2004.

22. Gaillard 2011.

23. In German, in Freud's German, the word used at the time is *Lehre*, which can be translated as "doctrine." Oddly enough, many French Lacanians have appropriated the term, even today, and are proud of what it means.

24. I will later return to the question of the relationship of the unconscious to time, and hence to history. It has actually haunted psychoanalysis and our psychoanalyses since Freud and Jung, and it gives direction to the observations I make in this book.

25. It's not that Freud himself did not grapple with the difficulties inherent to this approach. In 1915, that is, just after breaking off relations with Jung, he attempted a difficult hypothesis that he later developed very little of a "*Urverdrängung*," a primal repression, from which the unconscious would initially proceed. This is one of the fundamental questions that led Jung in his first clinical and theoretical works to differentiate himself so radically from Freudian psychoanalysis.

26. I have developed this analysis in various writings, particularly in a 2014 colloquium at the University of Strasbourg, organized by C. Maillard and V. Liard, entitled *Carl Gustav Jung. Pour une réévaluation de l'oeuvre* (Gaillard 2014).

27. Once again, I am speaking of what Jung called the individuation processes.

Charles Perrault (1628–1703)

Blue Beard

There was, some time ago, a gentleman who was very rich. He had fine town and country houses, his dishes and plates were all of gold or silver, his rooms were hung with damask, his chairs and sofas were covered with the richest silks, and his carriages were all gilt with gold in a grand style. But it happened that this gentleman had a blue beard, which made him so very frightful and ugly, that none of the ladies, in the parts where he lived, would venture to go into his company. Now there was a certain lady of rank, who lived very near him, and had two daughters, both of them of very great beauty. Blue Beard asked her to bestow one of them upon him for a wife, and left it to herself to choose which of the two it should be. But both the young ladies again and again said they would never marry Blue Beard; yet, to be as civil as they could, each of them said, the only reason why she would not have him was, because she was loath to hinder her sister from the match, which would be such a good one for her. Still the truth of the matter was, they could neither of them bear the thoughts of having a husband with a blue beard; and besides, they had heard of his having been married to several wives before, and nobody could tell what had ever become of any of them. As Blue Beard wished very much to gain their favour, he asked the lady and her daughters, and some ladies who were on a visit at their house, to go with him to one of his country seats, where they spent a whole week, during which they passed all their time in nothing but parties for hunting and fishing, music, dancing, and feasts. No one even thought of going to bed, and the nights were passed in merry-makings of all kinds. In short, the time rolled on in so much pleasure, that the youngest of the two sisters began to think that the beard which she had been so much afraid of, was not so very blue, and that the gentleman who owned it was vastly civil and pleasing. Soon after their return home, she told her mother that she had no longer any dislike to accept of Blue Beard for her husband; and in a very short time they were married.

About a month after the marriage had taken place, Blue Beard told his wife that he should be forced to leave her for a few weeks, as he had some affairs to attend to in the country. He desired her to be sure to indulge herself in every kind of pleasure, to invite as many of her friends as she liked, and to treat them with all sorts of dainties, that her time might pass pleasantly till he came back again. "Here," said he, "are the keys of the two large wardrobes. This is the key of the great box that contains the best plate, which we use for company, this belongs to my strong box, where I keep my money, and this belongs to the casket, in which are all my jewels. Here also is a master-key to all the rooms in the house; but this small key belongs to the closet at the end of the long gallery on the ground floor. I give you leave," said he, "to open, or to do what you like with all the rest except this closet. This, my dear, you must not enter, nor even put the key into the lock, for all the world. If you do not obey me in this one thing, you must expect the most dreadful punishments." She promised to obey his orders in the most faithful manner; and Blue Beard, after kissing her tenderly, stepped into his coach, and drove away.

When Blue Beard was gone, the friends of his wife did not wait to be asked, so eager were they to see all the riches and fine things she had gained by marriage; for they had none of them gone to the wedding, on account of their dislike to the blue beard of the bridegroom. As soon as ever they came to the house, they ran about from room to room, from closet to closet, and then from wardrobe to wardrobe, looking into each with wonder and delight, and said, that every fresh one they came to, was richer and finer than what they had seen the moment before. At last they came to the drawing-rooms, where their surprise was made still greater by the costly grandeur of the hangings, the sofas, the chairs, carpets, tables, sideboards, and looking-glasses; the frames of these last were silver-gilt, most richly adorned, and in the glasses they saw themselves from head to foot. In short, nothing could exceed the richness of what they saw; and they all did not fail to admire and envy the good fortune of their friend. But all this time the bride herself was far from thinking about the fine speeches they made to her, for she was eager to see what was in the closet her husband had told her not to open. So great, indeed, was her desire to do this, that, without once thinking how rude it would be to leave her guests, she slipped away down a private staircase that led to this forbidden closet, and in such a hurry, that she was two or three times in danger of falling down stairs and breaking her neck.

When she reached the door of the closet, she stopped for a few moments to think of the order her husband had given her, and how he had told her that he would not fail to keep his word and punish her very severely, if she did not obey him. But she was so very curious to know what was inside, that she made up her mind to venture in spite of every thing. She then, with a trembling hand, put the key into the lock, and the door straight flew open. As the window shutters were closed, she at first could see nothing; but in a short time she saw that the floor was covered with clotted blood, on which the bodies of several dead women were lying.

These were all the wives whom Blue Beard had married, and killed one after another. At this sight she was ready to sink with fear, and the key of the closet door, which she held in her hand, fell on the floor. When she had a little got the better of her fright, she took it up, locked the door, and made haste back to her own room, that she might have a little time to get into a humour to amuse her company; but this she could not do, so great was her fright at what she had seen. As she found that the key of the closet had got stained with blood in falling on the floor, she wiped it two or three times over to clean it; yet still the blood kept on it the same as before. She next washed it, but the blood did not move at all. She then scoured it with brick dust, and after with sand, but in spite of all she could do, the blood was still there; for the key was a fairy who was Blue Beard's friend; so that as fast as she got off the blood on one side, it came again on the other. Early in the same evening Blue Beard came home, saying, that before he had gone far on his journey he was met by a horseman, who was coming to tell him that his affair in the country was settled without his being present; upon which his wife said every thing she could think of, to make him believe she was in a transport of joy at his sudden return.

The next morning he asked her for the keys: she gave them to him; but as she could not help showing her fright, Blue Beard easily guessed what had been the matter. "How is it," said he, "that the key of the closet upon the ground floor is not here?" "Is it not?" said the wife, "then I must have left it on my dressing-table." "Be sure you give it me by and by," replied Blue Beard. After going a good many times backwards and forwards, as if she was looking for the key, she was at last forced to give it to Blue Beard. He looked hard at it, and then said: "How came this blood upon the key?" "I am sure I do not know," replied the poor lady, at the same time turning as white as a sheet. "You do not know?" said Blue Beard sternly, "but I know well enough. You have been in the closet on the ground floor! Very well, madam: since you are so mighty fond of this closet, you shall be sure to take your place among the ladies you saw there." His wife, who was almost dead with fear, now fell upon her knees, asked his pardon a thousand times for her fault, and begged him to forgive her, looking all the time so very mournful and lovely, that she would have melted any heart that was not harder than a rock. But Blue Beard only said, "No, no, madam; you shall die this very minute!" "Alas!" said the poor trembling creature, "if I must die, give me, as least, a little time to say my prayers." "I give you," replied the cruel Blue Beard, "half a quarter of an hour: not a moment longer." When Blue Beard had left her to herself, she called her sister; and after telling her, as well as she could for sobbing, that she had but half a quarter of an hour to live; "Prithee," said she, "sister Anne," (this was her sister's name), "run up to the top of the tower, and see if my brothers are not in sight, for they said they would visit me to-day, and if you see them, make a sign for them to gallop on as fast as ever they can." Her sister straight did as she was desired; and the poor trembling lady every minute cried out to her: "Anne! sister Anne! do you see any one coming?" Her sister said, "I see nothing but the sun, which makes a dust, and the grass, which looks green."

In the meanwhile, Blue Beard, with a great cimeter in his hand, bawled as loud as he could to his wife, "Come down at once, or I will fetch you." "One moment longer, I beseech you," replied she, and again called softly to her sister, "Sister Anne, do you see any one coming?" To which she answered, "I see nothing but the sun, which makes a dust, and the grass, which looks green." Blue Beard now again bawled out, "Come down, I say, this very moment, or I shall come to fetch you." "I am coming; indeed I will come in one minute," sobbed his wretched wife. Then she once more cried out, "Anne! sister Anne! do you see any one coming?" "I see," said her sister, "a cloud of dust a little to the left." "Do you think it is my brothers?" said the wife. "Alas! no, dear sister," replied she, "it is only a flock of sheep." "Will you come down, madam?" said Blue Beard, in the greatest rage. "Only one single mo-

ment more," said she. And then she called out for the last time, "Sister Anne! sister Anne! do you see no one coming?" "I see," replied her sister, "two men on horseback coming; but they are still a great way off." "Thank God," cried she, "they are my brothers; beckon them to make haste." Blue Beard now cried out so loud for her to come down, that his voice shook the whole house. The poor lady, with her hair loose, and all in tears, now came down, and fell on her knees, begging him to spare her life; but he stopped her, saying, "All this is of no use, for you shall die," and then, seizing her by the hair, raised his cimeter to strike off her head. The poor woman now begged a single moment to say one prayer. "No, no," said Blue Beard, "I will give you no more time. You have had too much already." And again he raised his arm. Just at this instant a loud knocking was heard at the gates, which made Blue Beard wait for a moment to see who it was. The gates now flew open, and two officers, dressed in their uniform, came in, and, with their swords in their hands, ran straight to Blue Beard, who, seeing they were his wife's brothers, tried to escape from their presence; but they pursued and seized him before he had gone twenty steps, and plunging their swords into his body he fell down dead at their feet.

The poor wife, who was almost as dead as her husband, was not able at first to rise and embrace her brothers; but she soon came to herself; and, as Blue Beard had no heirs, she found herself the owner of his great riches. She gave a part of his vast fortune as a marriage dowry to her sister Anne, who soon after became the wife of a young gentleman who had long loved her. Some of the money she laid out in buying captains' commissions for her two brothers, and the rest she gave to a worthy gentleman whom she married shortly after, and whose kind treatment soon made her forget Blue Beard's cruelty.

Chapter 7

1. I do not know the analysand personally. Her analyst allowed us to report on his work with her. Naturally, I have changed some of the data concerning her, especially biographical details.

2. The letters CB and the figures following them refer to the original case history of this analysis.

3. She noted that as a child and even more in adolescence, she enjoyed behaving like her father, even going so far as to adopt or imitate the way he spoke (CB 3).

4. The scene is reminiscent of the joyous lovemaking Boccaccio describes

in the introduction to the *Decameron*. We are also reminded of Botticelli's four-panel representation of *The Story of Nastagio*, a tale he got from Boccaccio, described in an earlier chapter that invited us to see that what we call our love life is certainly subject to curious twists and turns.

5. We know this from the folktale that was familiar and widespread even before Perrault published this story. Moreover, Perrault specifies that the bevy of maidens from which Bluebeard wanted to choose a wife were frightened by the blue of his beard. Perrault goes on to note, "they were repelled even more by the fact that he had already married several women, and no one knew what had become of the wives."

6. "*Hilf*," the first part of this German word, is related to the English word "help," the call for assistance. The second part, "*losigkeit*," speaks of loss and implies a general loss—at the same time as it gives the word, which might be frightening, the auditory gentleness of a pain that can be accepted.

7. In her childhood, as well as later, especially in adolescence following the death of her boyfriend. In this regard, her analyst also wondered if the young woman was not reproducing or "reenacting" what she had perceived of her parents' arguments and disputes, with the father's rejection of the mother, particularly sexually (CB 3).

8. On the victimhood of women, fate, and the power of their liberation from it, cf. Clara Pinkola-Estés' dynamic interpretation of the Bluebeard story and many others (Pinkola-Estés 1996).

9. Today, some of our Freudian colleagues use the term "subjectivation" to describe this phenomenon. Cf. in particular Roussillon 2010.

10. Were we to express this in more theoretical terms, we might say that in these cases, there is a disconnect between the representation and the affect that is nevertheless associated with it.

11. On these steps, these different moments, which are also different modalities of relating to the unconscious—faire place, faire face, and faire trace (making room, confronting, and, in this case, making a trace—cf. my book about Jung's relationship to the arts, Gaillard 1998.

12. Again, I am summarizing. By nature, we might say, these scenes tend to proliferate. Nevertheless, a two-part detail of these dreams deserves our attention in passing: the destructive woman who is in question is attacking cats and kittens she wants to eliminate, and she resembles an old acquaintance of the dreamer who used to say she was a psychoanalyst… As for the presence of the

brothers in the young woman's dream, perhaps we will dare to wonder if they might reflect the intervention of the brother knights in Perrault's fairy tale. I will take up this question again soon.

13. Cf. Freud 2010, de M'Uzan 2015.

14. Cf. Laplanche et Pontalis 1964. As early as 1911–12, which was at the time of Jung's tensest exchanges and debates with Freud, Jung explored in this direction, trying to capture what makes incest both attractive and repulsive. This thinking drew his attention to dreams of inclusion in the mother, which in reality can be deadly, like inclusion in the primal material from which we all come (Cf. Jung GW/CW 5, Humbert 2004, Guy-Gillet 1984, Gaillard 2013a, chap. IV, and 1998a, the chapter entitled "*L'Origine del mondo*," p. 144 sq.)

15. Here, we come back to Jung's findings in the latter part of his life and work, when he was studying the manuscripts of the alchemists and wondering about their *materia prima.*

16. Jung GW/CW 8.

17. In relation to the blood, many more or less expert commentators on the tale are careful to refer today's reader to menstrual blood, or to the blood shed at defloration. Evidently this is not necessarily untrue. The transition from girlhood to womanhood involves some loss, especially under the conditions in this particular story. But this approach is still relatively superficial. Christian Delourmel goes beyond this type of interpretation, drawing our attention to the pool of blood on the floor, glistening like a mirror (Delourmel 2005).

18. In other versions of this story, oral versions that date to an earlier time than Perrault's text, she asks him to let her change clothes—to remove the robe she is wearing, and put on something else. This might veil another intention on her part: to appeal to Bluebeard's lust rather than his pity, or to gain a little more time. Cf. Soriano 1968, and Soriano's interview with historians Jacques Le Goff, Emmanuel Le Roy Ladurie, and Louis Bruguière in1970, regarding Soriano's book on Perrault's fairy tales.

19. With some regret, I must depart from what Clarissa Pinkola-Estés writes about the key in this tale and in psychoanalysis. Certainly, the young woman's curiosities led her toward fields of reflection and knowledge that helped extricate her from the recurrent tragedies in which she was trapped. This curiosity led her to psychoanalysis, and to a personal commitment to an analysis. But, although these curiosities ultimately led her to confront the depths she was dealing with, they also confine her, literally and inevitably, to her fate. In itself,

curiosity is not a key that would open the door to another becoming. The possibility of salvation really does come from elsewhere, an elsewhere that, in this tale, is represented by her sister Anne and the two brothers.

20. Here, Verena Kast takes the text at its word. When Perrault has sister Anne say, "All I see is the sun beaming and the grass greening," Kast makes us understand that these words, the expression of an expectation and an almost desperate need for help that would finally come to save the poor young woman struggling with Bluebeard, also speak plainly of natural life, the real life that the young woman had lost, a life which had to be restored to her. (Kast 2010, p. 26 sq.).

21. The reader will have recognized the practice called "amplification," which I have mentioned more than once earlier. As to the distinction that should be made between imaginary and symbolic life, let us simply say that one serves the needs of the ego and obeys the pleasure principle, whereas the other imposes itself by its interpellatory power and resistance to the uses and abuses, including interpretative ones, to which one is tempted to put it.

22. I have already pointed out that I think it is more accurate to speak of an "analytic relationship" instead of confining oneself to the more classical terms "transference" and "countertransference." True, the latter do have the virtue of referring each of the protagonists in an analysis to what inhabits, animates, or sometimes unpredictably agitates them. However, the drawback with these terms is that they prevent us from emphasizing the fact that a relationship is really growing and flowing between the two of them. This relationship has its dissymmetry, misunderstandings, and improper investments on both sides. But it also has its own evolution and possible transformation, its own history, which might lend itself to analysis.

23. This happened in the study group where the analysis I am currently discussing was presented.

24. Our study group discussed Jean Cocteau's film about Beauty and the Beast at length, comparing it to the tale of Bluebeard and noting the contrasts. We also attended a performance of Bela Bartók's opera *Bluebeard's Castle.* After some lively debate, we realized it reinforced us in our approach to the story.

25. Actually, is this story just a fairy tale? Is the story of Bluebeard really fictitious? There is no sign of magic anywhere, not in the beginning, or at the end, or in the course of the events told by Perrault and illustrated by Doré. There is no fairy, spell, or object with miraculous powers. But what about the key? Isn't

it magical? No. Instead of being a curse, it is, on the contrary, a fact and effect that remains indelible—which is realistic in sum. As for the moral or morals of the story, a subterfuge to which Perrault resorts as an artist, they should not be taken at face value for the simple reason that appending a moral to the story was evidently an unobtrusive strategy for getting people to listen to it. The tale was disguised as a fable for children.

26. Regarding eyes that open, and the possibility to see or not, French Freudian psychoanalyst Christian Delourmel, whom I have already mentioned, reconsiders the scene where the young woman discovers the row of corpses hanging in the forbidden closet, as Perrault wrote it. Delourmel analyzes the pool of blood on the floor in light of the myth of Perseus overcoming the Gorgon by doing battle with her reflection in a polished shield, thereby avoiding a direct and deadly clash with the monster (Delourmel, 2005). This is an interesting approach to the story that provides much food for thought. However, it is challenged by the narrative unfolding and ultimately the structure of the story. Delourmel's analysis would be accurate and useful if the young woman could and did attack Bluebeard, which does not fit into the flow or meaning of the story, either in Perrault or in Doré. The only way for her to escape Bluebeard, however, is to obtain the help of her sister, and through her sister, her brothers, as we will see more clearly in the following notes. On the subject of the Gorgon, I have suggested my own analysis that is congruent with the one I develop here regarding "Bluebeard." (Gaillard 1998a, Part II).

27. On this subject, following in the footsteps of the Chomskian and post-Chomskian approach to linguistics, we might cite the "competence" of the unconscious to learn a language. This would clearly situate the clinical and theoretical work of psychoanalysis within the field and dynamic of structuralist approaches.

28. The reader familiar with Jung's writings will have recognized the thrust of his founding essay written in 1916, *Die transcendente Function.*

29. A parallel can be drawn between her consideration of the women from earlier generations of her family and Bluebeard's earlier wives and victims, in Perrault's tale.

30. Note that the analysis we have just followed proceeded in four directions. These four directions intersect and interweave, but can still be differentiated. For the young woman, the analysis engaged with reuniting her, as circumstantially and emotionally as possible, with the facts, gestures, and circumstances—

in this case, rather terrifying ones—that marked her infancy and childhood and, as a result, the later years of her adolescence. This analysis drew her attention and ours to the dreams, the inner life, the transformations of imaginary and symbolic life that dwell within her and animate her. The analysis also made her attentive to what was becoming of her life, while from session to session and year to year, the analysis continued to progress. And it led her to wonder what had been acted out and what was being acted out in her relationship with her analyst, ordinarily called the transference and countertransference, although as we noted in passing, it would be more appropriate to call it the transference relationship, or analytic relationship. I have published several articles suggesting that these four "dimensions" of an analysis deserve greater attention from us (Gaillard 2003). In the last chapter of this book, we will return to the subject, as we consider with and after Jung the need to consider a fifth "dimension" of analysis.

31. We could say that psychoanalysis "explicates," provided that we understand the verb in the Latin sense of "*ex-plicare*." In this case, it literally means to unfold, to spread out, or to smooth out that which is so compactly folded, densely distilled, and wrapped up in itself that the meaning is hidden, kept out of sight. Naturally, this type of "explication" would not involve any pedantry, nor would it have anything to do with dogmatic teachings that claim to know the truth. As I said, the work involves differentiation; that is, strictly speaking, "analysis." Techniques like "association" and "amplification" are the tools we use.

32. It is important to differentiate between the *nekyia,* which is a descent into Hell you are not sure you are ever going to emerge from, and the *catabasis,* which is the emergence from these realms or states which, as we clearly see in the tale of Bluebeard and many more, are far from human. I have discussed this question at length in my analysis of Picasso's work in light of Jung's 1932 essay on this artist (Gaillard 2013).

Chapter 8

1. On the distinction it is useful to make between modern and contemporary art, cf. Heinrich 2014.

2. Hans Namuth, born in Germany in 1915, traveled to Paris in 1933, and from there went to Spain to shoot his first photo essays, during the Spanish Civil War, on the Republicans' side. Returning to France, he joined the French

Foreign Legion to escape confinement as a German national. In 1940, he fled to the United States. Drafted in 1943, he served as an intelligence officer in Europe. After the war, he settled in New York. His photographs of Pollock helped him gain access to a series of other artists on whom he published books: de Kooning, Brancusi, Albers, Matisse, and Calder, among others.

3. Namuth 1978a and 1978b. Namuth's book *Pollock Painting* was published only in 1978. The French edition, *L'Atelier de Jackson Pollock* (published by Macula the same year), supplemented with a different version of Namuth's memories, many more of Namuth's 1950s photographs of Pollock in his studio, and enlightening essays by E. A. Carmean, J. Clay, R. Krauss, F. V. O'Connor, and Barbara Rose, as well as two interviews with Lee Krasner Pollock, is irreplaceable on Pollock as an action painter and, generally, on the creative processes and their flows.

4. Namuth means Pollock's wife Lee Krasner, whom we will speak of later. Namuth 1978a, page not numbered.

5. Namuth 1978b, page not numbered.

6. Ovid, *The Metamorphoses.* Book III, v. 380.

7. Betty Parsons (1900–82), a painter, had opened her own art gallery on West 57th Street in Manhattan in 1946, representing contemporary American artists. Peggy Guggenheim (1898–1979), a woman of the same generation, had been initiated to contemporary art by Duchamp, Cocteau, and Mondrian, who acted as her consultants. She had opened her gallery *Art of this Century*, also on West 57th Street, in 1942. Helen Marot, a friend of the Thomas Hart Benton, befriended Pollock upon his arrival in New York City in 1934. She later introduced him to Dr. Joseph Henderson.

8. Ovid wrote this description of Narcissus: "*Poteratque puer iuvenisque videri. Multi illum juvenes multae cupiere puellae.*" / "He looked as much like a child as like a young man, awakening desire in many a youth and young woman." *The Metamorphoses*, Book III, verses 352–3. It is just as Caravaggio painted him.

9. If we indulge a little in the literary reminiscences associated with such scenes, we might think of Baudelaire's famous poem *The Albatross*: he depicts the bird's collapse on the ship's deck, after having been so utterly free in the skies. His flight is interrupted, and he is weighed down by his own wings, defenseless and unable to take off again.

10. Betty Parsons gave him eight one-man shows at her 57th Street gallery

and continued to pay him a monthly stipend, but this did not solve his financial problems. He also showed his work at the Venice Biennale, at the Museo Correr in Venice, and at the Stedelijk Museum in Amsterdam, among other prestigious institutions. Art critics acclaimed him, especially Clement Greenberg, who long championed his work. Articles about him appeared in the popular picture weeklies *Time*, *Life*, and even *Vogue*.

11. Cf. Geldzahler 1965. I owe much of my introduction to American painting to Marcelin Pleynet, who was on the faculty with me at the National Academy of Fine Arts in Paris, where he taught esthetics. A great connoisseur of this painting, in 1982 he developed a detailed analysis of Pollock's artistic, family, and educational background, entitled "Jack'son Pollock." I published the essay in the *Cahiers de psychologie de l'art et de la culture*, a journal I founded and directed at the Academy (Pleynet 1982b).

12. Cf. Pleynet 1982b, p. 46.

13. In the last part of this book, we will see how the theme of a powerful, radiant, and invasive fire also for a time pervaded the work of the German artist Anselm Kiefer.

14. Now a common term in art history, tondo is actually an abbreviation of the Italian word rotondo, meaning "round." The *tondos* by Fra Angelico or Botticelli come to mind—but also those by Hieronymus Bosch. And is it possible to avoid thinking again of the circular composition of Caravaggio's *Narcissus*?

15. Marcelin Pleynet describes curls and twists around "an empty center." He sees these wavy swirls as spinning downward "into the funnel of a maelström" (Pleynet 1982b, p. 47), "in the vortex of a whirlpool." He goes so far as to mention "a psychological abyss."

16. We will later see the turn taken by this composition and the movement in the canvas in Pollock's later work.

17. For an analysis of Uccello's *Battles* by a contemporary painter, cf. Bloedé 1980.

18. When we are trying to determine the issues Pollock was dealing with from one decade to the next in his brief career, particularly his debates with figurative representation and the dripped or poured paintings he made between 1947 and 1950, the term "abstract" tends to obscure more than it reveals.

19. I developed elsewhere an analysis of the difficult years Picasso lived in the thirties (Gaillard 2013).

20. Jackson Pollock and his brother Sanford were suspected of conspiring or collaborating with the Communist Party (cf. Pleynet 1982b).

21. You may recall that I have described our deepest depths from which we come as inhuman.

22. Cf. Pleynet 1982a, p. 44–45, who claims Pollock's battles against his "fathers" are one of the decisive sources of his creative drive.

23. Critics sometimes described these as "psychoanalytic drawings." Cf. Wysuph 1970.

24. Pollock had spent several evenings writing automatic poetry with the painters Baziotès, Matta, and Motherwell. In 1943 and 1944, he showed his work alongside that of Salvador Dali, Max Ernst, Masson, Miró, Motherwell, Picasso, Rothko, and Tanguy. On more than one occasion, the Jungian and Freudian approaches to psychoanalysis have been combined with modern and contemporary art in the United States, in this case as they relate to surrealism.

25. Already a concept in 1890, when Denis published in *Art et Critique.*

26. Recall what Jung wrote in 1932, when on seeing Picasso's work, he attempted to describe what was at work in modern art, in comparison and contrast to earlier representations of the world. Cf. Jung GW/CW 15, Gaillard 2013.

27. This *Tondo* certainly appears to be a second effort to deepen the concept approached in the canvas *Circle*, discussed earlier in the sections entitled *Before 1950, Figuration awhirl*, and thc notes 14 and 15.

28. If a ritual can be said to be a regulated approach to the extraordinary.

29. Again, think of Ovid's description of Narcissus: "Hic puer, and studio uenandi lassus and aestu, procubuit faciemque loci fontemque secutus." ("There, the youth, wearied by the heat of the hunt and the day, came and lay on the ground, charmed by the beauty of the surroundings and the refreshing spring.") *The Metamorphoses*, Book III, verses 413–4b.

30. Note in passing that when Pollock painted the bare, black branches of *Number 32,* the trees in East Hampton were lush with green foliage.

31. A theme throughout this book, the question was at the heart of chapter 1.

32. If you will recall, we experimented with turning Caravaggio's *Narcissus* upside-down, only to conclude that looking at the painting right-side up makes all the difference in the world.

33. Pollock sometimes raised his canvas when he was in the middle of painting it, to maintain his distance from the work—a distance that had escaped Narcissus.

34. This observation and the question it raises oppose the "shamanistic" hypotheses of Lewis-Williams and Jean Clottes, mentioned in chapter 1 of this book. Here, the question arising is that of the grip man gives himself on powers that surpass him, rather than that of participation, headlong, in this case in the animated world of nature.

35. A gesture Caravaggio's Narcissus may have attempted when his left hand crossed the middle line between himself and the Beyond—or the Beneath—and dooming him to fall over the edge and drown. Regarding the left hand, cf. Gaillard 2001.

36. William Rubin speaks about the victory of Pollock over Picasso (Rubin 1974).

37. Cf. Pleynet in the interview published in the catalogue of the 1982 show at Centre Georges Pompidou.

38. On this approach to art and artists, which analyzes works in relation to events from the past of the individual artist, cf. Gaillard 1984.

39. Pollock's practice of numbering and dating his works could be interpreted as a sign of some inner individual resistance to the absolute and almost timeless commitment of action painting by opposing order and time to it, in his pieces. Even *One* is numbered in this way: *Number 31, 1950.* On time and timelessness, a question that leads to the heart of our experiences of the unconscious, cf. the excellent book by Angeliki Yassemidès (2014) and the article I devoted to it, entitled "*Le temps, l'intemporel et l'histoire*" (Gaillard 2015).

40. The "Chapel" commissioned by John and Dominique de Menil in 1964 opened in 1971, one year after Rothko's death. Early in his career as a painter, Rothko did "figurative expressionism."

41. We have seen how the painter Poussin protested against the risks Caravaggio took in and for art, saying that the latter was "born to destroy painting."

42. These two photographs were published on the back cover of the French edition of Namuth's book, entitled *L'Atelier de Jackson Pollock.* They illustrated my 1984 essay on the painter, p. 109.

43. Ges. Werke, vol. 10, Imago, London, 1946. This text is from 1914.

44. Ges. Werke, vol. V, Imago, London, 1942, p. 44, note 1. This text is from 1910.

45. Here, it is relevant to recall that Freud's essay on Leonardo da Vinci had left Jung pensive. It prompted a series of thoughts that engaged Jung in thinking differently from Freud about the relationship to the unconscious and the cre-

ative processes (cf. Gaillard 1994). The writings by Jung I have just quoted arose from the debate between Freud and Jung about Jung's findings in psychoanalysis.

46. It would be helpful to gain some insight into the role of the double in this question of "sufficiently similar, sufficiently different." Based on an approach that considers complementarity and compensation, this question opens that of the *shadow.* I made an attempt in my essay on Dostoyevsky's novella *The Double* (Gaillard 1980).

47. Namuth 1978b, page not numbered.

48. Earlier, I discussed an experiment with turning Caravaggio's *Narcissus* upside-down, proving that the work definitely has a top and bottom.

49. Cf. *Jackson Pollock: Drawing into Painting*, catalogue of the exhibition in November to December 1979 at the Centre Georges Pompidou, Musée d'art moderne de la Ville de Paris, particularly the article by Bernice Rose (Rose 1979).

50. Here, I am speaking of the "nigredo" experienced by the alchemists and then by Jung, who showed its place and role in the various processes, particularly the creation process, which befall us (Gaillard 2015).

51. Carmean 1978.

52. Clay 1978, Krauss 1978.

53. Cf. Carmean 1982a, in his debate with Rosalind Krauss on this subject.

54. Ovid, *The Metamorphoses*, Book III, verses 386 and 455.

55. Verses 430–1.

56. Verses 478–9.

57. In 1954, Jung developed the ambiguity of these figures of the "anima" at length, when they are not differentiated from those of the mother—which should be written with a capital M: Mother (Jung GW/CW, 9/1). Very early in his writing, in the first printing of his *Wandlungen und Symbole der Libido*, in 1911–12, he focused his attention on these modalities of incest, which have very little to do with sexual desire for the "domestic" mother. They would actually be a return, attempted return, or the temptation to return, to being buried in the primal wholeness from which we are all obliged to separate ourselves.

58. Like the "*pali*" of Venice, also often painted blue. They enable vessels to navigate the city's canals and lagoons, indicating depth and direction, and also serve to tie up boats when it is time for the passengers to alight.

59. Here, I am reminded of an even more recent piece by Anselm Kiefer.

It features skis, not "poles." These skis are almost real, and one can imagine putting them on, standing up, and gliding over rough terrain that would be extremely dangerous to tread without them. They appear in Kiefer's 1986 object–canvas *Jerusalem.* We will be meeting Kiefer again in the conclusion to this book.

60. Cf. Wysuph 1970a and 1970b, and also Wolfe 1972. In 1979, in a two-part article in *Art in America,* William Rubin discussed them, criticizing them sharply, as did E. A. Carmean, who nevertheless integrated certain Jungian concepts into his analyses (cf. the article printed in the catalogue for the 1982 Pollock show at the Centre Pompidou).

61. Cf. O'Connor 1978.

62. Quoted in Friedman 1972 and also in Carmean's essay in the Pompidou catalogue (p. 58, note 14).

63. Dr. Joseph Henderson, in Wysuph 1970a, p. 55.

64. This analysis is mainly that of Francis O'Connor. Howard Devree also has pointed out these inner conflicts and debates tormenting the painter struggling to escape from dead ends.

65. Wysuph had already raised the question of more or less concealed representation of such iconographic themes. However, Francis O'Connor, in his essay "Hans Namuth's Photographs of Jackson Pollock as an Art Historical Document," published in *Pollock Painting: Photographs by Hans Namuth* (Namuth 1978), who explicitly speaks of Pollock's "iconography." In *Black Pourings,* O'Connor commits to tracking them down. E. A. Carmean resumed the investigation in his discussion of the stained-glass plans for Tony Smith's church project.

66. We cannot rule out the fact that he may have known about it. The *Crucifixion* had been published by Alfred Barr, but only in 1946 in the catalogue for the exhibition *Picasso: Fifty Years of His Art.*

67. Because of its ambivalent character, partly infernal and partly heavenly, I have also qualified it as "inhuman," in this book. True, this is a lesson that one learns from Jung's work only gradually, from one decade to the next of his journey. For a presentation of this elaboration of Jung's thought in both theory and practice, cf. my *Jung* (Gaillard 2013 [1995]), and, first, that by E. G. Humbert, to which I was honored to write the introduction for the latest paperback edition (Humbert 2004 [1982]).

68. Carmean, in Namuth 1978b.

69. Rosalind Krauss, in her paper entitled in French "*Emblèmes et lexies: le*

texte photographique," analyzing how Namuth proceeded to photograph Pollock by moving the camera in unison with the artist's movement as he danced around dripping paint on the canvas, applies the term "analogon." In Namuth 1978b.

Conclusion

1. For the German text, cf. Jung 1962, p. 179 ff ; for the English, cf. Jung 1967, p. 177; for the French translation, cf. Jung 1966, p. 206. These pages should be read and reread closely, so impressively rich are they in clinical and theoretical lessons.

2. "My enduring these storms was a question of brute strength." (Jung actually wrote these words.). "*Dass ich es aushielt, war eine Frage der brutalen Kraf.*" And the French translator wrote: "'*Tenir le coup' dans cette épreuve fut une question de force brutale,*" which is fairly accurate. "*Aushalten*" does mean to endure or weather an ordeal, or to bear a trying difficulty. As for the determination required, in 1916, in a fundamental essay he entitled "*Die transcendente Funktion,*" Jung emphatically applied the German terms "Bestimmheit " and "Gerichtetheit" to express what characterizes the consciousness.

3. Cf. the article entitled "The Effectiveness of Symbols" Lévi-Strauss published in 1958 in the first volume of his *Structural Anthropology.*

4. Earlier, we discussed how Jung uses the dynamic German word "*Wirklichkeit*" to speak of psychic reality, or the reality of the soul. The verb "wirken," which means to act, to be effective, at the root of the word, concretely speaks of action and effectiveness.

5. Cf. Jung, 1933, von Franz, 1991.

6. Nicholas of Fluë was made the patron saint of Switzerland.

7. French psychoanalyst Murielle Gagnebin, who has focused to a great extent on psychoanalytical approaches to the arts, devotes particular attention to the relationships between figuration and that which escapes it. Cf. Gagnebin 1984, especially.

8. On this subject, refer to the photographic portraits published by Jaffé, 1977, and Wehr, 1979.

9. To all appearances, for it is also known that, no longer at all sure of what he could teach, he resigned from his position at the university—which is quite unusual for an academic. When I visited the Jung house at Küsnacht, I was

privileged to discover and read carefully, with Jung's son Franz, a collection of family documents that included the letter of resignation Jung sent to the university. As for his emotional life, we are aware of the close relationships he had formed with Sabina Spielrein, and then with Antonia Wolff (Bair 2004, chap 17, Gaillard 2006, 2009, 2012).

10. Only Antonia Wolff occasionally joined him, but she never took any part in the building itself. Jung writes about how the play reminded him of times in his childhood: cf. Jung 1962a, chap. VI, Gaillard 2013b, chap. IV.

11. We owe it to Sonu Shamdasani to have organized several exhibitions of certain of Jung's sculptures, especially in 2010, when the *Red Book* was presented for the first time at the Rietberg Museum in Zurich.

12. His 1916 essay on the "transcendent function" could be read as a development of the theme that was simultaneously theoretical and very concrete.

13. I like the definition of "ritual" that says it is an organized approach to the extraordinary. It compels us to consider rituals and rites as steps forward, as opposed to Freud's evaluation of them as defense mechanisms. The concept renews the approach to religions considerably.

14. Freud's strength was to have encouraged his patients to express themselves in analysis through "free association" as a way of circumventing the inhibitions of the conscious mind. Freud also showed that regression involves three dimensions at once: the temporal one, leading back through reminiscence and reliving to the past and bygone times of childhood; the formal dimension, in that it allows more sensual or pictorial means of expression; and lastly, its topical aspect, in that it activates a form of psychic functioning in which the tone is set by perception. All of these characteristics are common to the Jungian practice of "amplification," which, in its own way, as we saw earlier, also enables a person to experience emotions usually repressed or held at bay, being too difficult to approach.

15. Note moreover that the written pages are also punctuated by miniature figures and scenes, especially on the first pages of chapters. These illustrations open the reading to a dreamier, more lively and colorful process.

16. Another instance where Jung prefers the term "*Wirklichkeit*" to "*Realität*" when he wishes to emphasize the lively, active nature of psychic reality.

17. Note that each of these verbs (impress, compel, mobilize, animate, engage, escape, haunt, strike, obsess, agitate) tells us something about what we agreed to call "the unconscious." For a more detailed approach to the distinction to make between "figures," "configurations," "scènes," and "scénarios," cf.

Gaillard 2012b. I have developed this distinction in a book written with a group of prehistorians and anthropologists, to be published shortly, and dedicated to certain enigmas of prehistory.

18. In their 1967 *Vocabulaire*, under the entry "primal fantasies," Laplanche and Pontalis presented and analyzed the question.

19. Please refer here to page 122 of *Liber Novus*.

20. Elsewhere, I published a comparative analysis of this essay of Freud's on the *Moses* of Michelangelo and of Jung's on the novel *Ulysses* by James Joyce (Gaillard 1978, 1979).

21. Pomerania is the part of the former East Germany where Kiefer grew up.

22. Here, one might quote from Bachelard's *Poétique de la rêverie*, "*L'être est rond*." (The being is round.) But Bachelard himself admits the phrase is his own daring translation of Karl Jaspers: "*Jedes Dasein scheint in sich rund*."

23. The various themes found in Kiefer's work are transformed at different periods in his life as an artist, but some of them cross paths in the same period. In fact, Kiefer often reworks pieces up to a decade after their first creation.

24. Recall that the concept of the "self," so central and axial to his psychology and clinical practice, did not appear in his writings until 1919.

25. Cf. "the Liverpool dream" in *Memories, Dreams, Reflections*.

26. This question of the "self" is one of those that quickly emerged in a majority of the various schools that make up today's psychoanalytic movement, but not without some serious misunderstandings on all sides.

27. This is an experience that occurs constantly in clinical work, and it can also be observed in the arts. I wrote an essay on Federico Fellini's *Libro dei miei sogni (The Book of My Dreams)*, and to the relationship between his creations as a filmmaker and the dreams he noted, particularly during his analysis with Dr. Ernst Bernhard, founder of the Jungian movement in Italy (Gaillard & Ravasi Bellocchio 2009).

28. Regarding the vocabulary of totality, I have pointed out the distinction Jung makes between "*Vollkommenheit*" and "*Vollständigkeit*" elsewhere (Gaillard 2013b, chap. V).

29. The reader will recognize here another aspect of what we said earlier about the "emergentist" nature of the Jungian approach to psychoanalysis. This emergence is one that can be grasped at different scales: personal or transgenerational, or on the scale of cultural transformations—a subject I will return to again in this chapter.

30. This decentration is no lesser than the one in earlier times that led us to conclude, not without difficulty, that the Earth is definitely not the center of the universe, but revolves around the Sun. This is a blow to the ego, which tries to cling to its old position. Cf. Humbert 2004 on the "*Ichhaftigkeit*" Jung mentions, and on the defeat of the ego, *Mysterium Conjunctionis II,* § 232, 351, as well as Rosen 2002, who speaks of "egocide."

31. It is worth repeating that Kiefer often does variations on his themes, interpreting them in several successive pieces. The materials and figuration may be quite different, but the theme will reappear. Also, Kiefer is prone to rework these pieces several years after he has created them. This is the case with the different states of *Midsummernacht*: one version dating from 1977 was reworked in 1985; another piece on the same theme was done in 1979 and reworked in 1981; there is also another 1981 *Midsummernacht,* and still others from 1986 and 1987. This is because the work is carried by deep waves, or thrusts. They come in series, but they are often interrelated, generating or reenergizing each other.

32. In the catalogue of the 2015 Kiefer exhibition at Centre Georges Pompidou, museographer Doïna Lemmy, commenting on the work, speaks of poetry and apparition, salutary power, a guardian angel watching over an abandoned grave, and of the light of hope. Oddly enough, she also quotes Daniel Arasse, author of a monograph on Kiefer. Exploring the theme of the Palette, Arasse discusses the "reappropriation of images" from the Catholic tradition in which Kiefer was raised (Bouhours, 2015, p. 128, Arasse, 2001, p. 99).

33. Unless these objects are actually caricatures of tanks, or miniatures military leaders use to plan a battle.

34. At this point, we are reminded of the flightless wings of the earthbound angel in Dürer's engraving entitled *Melancolia.* All the more, knowing that Kiefer refers specifically to the print in several of his works. In fact, the polyhedron Dürer put beside his fallen angel reappears in Kiefer's prints dating from 1982–2013, published in BNF catalogue form and others. Kiefer called them *The Rhine* (Minssieux-Chamonard 2015, p. 64–5). Even more explicitly, it figures in a 1988 work entitled *Melancholia* (Arasse 2001, p. 229).

35. These pages have been made of lead since the mid-1980s. Lead has an affinity with Saturn and melancholy, as well as with the "*materia prima*" of the alchemists (Klibansky, Panofsky, Saxl 1989).

36. Fortunately, the exhibition of these books in Paris was accompanied by a video in an adjacent room where the viewer could see some of the pages of the

books—but the individual viewer could not select which pages to view, since they had been filmed long beforehand, or pause the video to view one of the pages at length.

37. Cf. his interview in Minssieux-Chamonard 2015.

38. In *Die Wege des Weltweissheit*, recall the great minds of German thought are presented in a very different light, as errant souls, as empty and hollow as ghosts. It is impossible to see how they could ever come to life and speak again.

39. On this subject, it is interesting to reread the artist's 2010–11 lectures at the Collège de France, Kiefer 2011, p. 86. He has long been fascinated by the perspective of old, half-buried railroad tracks. They lead him in two directions: toward the Brünhilde of Germanic legend and Wagner, and to the Nazi German concentration camps, which the artist brings to our attention.

40. It is actually a photograph of the French actress Catherine Deneuve, taken by Kiefer at a 1969 screening of François Truffaut's film *Mississippi Mermaid* and then reworked, a technique he often uses. Lest we forget, Brünhilde was put to sleep by Wotan as punishment for treachery, until Siegfried rescued her.

41. Likewise, in pieces from the *Shevirat ha-Kelim* series, we see figurations that range far and wide from the theme of broken vessels—in the form of fixed, uninhabited children's dresses; or locks of hair perhaps. We can read the names of the sephirot. The paintings entitled *Sulamith* also go through a number of different expressions. Kiefer's 1990 book entitled *Sulamith* is actually devoted to Céline's novel *Voyage au bout de la nuit*. It contains pages made of lead that are also punctuated by locks of hair.

42. For Celan's *Todesfuge*, cf. the bilingual French-German edition, published by Gallimard, Paris, 1998, p. 53, and Lauterwein, 2006.

43. In 1983, Kiefer made a first piece called *Sulamith*, a very large canvas covered with dark-colored paints mixed with various charred materials. It looks like an underground vault, swallowing up the viewer. On the use of ashes in Kiefer's work, cf. in particular his comments for the catalogue of the Milan exhibition, Macciari 2007, p. 432.

44. These pages and books are one of the greatest discoveries to which the exhibition of Kiefer's latest works at the French National Library in 2015–16 gave us access.

45. Bonnefoy 2010, p. 29, 46. The writings collected in this little book were intended to accompany a show of works by artists who are also his friends.

46. It is important to linger here and observe the vases closely. They figure

prominently in his *Red Book.* One is being used to pour water onto big flowers and dragons, on page 123, and another is being held over a person's head, with an urban/rural landscape below, p. 125. The same observation and reflection could be applied to the explosive transition from the egg to the volcano, on page 64 (cf. Gaillard 2012b).

47. Bair 2003, p. 775, Shamdasani 1999, p. 43, Van den Berk 2012, p. 74, Gaillard 2013b, p. 72.

48. With the exception of Melanie Klein, Winnicott, or Bion, but only to a certain degree and in another form.

49. On this concept, which I see as crucial, cf. Green 2002, Waren 2007, Gaillard 2014.

50. Artists, especially contemporary ones, are not especially afraid of the nekyia. Neither is an analyst. It would seem as though artists and analysts both trust in a catabasis. In the chapter above on the tale of Bluebeard, I defined the distinction between nekyia and catabasis, as applied to an analysis today.

51. Both Kiefer and Jung, from their very first steps, almost, are men of the book and written word. One of the pieces Kiefer showed at the French National Library in 2015–16, was his very first book, which he wrote at the age of nine. It is a story with illustrations. Jung, in his *Memories, Dreams, Reflections,* mentions his secret writings as a child, hidden in a box in the attic of his family's home. The artist–books Kiefer shows us today derive from his first experiences with books. If I were to choose one decisive book from all of Jung's writings, it would be the *Answer to Job,* because of the way it encompasses his sense of history and heritage, along with his views on and commitment to the future.

Bibliography

Anzieu, Didier. *Le Corps de l'Oeuvre.* Paris: Gallimard, 1981.

Arasse, Daniel. *Anselm Kiefer.* Paris: Editions du Regard, 2001.

Attali, Jacques. *1492.* Paris: Fayard, 1991.

Bair, Deirdre. *Jung. A Biography.* London: Little, Brown and Company, 2004.

Barbet, Alix. *La Peinture Murale Romaine.* Paris: Picard, 1985.

Beaussant, Philippe. *Vous Avez Dit Baroque?* Arles: Actes Sud, 1988.

Beebe, John. *Integrity in Depth.* College Station, TX: Texas A&M University Press, 1992.

Bellemin-Noël, Jean. *Les Contes et Leurs Fantasmes.* Paris: Presses Universitaires de France, 1983.

Belmont, Nicole. *Poétique du Conte.* Paris: Gallimard, 2001.

Berne-Joffroy, André. *Le Dossier Caravage.* Paris: Éditions de Minuit, 1959.

Bettelheim, Bruno. *The Uses of Enchantement.* New York: Alfred A. Knopf, 1976.

Bishop, Paul. *Jung in Contexts.* London/New York: Routledge, 1999a.

——. "Epistemological Problems and Aesthetic Solutions in Goethe and Jung." In *The Goethe Yearbook.* Vol. 4. New York: Boydell & Brewer, 1999b.

Bloedé, James. "Essai sur la Representation du Mouvement dans les Batailles d'Uccello," *Cahiers de psychologie de l'art et de la culture,* n° 6, Paris: Ecole Nationale Supérieure des Beaux-arts, 1980.

Boccacio, Giovanni. *Il Decamerone,* Paris: Firmin Didot Frères, 1849.

Bonardel, Françoise. *Triptyque pour Albrecht Dürer. La Conversation Sacrée.* Paris: Editions de la Transparence, 2012.

Bonnefoy, Yves. *Pensées d'étoffe ou d'argile / Thoughts on Fabric or Clay,* Paris: L'Herne, 2010.

Botella César, and Sara Botella. *La Figurabilité Psychique*. Paris: InPress, 2001.

Bouhours, Jean-Michel. *Anselm Kiefer*. Paris: Centre Pompidou, 2015.

Braudel, Fernand. *On History*. Chicago: The University of Chicago Press, 1980.

Bricout, Bernadetta. *La Clé des Contes*. Paris: Seuil, 2005.

Brikmann Bodo, and Stephan Kemperdick. Deitscje Gemälde in Städel. Mainz: Phillip von Zabern, 2002.

Cacciari, Massimo. *Anselm Kiefer*. Milano: Charta, 2007.

Cambray, Joseph, and Linda Carter. *Analytical Psychology. Contemporary Perspectives in Jungian Analysis*. East Sussex/New York: Brunner Routledge, 2004.

Carmean, Elizabeth A. "The Church Project: Pollock's Passion Themes," *Art in America*, n° 6, Summer 1982, 1982a.

——. "Les Peintures Noires de Jackson Pollock and le Projet d'Eglise de Tony Smith," in *Jackson Pollock*, catalogue de l'expositon Pollock at the Centre Georges Pompidou. Musée national d'Art Moderne, 1982b.

Carotenuto, Aldo. *Diario di una Segreta Simmetria*. Rome: Astrolabio, 1980.

Casement, Ann, ed. *Post-Jungians today. Key Papers in Contemporary Analytical Psychology*. London/New York: Routledge, 1998.

Castiglione Morelli, Vincenzina. (1996). *Pompei. Abitare sotto il Vesuvio*, cat. exhibition Ferrara, 1996.

Celan, Paul. *Die Gedichte*. Frankfurt am Main: Suhrkamp, 2003.

Clay, Jean. 1978. "Pollock, Mondrian, Seurat: la Profondeur Plate," and "Quelques Remarques sur les Propos de Rosalind Kraus Soulignant les Rapports de la photo et de la Peinture et sur la Photo en Général," in Namuth, 1978b.

Clottes, Jean, and Jean Courtin. *La grotte Cosquer. Peintures et Gravures de la Caverne Engloutie*. Paris: Seuil, 1994.

Clottes, Jean, and David Lewis-Williams. *Les Chamanes de la Préhistoire. Texte Intégral, Polémique et R*éponse. Paris: La Maison des Roches, 2001.

Colman, Warren. "Symbolic conceptions: the idea of the third." *The*

Journal of Analytical Psychology, n° 52 (2007).
Covington, Coline, and Barbara Wharton. *Sabina Spielrein. Forgotten Pioneer of Psychoanalysis.* Hove and New York: Brunner-Routledge, 2003.
Damisch, Hubert. *D'un Narcisse l'Autre. Nouvelle Revue de Psychanalyse*, n° 13 (1976).
De Caro, Stefano. *Il Museo Archeologico di Napoli*, 1994.
——. Pompei. *Un art de Vivre.* Paris: Gallimard, 2011.
De M'Uzan, Michel. *De l'art à la Mort.* Paris: Payot, 1972.
De Mijolla, Alain. *Dictionnaire International de la Psychanalyse.* Paris: Calmann-Lévy, 2002.
De Mijolla, Sophie. *Le Besoin de Croire. Métapsychologie du Fait Religieux.* Paris: Dunod, 2004.
De Mijolla-Melor, Sophie. *Le Choix de la Sublimation.* Paris: Presses Universitaires de France, 2009.
Delourmel, Christian. "Tiers Analytique et Pouvoir Autoréflexif du Psychisme: de Quelques Aléas," *Revue Française de Psychanalyse*, Tome LXIX, n° 3 (2005).
Delumeau, Jean. *La Peur en Occident.* Paris: Fayard, 1978.
Descamps, Marc Alain. *Psychanalyse des Contes de Fées*, http://www.europsy.org/marc-alain/contedefee.html.
Durand, Gilbert. *Les Structures Anthropologiques de l'Imaginaire.* Paris: Presses Universitaires de France, 1963.
Ebert-Schifferer, Sybille. *Caravage*, Paris: Hazan, 2009.
Ehrenzweig, Anton. *The Hidden Order of Art. A Study in the Psychology of Artistic Imagination.* Oakland, Ca.: University of California Press, 1971.
Eliade, Mircea. *Le Chamanisme et les Techniques Archaïques de l'Extase*, Paris: Payot, 1968.
Eörsi, Anna. *La Peinture de Style Gothique International.* Budapest, Paris: I.A.M, 1984.
Flahault, François. *L'Interprétation des Contes.* Paris, 1988.
Fonseca, Claudio, Giovanna Galdo, and Flore Delapalme. "L'Animal en Soi," *Cahiers Jungiens de Psychanalyse*, n° 126 (2008).
Frachi Dell'Orto, Luisa. Rediscovering Pompeii, cat. exhib. New York, Rome, 1990.

Freud, Sigmund. *Die Traumdeutung. Gesammelte Werke V*, 1900.
Friedman, Bernard Harper. *Jackson Pollock: Energy Made Visible.* New York: McGraw-Hill, 1972.
Gagnebin, Murielle. *L'Irreprésentable ou les Silences de l'Oeuvre.* Paris: Presse Universitaires de France, 1984.
Gaillard, Christian. "Ulysse et Moïse I," "Ulysse et Moïse II," *Cahiers de Psychologie de l'art et de la culture*, n° 3, n° 5, Paris: Ecole Nationale Supérieure des Beaux-arts (1978, 1979).
——. "Le Séraphin Panique. Quatre Tableaux de Botticelli." *Cahiers de psychologie de l'art et de la culture.* Paris: Ecole nationale Supérieure des Beaux-arts, n° 4 (1979).
——. "L'Étrange Histoire d'un Petit Pétersbourgeois," *Cahiers de psychologie jungienne*, n° 26 (1980).
——. "La Femme et la loi," *Cahiers de psychologie de l'art et de la culture*, n° 7 (1981).
——, editor. *Cahiers de Psychologie de l'art et de la Culture*, n° 8, "Incroyable, ou si l'on Veut Art et Croyance Aujourd'hui." Paris: Ecole Nationale Supérieure des Beaux-arts, 1982.
——. "Psychanalyse à l'Ecole?," in *La mémoire de l'art*, Edited by J. Gatard. Paris: Sgraffite, 1984.
——. "Pollock et Narcisse." *Cahiers de psychologie de l'art et de la culture.* Paris: Ecole Nationale Supérieure des Beaux-arts, 1984.
——. "Et in Arcadia ego. Un Rêve pictural à Herculaneum," *Cahiers de psychologie jungienne*, n° 46, 1985.
——. "Narcisse Spectateur et Peintre." *Cahiers de psychologie de l'art et de la culture*, n° 11, Paris: Ecole Nationale Supérieure des Beaux-arts, 1985.
——. "Espace Pictural et Espace Intérieur." *Cahiers de psychologie Jungienne*, n° 50 (1986).
——. "Ovid's Narcissus and Caravaggio's Narcissus," in *The Archetype of Shadow in a Split World*, Proceedings of the 10th International Congress for Analytical Psychology, Berlin, 1986, M. A. Matton, ed. Einsiedeln: Daimon Verlag, 1987.
——. "De la Mère de Léonard à Motherwell." *Cahiers Jungiens de Psychanalyse*, n° 79 (1994).
——. "Accord Perdu ? Le Jardin du Paradis de Frankfort," "Noces. La

Chasse Infernale de Botticelli." *Revue d'esthétique*, n° 27 (1995).
——. "Origine d'Une Oeuvre. La Palette d'Anselm Kiefer," *Corps Ecrit*, n° 32, Paris: Presses Universitaires de France, 1996.
——. "Whatever Happened to Paradise?" *The San Francisco Jung Institute Library Journal*, vol. 16, n° 2 (1997).
——. *Le Musée Imaginaire de Carl Gustav Jung*. Paris: Flammarion, 1998.
——. *Le Musée Imaginaire de Carl Gustav Jung*. Paris: Stock, 1998.
——. *Donne in Mutazione. Saggi di Psicoanalisi dell'arte*. Bergamo: Moretti & Vitali, 1998a.
——. *Donne in Mutazione*. Bergamo: Moretti & Vitali, 2000.
——. *Donne in Mutazione. Saggi di Psicoanalisi dell'arte*. Bergamo: Moretti & Vitali, 2000.
——. "Amplification et Pensée Après Jung," *Topique, Revue Freudienne*, n° 76 (2001).
——. "Le Rêve est-il Créatif?" in *Des interprétations du* Rêve. Psychanalyse, Herméneutique, Daseinanalyse. Edited by H. Mésot. Paris: Presses Universitaires de France, 2001.
——. "For a Measure of Left-Handed Thinking," *Harvest*, Fall 2001, vol. 3 (2001).
——. "La Psychanalyse Jungienne," in *Psychanalyses, Psychothérapies: les Principales Approches*. Edited by M. Elkaim. Paris: Seuil, 2003.
——. "Le Goût du Sens," in *Humbert*, 2004 (1982).
——. "The Arts," in *The Handbook of Jungian Psychology*, R. Papadopoulos, ed. London/New York: Routledge, 2006.
——. "Anima ou Sabina?," *La Vouivre. Culture et Pensée Jungienne*, vol. 15 (2006).
——. Le Bipède s'Étonne," *Cahiers Jungiens de Psychanalyse*, n° 127 (2008).
——. "The Biped Surprised," in *Cape Town 2007. Journeys, Encounters: Clinical, Communal, Cultural. Proceedings of the 17th Congress for Analytical Psychology*. P. Bennett, ed. Einsiedeln: Daimon Verlag, 2009.
——. "Revisiter le Passé au Cinéma et en Psychanalyse," *Le Coq Héron*, n° 197, Juin 2009, *Sabina Spielrein, une Oeuvre Pionnière, un Destin Singulier*.

——. "Panel Archetypes and/or primal phantasies: an Encounter and a Debate Between Freudian and Jungian analysts. Introduction" and "A Thematic Dialogue: Towards a Conclusion and a Follow-up," with Alain Gibeault, *Journal of Analytical Psychology*, vol. 56, n° 3, June 2011.

——. "Sabina Spielrein Entre un Analyste et l'Autre, et Entre un Film et l'Autre," *Les Lettres de la Société de Psychanalyse Freudienne*, n° 27 (2012).

——. "Rivisitare il Passato al Cinema e in Psicoanalisi. Note e Riflessioni sul Film di Elisabeth Marton Mi Chiamavo Sabina Spielrein," *Anima e Terra*, n° 1, April 2012 (2012a).

——. "The egg, the Vessels and the Words. From Izdubar to Answer to Job. For an imaging thinking," *Journal of Analytical Psychology*, vol. 57, n° 3 (2012b).

——. *Jung*. 6th ed. Paris: Presses Universitaires de France, 2013 (1995).

——. "Jung, Picasso et le Bleu," *Revue de Psychologie Analytique. Psychanalyse jungienne: cliniques et théories*, n° 1 (2013).

——. "A dream in Arcadia," in *The dream and its Amplification*. Edited by E. Shalit, and N. Swift Furlotti. Skiatook: Fisher King Press (2013b).

——. "Penser la Psychanalyse Hier et Aujourd'hui. Quelques Thèmes de Recherche et Débats Actuels," in *Carl Gustav Jung. Pour une Réévaluation de l'Oeuvre*. Edited by C. Maillard. Strasbourg: Etudes Germaniques, n° 9. Hors-série (2014).

——. "Alchimie et Modernité," *L'Herne*, n° 46, special Jung issue, 2015 (1984).

——. "Le Temps, l'Intemporel et l'Histoire." *Cahiers Jungiens de Psychanalyse*, n° 141 (2015).

Gaillard, Christian, and Claude Bourreille. "Le Giron d'Arcadie," *Cahiers de psychologie de l'art et de la culture*, n° 12 (1987).

Gaillard, Christian, and Gilles Sauron. "Propos Croisés sur la Villa des Mystères à Pompéi." *Cahiers de psychologie de l'art et de la culture*, n° 11 (1985).

Gaillard, Christian, and Lella Ravasi Bellochio. *L'Inconscio Creatore. Attorno al Libro dei Sogni di Federico Fellini*. Bergamo: Moretti & Vitali, 2009.

Geldzahler, Henry. *American Painting in the 20th Century*. New York: The Metropolitan Museum, 1965.
Gibeault, Alain. *Chemins de la Symbolisation*. Paris: Presses Universitaires de France, 2010.
Gougaud, Henri. *Le Murmure des Contes*. Paris: Desclée de Brouwer, 2002.
Green, André. (2002). *Idées Directrices Pour une Psychanalyse Contemporaine*. Paris: Presses Universitaires de France, 2002.
Guy-Gillet, Geneviève. "Inceste et Sacrifice." In *Carl G. Jung*. Paris: L'Herne, 1984.
Heinich, Nathalie. *Le Paradigme de l'art Contemporain*. Paris: Gallimard, 2014.
Hersant, Yves. "Mélancolie Rouge." In *Questions de Couleurs*. Paris: Les Belles Lettres, 1991.
Hillman, James. *Pan and the Nightmare*. New York: Spring, 1972.
Hillman, James, and Sonu Shamdasani. *Lament of the Dead. Psychology after Jung's Red Book*. New York: Norton & Company, 2013.
Homans, Peter. *Jung in Context. Modernity and the Making of Modern Psychology*. Chicago: The University of Chicago Press, 1979.
Humbert, Elie G. *Ecrits sur Jung*. Paris: Retz, 1993.
——. *Jung*. Paris: Hachette, 2004 (1982).
Jacobi, Jolan. *The Way to Individuation*. New York: Harcourt, Brace and World, 1967.
Jaffé, Aniela. *C. G. Jung. Bild und Wort*. Olten: Walter Verlag, 1977.
Jamet, Christian. Botticelli. *Le Sacré et le Profane*. Paris: Herscher, 1996.
Jung, Carl G. "Bruder Klaus," GW 11, 1933.
——(1962a), *Erinnerungen, Träume, Gedanken*, Aufgezeichnet und Herausgegeben von Aniela Jaffé. Olten und Freiburg in Brisgau: Walter Verlag, 1962a.
——. *Memories, Dreams, Reflections*, recorded and edited by Aniela Jaffé, 1962b.
——. *Memories, Dreams, Reflections*, recorded and edited by Aniela Jaffé. New York: Pantheon Books, 1964 (1961).
——. *"Ma vie." Souvenirs*, Rêves et *Pensées, Recueillis* par Aniela Jaffé. Paris: Gallimard, 1966.

Jung, Carl G., and Sonu Shamdasani. *The Red Book. Liber Novus.* New York/London: Norton, 2009.

Kast, Verena. *Abschied von der Opferrolle. Das Eigene Leben Leben.* Freiburg im Breisgau: Herder, 1998.

Kenneth, Clark. *L'art du Paysage.* Paris: Julliard, 1962.

Kerr, John. *A Most Dangerous Method.* New York: Random House, 1993.

Kiefer, Anselm. *L'art Survivra à ses Ruines. Art Will Survive its Ruins.* Paris: Regard, 2011.

Klibansky, Raymond, Erwin Panofsky, and Fritz Saxl. *Saturne et la M*élancolie. Paris: Gallimard, 1989 (1864).

Knoepfer, D. *La Patrie de Narcisse: un* Héros *Mythique Enraciné Dans le sol et Dans l'Histoire d'une Cité Grecque.* Paris : Odile Jacob/Collège de France, 2010.

Kohut, Heinz. *The restoration of the self.* New York: International University Press, 1977.

Kraus, Theodor, and Leonard von Matt. *Lebendiges Pompeji. Pompeji und Herculunum. Antlitz und Schiksal Zweir Antike Städte.* Köln: Dumont/Shauberg, 1982.

Krauss, Rosalind. "Emblèmes and Lexies: le Texte Photographique," in Namuth, 1978b.

——. "Contra Carmean: The Abstract Pollock," *Art in America*, n° 6 (1982).

Kristeva, Julia. *Soleil Noir. Dépression et M*élancolie. Paris: Gallimard, 1987.

Lacan, Jacques. *Le Séminaire. Livre II. Le Moi Dans la Théorie de Freud et Dans la Technique de la Psychanalyse.* Paris: Seuil, 1977 (1954–1955).

Langaney, André. *Les Hommes: Passé, Présent, Conditionnel.* Paris: Armand Colin, 1989.

Laplanche, Jean, and Jean-Bertrand Pontalis. "Fantasmes Originaires, Fantasmes des Origines, Origine des Fantasmes." *Les temps Modernes*, n° 215 (1964).

Lauterwein, Andrea. *Anselm Kiefer et la poésie de Celan,* Paris: Regard, 2006.

Leroi-Gourhan, André, Brigitte Delluc, and Giles Delluc. *Préhistoire de l'Art Occidental.* Paris: Mazenod, 1995.

Lewis-Williams, David. *The Mind in the Cave.* London: Thames and Hudson, 2003.

———. "Mobiliser le Cerveau: Vison et Chamanisme au Paléolithique Supérieure en Europe de l'Ouest." *Cahiers Jungiens de Psychanalyse*, n° 127 (2008).

Lewis-Williams, David, and David Pearce. *Inside the Neolithic Mind: Consciousness, Cosmos and the Realm of the Gods.* London: Thames and Hudson, 2005.

Liard, Véronique. *Carl Gustav Jung: Kulturphilosoph.* Paris: Presses de l'Université Paris-Sorbonne, 2007.

Longhi, Roberto. *Le Caravage.* Paris: Regards, 2004 (1927).

Lopez-Pedraza, Raphael. *Anselm Kiefer. After the Catastrophe.* London: Thames and Hudson, 1996.

———. *Herms y sus Hijos.* Caracas: Festina Lente, 2001.

Lorblanchet, Michel. *Les Grottes Ornées de la Préhistoire. Nouveaux regards.* Paris: Errance, 1995.

Lorblanchet, Michel, Jean-Philippe Le Quellec, Paul Bahn, Henri-Paul Francfort, Brigitte Delluc, and Giles Delluc. *Chamanismes et Arts Préhistoriques. Vision critique.* Paris: Errance, 2006.

Maillard, Christine. *Les Sept Sermons aux Morts de Carl Gustav Jung.* Nancy: Presse Universitaires de Nancy, 1993.

Marin, Louis. *Détruire la Peinture.* Paris: Editions Galilée, 1977.

Minssieux-Chamonard, Marie. *Anselm Kiefer. L'Alchimie du Livre.* Paris: Bibliothèque Nationale de France/Editions du Regard, 2015.

Mondzain, Marie-José. *Image, Icon, Economy. The Byzantine origins of the contemporary imaginary.* Redwood City: Stanford University Press, 2004.

Namuth, Hans. *Pollock Painting.* New York: Agrinde Publications, 1978a.

———. *L'Atelier de Jackson Pollock.* Paris: Macula, 1978b.

———. "Les Photographies de Hans Namuth Comme Documents d'Histoire de l'art," in Namuth 1978b.

Nava, Maria Luisa. *Rosso Pompeiano. La Decorazione Pittorica Nelle Collezioni del Museo di Napoli,* cat exhib. Roma, 2007.

O'Connor, Francis V. *Jackson Pollock. A Catalogue Raisonné of Paintings, Drawings, and Other Works.* New Haven, London: Yale University Press. Vol 4, 1978a.
Ogden, Thomas H. *Les Sujets de l'Analyse.* Paris: Ithaque, 2014 (1994).
Ovid. *The Metamorphoses, III.*
Papadopoulos, Renos K. *The Handbook of Jungian Psychology: Theory, Practice and Applications.* London and New York: Routledge, 2006.
Papet, Édouard. *Gustave Doré. L'Imaginaire au Pouvoir.* Paris: Flammarion, 2014
Parkington, John. *The Mantis, the Eland and the Hunter.* Cape Town: Creda Communications, 2002.
——. *Cederberg Rock Paintings,* Cape Town: Creda Communications, 2003.
Pastoureau, Michel. *Bleu. Histoire d'Une Couleur.* Paris: Seuil, 2000.
Perrault, Charles. *Contes.* Paris: Flammarion, 1989.
Perry, John Weir. *The Self in the Psychotic Process.* Berkeley: University of California Press, 1953.
Philipson, Morris H. *An Outline of Jungian Aesthetics.* Boston: Sigo Press, 1994.
Pinkola Estés, Clarissa. Femme qui Court Avec les Loups. Paris: Grasset, 1996 (1992).
Pleynet, Marcelin. "Pollock, Jung et Picasso," in Jackson Pollock. Paris: Centre Georges Pompidou. Musée National d'Art Moderne, 1982a.
——. "'Jack'son Pollock,' Cahiers de Psychologie de l'art et de la culture, n° 8, Paris: Ecole Nationale Supérieure des Beaux-arts, 1982b.
Puglisi, Catherine. Le Caravage. Paris: Gallimard, 2008.
Ragon, Michel. Journal de l'art Abstrait. Lausanne: Skira, 1992.
Raphoz, Fabienne. Les femmes de Barbe Bleue. Une histoire de curieuses. Paris: Métropolis, 1995.
Reinach, Salomon. Repertorio di Dipinti Greci e Romani. Roma: L'Erma di Bretschmer, 1970.
Renouart de Bussière, Sophie. L'Europe du Nord au Quinzième Siècle. Entre Mysticisme et Réforme," in Martin Schongauer. Paris: RMN, 1991.

Richebächer, Sabine. Sabina Spielrein. Eine Fast Grausame Liebe sur Wissenchaft. Zurich: Dörlemann, 2005.
Rose, Bernice. "Jackson Pollock: Drawing into painting," in Jackson Pollock: Drawing into painting. Catalogue of the Pollock exhibition at the Centre Georges Pompidou. Musée d'Art Moderne de la Ville de Paris, 1979.
Rosen, David H. *Transforming Depression. Healing the Soul Through Creativity.* York Beach: Nicolas-Hays, 2002.
Roussillon, René. "Précarité et vulnérabilité à l'adolescence." Adolescence, n° 72 (2010).
Rowland, Susan. *C. G. Jung and the Literary Theory: The Challenge From Fiction.* Basingstoke: Macmillan Press, 1999.
——. *Jung as a Writer.* London/New York: Routledge, 2005.
——. *Psyche and the Arts: Jungian Approaches to Music, Architecture, Literature, Painting and Film.* London/New York: Routledge, 2008.
Rubin, William. "Pollock was not accident." New York Times, New York Times, January 27, 1974.
——. "Pollock as Jungian Illustrator. The Limits of Psychological Criticism." Art in America, n° 7 and n° 8 (1979a, 1979b).
Sacco, François, and Georges Sauvet. *Le Propre de l'Homme. Psychanalyse et Préhistoire.* Neuchatel: Delachaux et Niestlé, 1998.
Salvy, Gérard-Julien. *Le Caravage.* Paris: Gallimard, 2008.
Samuels, Andrew. *Jung and the Post-Jungians.* London/New York: Routledge, 1985.
Samuels, Andrew, Bani Shorter, and Fred Plaut. *A Critical Dictionary of Jungian Analysis.* London, New York: Routledge, 1987.
Sauron, Gilles. "Nature et Signification de la Mégalographie Dionysiaque de Pompéi." Paris: Académie des inscriptions et Belles-Lettres, de Boccard, 1984.
——. La Grande Fresque de la Villa des Mystères à Pompei. Paris: Picard, 1998.
Schneider, Norbert. *Les Natures Mortes.* Cologne: Taschen, 1991.
Shamdasani, Sonu. (1999). "Jung in Historical Context. Memories, Dreams, Omissions." In *Jung in Contexts: a Reader.* Edited by Paul Bishop. London, New York: Routledge, 1999a.

——. *Jung and the Making of Modern Psychology.* Cambridge: University Press, 2003.

——. *C. G. Jung. A Biography in Books.* New York, London: Norton, Bodmer Foundation, 2012.

Shefold, Karl. La Peinture Pompéienne. Essai sur l'Évolution de sa Signification, Brussels, 1972.

Simon, Erica. "Deutung and Künsterische Herkunft der Geflügelten," in "Zum Fries der Mysterien Villa bei Pompeji," *Jahrbuch des deutschen archäologischen Institut,* n° 76 (1961).

Singer, June. *Boundaries of the Soul: The Practice of Jung's Psychology.* New York: Doubleday, 1973.

Soriano, Marc S. *Les Contes de Perrault. Culture Savante et Traditions Populaires.* Paris: Gallimard, 1968.

——. *Les Contes de Perrault. Culture Savante et Traditions Populaires.* Paris: Gallimard, 1977.

Soriano Marc, Jacques Le Goff, Emmanuel Le Roy Ladurie, and André Burgière. "Table ronde sur le contes de Perrault." *Annales, Economie, Sociétés et Civilisations,* May–June, 1970.

Spike, John T. *Caravaggio.* New York: Abbeville Press, 2010.

Stein, Murray B. *Jung's Treatment of Christianity. The Psychotherapy of a Religious Tradition.* Wilmette, Ill.: Chiron, 1985.

——. *Jung's Map of the Soul. An introduction.* Chicago: Open Court/ La Salle, 2006.

Vaisse, Pierre. *Albrecht Dürer.* Paris: Fayard, 1995.

Van den Berk, Tjeu. *Jung on Art. The Autonomy of the Creative Drive.* London, New York: Routledge, 2012.

Vaudret, Rossella. *Caravage. L'Oeuvre Complet.* Milan: Silvana, 2010.

Vetter, Ewald. M. "Das Frankfurter Paradiesgärtlein." *Heidelberg Jahrbücher,* 9 (1988).

Veyne, Paul, François Lissarague, and Françoise Frontisi-Ducroux. *Les Mystères du Gynécée,* Paris: Gallimard, 1998.

Vialou, Denis. *Chasseurs et Artistes. Au* Cœur de la *Préhistoire.* Paris: Gallimard, 1996.

——, editor. *La Préhistoire. Histoire et Dictionnaire.* Paris: Laffont, 2004.

——. *La Préhistoire*. Paris: Gallimard, 2006.
Von Franz, Marie-Louise. 1978 (1970). *Interpretation of Fairy Tales*. New York: Spring.
——. *Individuation in Fairy Tales*. New York: Spring, 1978 (1977).
——. *Die Visionen des Niklaus von Flüe*. Einsiedeln: Daimon, 1991.
Von Goethe, Johann Wolfgang. Über Kunst und Altertum, 1818.
Wajeman, Gérard. *Narcisse ou le Fantasme de la Peinture*. In *Art et Fantasme*. Seyssel: Champ-Vallon, 1984.
——. "Narcisse Spectateur et Peintre." *Cahiers de psychologie de l'art et de la culture*, n° 11, Paris: Ecole Nationale Supérieure des Beaux-arts, 1985.
Waren, C. (2007). "Symbolic conceptions: the idea of the third." *The Journal of Analytical Psychology*, n° 52.
Wehr, Gerhard. *Jung*. Zurich: Shweizer verlagshaus; Geneva/Lucerne: Coeckelberghs, 1979.
——. *Jung*. Geneva, Lucerne: Coeckelberghs, 1989..
Wolfe, Judith. "Jungian Aspects of Jackson Pollock's Imagery." *Artforum*, vol. 11 (1972).
Wölflin, Heinrich. *Renaissance and Barock*, 1888.
Wysuph, C. L. *Jackson Pollock: Psychoanalytic Drawings*. New York: Horizon Press, 1970.
Yiassemides, Angeliki. *Time and Timelessness. Temporality in the Theory of Carl Jung*. London and New York: Routledge, 2014.
Zink, Jörg. *Komm in Meinem Garten. Verlag am Eschbach*, 1988.
Zuffi, Stefano. *Il Quattrocento*. Milano: Electra, 2004.

Index

Other Titles in the Carolyn and Ernest Fay Series in Analytical Psychology

The Stillness Shall Be the Dancing: Feminine and Masculine in Emerging Balance Marion Woodman
Buddhism and the Art of Psychotherapy Hayao Kawai
Gender and Desire: Uncursing Pandora Polly Young-Eisendrath
The Archetypal Imagination James Hollis
Soul and Culture Roberto Gambini
Joy, Inspiration, and Hope Verena Kast
Transformation: Emergence of the Self Murray Stein
Integrity in Depth John Beebe
The Two Million-Year-Old Self Anthony Stevens
Memories of Our Lost Hands Sonoko Toyoda
The Old Woman's Daughter: Transformative Wisdom for Men and Women Claire Douglas
Ethics and Analysis: Philosophical Perspectives and Their Application in Therapy Luigi Zoja
The Black Sun: The Alchemy and Art of Darkness Stanton Marlan
Synchronicity: Nature and Psyche in an Interconnected Universe Joseph Cambray
The Therapeutic Relationship: Transference, Countertransference, and the Making of Meaning Jan Wiener
Connecting with South Africa: Cultural Communication and Understanding Astrid Berg
Finding Jung: Frank N. McMillan Jr., a Life in Quest of the Lion Frank N. McMillan III
Madness and Creativity Ann B. Ulanov
Brothers and Sisters: Myth and Reality Henry Abramovitch